Asia

Europe

Africa

Pacific
Ocean

Indian
Ocean

Oceania

Berlin,
Germany

Damascus,
Syria

Iraq

Tarim River Basin
China

Jerusalem,
Israel

Awash Valley
Ethiopia

Berbera,
Somalia

Adam's Peak/Sri Pada Mountain
Sri Lanka

Praslin Island
The Seychelles

Lake Bangweulu
Zambia

The Location of
the Garden of Eden
on Earth

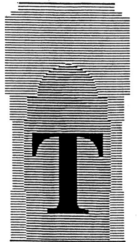

T H E
FRIENDS
of the
Beverly Hills
Public Library

SHIRLEY KERM

Paradise Lust

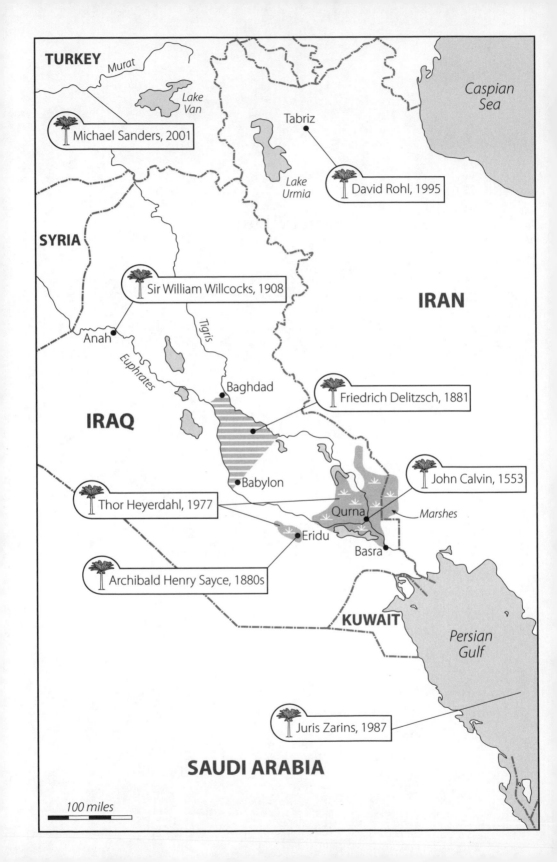

Paradise Lust

*Searching for
the Garden of Eden*

BROOK WILENSKY-LANFORD

Grove Press
New York

Excerpts from Chapter 3, 'The Serpent Lesson,' have appeared
In *The Common* (Issue No. 1), and from Chapter 6,
'Practically Paradise,' in *The Exquisite Corpse Annual #2*.

Endpaper and frontispiece maps by ML Design, London

Printed in the United States of America
Published simultaneously in Canada

ISBN: 978-0-8021-1980-3

Grove Press
an imprint of Grove/Atlantic Inc.
841 Broadway
New York, NY 10003

Distributed by Publishers Group West

www.groveatlantic.com

11 12 13 14   10 9 8 7 6 5 4 3 2 1

For Dad

Contents

Once upon a time there was a king's son; nobody had so many and such beautiful books as he. In these all that had ever happened in the world he could read and see depicted in splendid engravings. Of every people and every land could he get information, but as to where the Garden of Eden was, not a word was to be found therein; and this, just this it was, on which he meditated most of all.

       —Hans Christian Andersen, "The Garden of Paradise"

Prologue

In the beginning, I was just following a family rumor. Sometime in 2004, my father told me that my great-uncle William had been looking for the Garden of Eden. William had died in 1971, before I was born, and all I knew about him was that he had lived on the Upper East Side of Manhattan and was a highly regarded allergist at Columbia University's medical center, where *his* father, a member of the National Academy of Sciences, had discovered the structure of vitamin B$_1$. Most of my father's relatives were practicing scientists. If they really thought they could find a Biblical place on the rational Earth, the news was surprising, to say the least.

I had to know more. Was it all a joke? Where was the Garden of Eden supposed to be? How were they going to get there? Did they make the trip? What did they find? Dad didn't know, so I tracked down William's daughter Phoebe, my second cousin, who told me that the rumors were true: her father *had* been looking for the Garden of Eden. Phoebe's parents had both been interested in archaeology and frequently visited the collections of antiquities at the Metropolitan Museum of Art. Sometime in the 1950s, when Phoebe was a young girl, William and his cousin Dallas Sherman, a dashing Pan Am pilot, had hatched a plan to go to Eden, to "fly around the suspected area and look for signs of the site."

Phoebe didn't remember where the suspected area was, or what the signs of the site were supposed to be, and anyway the plan never materialized. "Needless to say," Phoebe wrote to me, "nothing happened beyond what I would have called cocktail chatter."

I admit my heart sank when I heard they never flew to Eden.

But something had happened: they believed that there *was* a place to search for. This was a mystery. If I'd thought about it at all, I'd assumed that people had stopped believing the Garden of Eden was a real place somewhere back in the Middle Ages, or certainly once the theory of evolution began to show that man had not been created, all at once, in a place mentioned in the Bible. Apparently not.

William and his family had belonged to the venerable Brick Presbyterian Church, and Dallas to St. Bartholomew's Episcopal, both of them on Park Avenue. These were surely not the kind of churches that required belief in a literal, six-day creation. And yet my great-uncle still believed in the Garden of Eden. I tried to find Dallas Sherman to see if he could help me understand how this was possible. I did find another elderly airplane pilot named Dallas Sherman who told me wonderful mistaken-identity stories about my great-uncle's cousin who, he'd just heard, had recently passed away. The trail seemed to have gone cold. But I couldn't get the story out of my head.

I imagined the two of them, William and Dallas, sitting down with a martini at the Union Club, loosening their ties, and mapping the Book of Genesis on a cocktail napkin. Perhaps an olive reminded them of the forbidden fruit and the Tree of Knowledge. Sticklers for scientific accuracy, they might have noticed that the Bible never says "apple," just "fruit." I could almost hear William discussing what species of fruit Adam and Eve might have eaten, in the same matter-of-fact tone he would have used to discuss "hypersensitivity mechanisms and management."

My hyperrational relatives still held out the possibility that science could find the Garden of Eden in the 1950s. Proving that the apple—or fruit—does not fall far from the tree, I, too, looked first to science. There must be some reasonable explanation. Some archaeological find must have been uncovered, some new scroll translated; it must have been in all the newspapers; it must have been huge. Maybe with a little digging of my own I could figure out what this major discovery was—and *where*. Maybe then I could imagine William and Dallas out of the Union Club and onto a plane.

I began with a subject search in the library catalog for "Garden of Eden." There were far too many titles to skim quickly. So I narrowed it down to books published after Darwin's *On the Origin of Species* in 1859 and before William's death in 1971. That didn't help.

Lo and behold, the Garden of Eden had been found in Iraq, Turkey, Sri Lanka, Mongolia, the Seychelles, Florida, California, Missouri, and Ohio; at the North Pole; under the Mediterranean near Crete; in Sweden, the Persian Gulf, and Egypt. And that list only goes back to the late nineteenth century. No sooner did one authoritative account come along than another popped up to supplant it.

Archaeologists did have theories. But so did college presidents, military officials, country preachers, and ordinary citizens. And every single one of them claimed he could prove—scientifically—that his was the one perfect spot described in the Book of Genesis. How could I tell whom to believe?

I kept reading—books, pamphlets, academic journals, and newspaper articles: *Want to Get into Garden of Eden for Buck, Ten Cents? Garden of Eden: Its Position on the Globe Definitely Located. Were There Two Gardens of Eden, or Only One?* And of course: *Paradise Found!*

Most of these works, I noticed, belonged only to the local library of their author. I found myself calling manifestos out of cold storage in Ohio and asking the University of Hong Kong to digitize crumbling memoirs for me. Columbia University had a noncirculating copy of the British engineer Sir William Willcocks's 1919 book on Eden, but it was still classified as an engineering title, so I was required to read *From the Garden of Eden to the Crossing of the Jordan* in the engineering library, next to exhausted undergraduates studying biomedicine or atomic energy.

I wished I could have heard the theories out loud from their authors the way their first audiences did, in grand theaters, elite clubs, and tiny churches. Some books arrived still bearing the literal marks of their creators, the next best thing. There was a dedication from the Floridian Elvy E. Callaway to his Baptist alma mater in Jacksonville; a greeting typed on letterhead from Boston University President William Warren to his colleague at Union Theological Seminary, requesting two dollars' payment for this copy of *Paradise Found.* Tse Tsan Tai's 1914 pamphlet *The Real Situation of Eden and the Origin of the Chinese* (tastefully library-bound in red) came with a bilingual English-Chinese map tucked in the back. The "route of Noah after the Flood" was inked across Mongolia in the author's own minute, spidery hand. Such traces of obsession proved contagious. How could someone possibly be so sure that they knew where Noah went after the flood? I became just as determined to understand the Eden seekers as they had been to put Eden on the map.

They all began with Genesis 2:10–14, the Bible's maddeningly terse geographical description of Eden. So I did too. I had already memorized the verses in their entirety:

> A river flows out of Eden to water the garden, and from there it divides and becomes four branches. The name of the first is Pishon; it is the one that flows around the whole land of Havilah, where there is gold; and the gold of that land is good; bdellium and onyx stone are there. The name of the second river is Gihon; it is the one that flows around the whole land of Cush. The name of the third river is Tigris, which flows east of Assyria. And the fourth river is the Euphrates.

The Bible sounds positively nonchalant: if you can pinpoint the four rivers, you can locate paradise. In fact, many Eden seekers claimed that the unusually matter-of-fact description was the reason they decided to look for Eden to begin with—it just *sounded* like a real place. Upon closer inspection, however, problems arose. Everyone knows that the Tigris and the Euphrates run from Turkey through Iraq, ending in the Persian Gulf. But no one knows for sure where the rivers Pishon and Gihon are, or were. The details don't necessarily help make sense of things.

Yes, Pishon circles a land called Havilah, where gold and a number of other valuable things can be found, but nobody knows where Havilah is either. The Gihon circles a land called Cush, but no one agrees on which ancient land used to be called Cush. Thus, to solve the Eden equation, you'd have to solve the Pishon-Gihon unknowns. To do that, you'd also have to solve for Havilah and Cush.

The Biblical algebra reached a level of detail that boggled my mind, which lacked training in Greek, Hebrew, or ancient geography. So I decided to back up, to find out where the search itself had begun. Who had first decided that Eden *could* be found? Not surprisingly, it's a very old story, with innumerable branches.

Among those people who believed that Eden could be located using Genesis as a map, there seemed to be two main camps, roughly aligned with the two pairs of rivers. Tigris-Euphrates seekers took it for granted that the Tigris and Euphrates named in the Bible were the same Tigris and Euphrates that we know now, and so the Pishon and Gihon would have to be somewhere nearby. That puts Eden in Iraq, or possibly Turkey, or Armenia.

Seekers more interested in the Pishon and Gihon than the Tigris and Euphrates tended to have more fanciful geography. Since we no longer knew where the Pishon and Gihon were, perhaps they were *not* near today's Tigris and Euphrates. Since the Bible mentions two rivers that are no longer known by those names, these seekers believed that we couldn't trust the names at all. Perhaps today's Tigris and Euphrates are simply named after Eden's *original* Tigris and Euphrates, much as Lebanon, New Hampshire, was named after Lebanon, Lebanon! For them, Eden could be anywhere.

Pishon-Gihon seekers liked to hark back to the first-century Roman historian Josephus. He had released the rivers from what would seem to be their geographical bounds in the Near East, insisting that Genesis must instead be referring to an arrangement called the Four Great Rivers of the World. In Josephus's theory, the Tigris and Euphrates stay where they're at, but the Pishon and Gihon wander. The Pishon becomes the Ganges, thus making Havilah India, and the Nile is the Gihon, making Cush Ethiopia. The genius of the Four Great Rivers formulation is that it assumes Eden to be earthly, but doesn't put a finger on its exact location. People could—and did—take off in any number of directions. Eden, the earthly paradise, was somewhere at the center of this mystical geography, probably enclosed by a tall stone wall. Jerusalem, the sacred center of the medieval Christian universe, was advocated by many as a location for Eden. One of the major sources of freshwater in the years of King David was known as the Gihon Spring. But there were infinite possibilities for Eden and the four rivers—the Gihon might also be the Thames, the Pishon the Rhône—whatever your idea of the known world was, there had to be four symmetrical rivers to divide it. The gardens in medieval monasteries were designed this way, with elaborate elevated fountains in the center and four straight paths leading outward to each corner.

After Josephus, the search for Eden was sustained by Saint Augustine, the bishop of Hippo, who spent a great deal of time before his death in A.D. 430 considering whether Eden was or was not a real place. Augustine laid out the options at the beginning of the eighth volume of his book *The Literal Meaning of Genesis*. (Apparently it had taken him the first seven volumes just to get through the six days of creation.) According to Augustine, Eden could be—wait for it—either real, or metaphorical, or both. Which did the great man favor? "I admit that the third interpretation appeals to me": that is to say, Eden was both a real *and* an unreal place. But by the end of Volume 8, Augustine had talked himself back into realism. The events in Eden happened. The Tree of Knowledge was "a real material tree." And the four rivers were "true rivers, not just figurative expressions." Augustine exercised a massive influence over all of Latin-speaking Christianity, and his ideas stuck around.

Augustine's permission and Josephus's geography brought on a torrent of medieval Eden theories. In the Middle Ages, the Garden was assumed to exist somewhere on Earth, probably in "the East." No doubt it was barred shut, still guarded by the angels with flaming swords that God placed at its gates to keep fallen man away from the Tree of Life. If it had survived Noah's Flood, it would have to be either on top of a very tall mountain, or on an island. Mountains were tall enough to outlast most floods; islands suggested the tip of an iceberg of land now underwater. In 1358, a Florentine monk found both: a very tall mountain on the island of Sri Lanka (Ceylon). At the top, he found a fossilized footprint he claimed was Adam's; today, it's a major hiking trail and tourist attraction called Adam's Peak.

Christopher Columbus, who thought he was in the East, came to believe that the earthly paradise lay somewhere in the interior of South America, at the end of the 1,700-mile Orinoco River. He passed by the river's enormous Atlantic mouth, in what's now Venezuela, on his third return voyage from the New World back to the Old, and he was immediately smitten. The sheer size of the river granted it status as one of the four rivers of paradise, as far as Columbus was concerned. He wrote to Ferdinand and Isabella, "If the water does *not* proceed from the earthly paradise, it seems to be a still greater wonder, for I do not believe that there is any river in the world so large and deep." The Orinoco, posited Columbus, must descend from a high point in the middle of the unknown continent. The Earth, he believed, was shaped exactly like a giant breast, and the Garden of Eden would be the nipple. If Spain could conquer this nipple of paradise, Columbus wrote to Ferdinand and Isabella, it would be an unbeatable weapon in the Crown's efforts to convert everyone to Christianity.

But the king and queen would not pay much attention to anything Columbus wrote on his third voyage; he was being expelled from the island of Hispaniola in shackles after a particularly brutal massacre of Indians, and suffering, most likely, from syphilis-induced madness.

The search for Eden, however, did not disappear in madness and fantasy, like the notion of the breast-shaped Earth. Quite the contrary. Later in the sixteenth century, the actual existence of an earthly Eden was entirely taken for granted by most Christians. That was all thanks to John Calvin, the Protestant theologian and patron saint of the more down-to-earth Tigris-Euphrates seekers. Not for Calvin the mystical symmetry of the Four Great Rivers of the World. In his 1553 commentary on Genesis, he included a map. This was a first, and it placed Calvin squarely in the "Eden is a real place" camp. The map, though geographically incorrect in many respects, depicted a fairly realistic Y-shaped junction of the

Tigris and Euphrates in the south of Mesopotamia. That's where Eden was supposed to be, Calvin wrote: "east of Babylon." Done. When the Church of England created its own English translation of the Bible in 1568, the Bishops' Bible, it borrowed Calvin's geography, and it became widely accepted. Calvin is the one we have to credit with making the original connection between Eden and Iraq. And something about his no-nonsense approach seems to have allowed the old religious quest to carry over into the new scientific era. Most of the Eden seekers, whether they followed fanciful or realistic maps, did not see themselves as opposed to science. In fact, new scientific discoveries and techniques seemed only to spur their old search forward.

By the early nineteenth century, fossil discoveries began to indicate a much older Earth than the Biblical chronology could account for. Naturalists such as Lamarck and Darwin proved that species changed over time, meaning that God did not create, say, the birds of the air all in one fell swoop. At every point in the process of the separation of science from religion, however, new ideas were slow to take hold.

In 1840, the famous Harvard naturalist Louis Agassiz published his theory that the Earth had gone through a relatively recent and entirely transformational ice age. This theory was controversial; many people assumed that the last great upheaval to form the Earth's surface had been Noah's Flood. Agassiz's ideas would revolutionize modern geology. Darwin took some of his writings as endorsements of evolutionary theory. But Agassiz himself was still a believer in what might now be called "intelligent design." He referred to a "species" as a "thought of God." He believed that glaciers had been created instantaneously and were of divine origin: he called them "God's great plough."

Agassiz was possibly the last venerable scientist of his generation to keep his reputation while disavowing evolution. After the publication of Darwin's *On the Origin of Species* in 1859, most scientific thinkers began to shift away from belief in a world that had been created—pouf—all at once at a particular spot on a map, with a man, a woman, an apple, and a snake. People did like to refer to the Galápagos islands as "Darwin's Eden," because Darwin's idea of natural selection originated there, but that's really a joke. Picturing the man who brought us natural selection standing in the Garden is like imagining a meteorologist who believes thunderbolts come from the hand of Zeus. Darwin himself did not want to commit to any geographical point of origin for *Homo sapiens*, let alone pinpoint sin or paradise on a map. In his 1871 *Descent of Man* he did allow that humans probably developed somewhere geographically near where our primate relatives still live: "It is somewhat more probable that our early progenitors lived on the African continent than elsewhere." But, Darwin declared, there was also a large ape that roamed Europe not so long ago, and anyway the Earth is old enough for primate species to have migrated all the way around it by now. So, "It is useless to speculate on this subject."

Darwin was diplomatic in his dismissal of the quest for Eden; the same could not be said of the nineteenth-century radical Victoria Woodhull, who advocated for women's suffrage, labor reform, and free love, and, in 1872, was the first female U. S. presidential candidate. In her epic speech of 1875, "The Garden of Eden," she saw no reason to tolerate such nonsense. "Any school boy of twelve years of age who should read the description of this garden and not discover that it has no geographical significance whatever, ought to be reprimanded for his stupidity."

But there were holdouts. Men much older than twelve—and they were mostly men—were still speculating on Eden, uselessly or not. Darwin, Woodhull, and the pace of the modern world didn't stop the missionary-explorer David Livingstone from declaring, in 1871, that Eden existed at the source of the Nile, which he judged to be in the Lake Bangweulu region of Zambia. (His theory, like Columbus's, was mired in madness, in his case from malaria.) Nor did modern science dissuade distinguished British general Charles "Chinese" Gordon from insisting in 1886 that the island of Praslin, in the Seychelles off the east coast of Africa, conformed exactly to the geography of Genesis.

The late nineteenth century was a tricky time for believers. The Book of Genesis was no longer considered by scholars to be historically true, and symbolic interpretations prevailed. Yet the Biblical view of the world had an extremely long half-life. Geologists had begun to override Noah's Flood, but writers of Biblical dictionaries still treated Adam as a real person. And people were still looking for Eden.

Even Victoria Woodhull was an Eden seeker of sorts—she did spend two hours and 16,000 words on the topic. She set out to prove that Eden wasn't a place on the map, but she did arrive at another, figurative destination for Eden. In Genesis, declared Woodhull, Moses had written an allegory of the human body before it was defiled by sin; the four "rivers" all branch out from the stomach.

What accounts for the amazing persistence of the quest? If the search for Eden is a centuries-long epic novel, the post-Darwin chapter is a major plot twist. For the first time, anyone seeking Eden did so in full knowledge that this Garden did not mean the same thing to everybody. Was it the *Origin of Species*? Or *Paradise Lost*? No longer could seekers count on their audience's familiarity with Augustine, Josephus, or Calvin.

Seekers might claim, demurely, that they just happened to read the names of those four rivers in Genesis and, much to their own surprise, came up with the location of Eden. But really, nobody stumbled upon the Pishon and the Gihon. Those who looked for Eden always had an urgent reason for doing so, even if they kept it to themselves. They would have to answer at least two questions: not only *where* was Eden, but, more important, *what* was Eden?

And answer they would. Eden is part paradise, but only part. Really, the story is much bigger. Eden is supposed to tell us where we came from, what we've done wrong, and where we go from here.

No wonder we keep looking. Ideas of Eden still flow on, long past Darwin, into the late twentieth century and beyond. I set out to follow Eden as far as it would take me. The terrain I covered along the way—bizarre, heartfelt, desperate—had yet to be explored.

PART I

Unity

I

The Last Giant Man of Eden

I N THE BEGINNING, millions of years ago, the Lord God planted a garden northward, in Eden. There was an abundance of sunlight, sequoias, and electricity, and all the biological conditions were most favorable.

William Fairfield Warren did not look like a candidate to discover the location of the Garden of Eden. He wasn't an explorer. He stood only five feet six, when he stood at all. In his role as the first president of Boston University, he spent much of his time sitting behind his desk, speaking with the faculty, students, and trustees in a soft, husky voice. Though he was only forty when appointed to the position, his pale bespectacled face, framed by thinning gray hair and a trim beard, made him look much older. Known as a diplomat, Warren insisted on perfect courtesy and friendship between faculty and students. He held the job for thirty years.

But Warren was also a trained Methodist minister, and he continued teaching in the School of Theology throughout his tenure as president. In his classroom, behind the podium, William Warren seemed to grow. His usually restrained speaking voice became louder and more resonant. His prominent forehead began to flush. He made bad jokes. He had a penchant for creating and acting out fake Socratic dialogues and reciting long passages from Emerson. And instead of playing the courteous diplomat, Warren became a defender of the faith.

The faith needed defending after 1859, when the post–Darwin furor over human origins was in full blaze. Evolution suggested that man had *ascended* over time from our less intelligent and more animalistic primate origins. Christianity had been insisting for millennia that man had *descended,* through original sin, from near-divine heights in the Garden of Eden to the miserable, depraved society of the late nineteenth century.

In 1872, an overeager German philosopher proclaimed that man *was* an animal, no different from a monkey; human thoughts were just emanations of the brain, "like bile from the liver." These shock tactics gave Warren ammunition against the evolutionist heresy, and his already scheduled lecture on "Scripture Inspiration" provided him with an opportunity to attack.

Warren began with an ultimatum. If any human in the audience believed himself to be an animal, he declared, "it will be eminently fitting to postpone all arguments with him until he shall become a man. Lunatics, we are told, should never be contradicted." Man is a spiritual creature, Warren declared, created by God. And God hadn't just stepped back after the creation, exhausted, and "sunk into an eternal swoon." Nor was He "locked up in the sky-parlor of the universe." No, the Creator God was still around, and he was keeping busy. "I assume that, as the air inspheres all trees, so God all souls."

Warren's own faith never wavered, but his position had him trapped. As a modern man, the president of a major university, he knew science was coming. But his Methodist theology, like that of most Christian denominations, required humans to be sinners always reaching backward toward a more perfect, Edenic past. How could he maintain both points of view?

He refused to take the easy way, refused to shake the Bible in the face of the heathens. Dogmatic, overanxious defense of Christianity was to his mind worse than no defense at all. Besides, he'd served as a missionary himself in Germany, and he knew those blunt tactics wouldn't work. Make transparent arguments based on a literal reading of the Bible, Warren warned, and you'll "fatally disgust many an ingenious mind."

Within the theology department, Warren specialized in comparative mythology, which he described as "the science of the oldest traditional beliefs and memories of mankind." He knew the great epic folklore of the Hindus, the Celts, the Chinese, and the Persians. In the nineteenth century, this was a rare, esoteric body of knowledge, full of metaphoric echoes of Bible stories. So Warren didn't have to point to the Bible and say, "God said so"; he had corroborating evidence from all over the world.

Warren knew that to have the best chance at conversion, you needed to speak in the language of the potential convert. So he began to learn the language of science. He would examine fossils, not just Bible verses. He quoted Darwin, not just Augustine. And he always kept an eye toward the gaps in the young body of knowledge accumulating around Darwin. What did the Darwinists *not* know?

What they didn't know, and wouldn't for almost a century after Darwin, was *where* on Earth the first *Homo sapiens* had appeared. How could you know *how* man began unless you knew *where* man began? How could you move into a brave new future with so many questions about the past? The archaeologists, historians, and anthropologists, though they continued working, tentatively, found themselves "in the dark," and Warren saw his opportunity to shine some theological light.

He promised his students not to try to defend "metaphysical absurdities" like angels and hellfire. Christianity didn't need fire and brimstone; it could simply state the truth. "Nothing is so persuasive as honesty."

And God's honest scientific truth was: the Garden of Eden is at the North Pole.

Or at least it *had* been, before the Flood. Warren's theory began with one true scientific premise. Millions of years ago, the Earth had been much warmer. Back then, the North Pole would not have been frozen. It might have been, if not tropical, then at least, perhaps, habitable. And as all the paleontologists of Warren's time could confirm, the oldest life-forms on Earth seemed to emerge directly out of a primeval paradise—fantastic creatures at once familiar and mythical, like the woolly mammoth, the dinosaur, and the giant sequoia—"flora and fauna of almost unimagined vigor and luxuriousness." The North Pole must have been a place of abundance and perfection, just as the Garden of Eden should be: Genesis says that Eden contains "every tree that is pleasant to the eye or good for food." Warren translated the Bible into science: Eden was "the one spot on Earth where the biological conditions are the most favorable."

Warren could not have picked a more perfect moment for a Polar Eden. At the end of the nineteenth century, the North Pole was a rare blank spot on the world map. Despite numerous attempts, no one had been there. No one knew what it looked like. There could be an open sea, or there could be a whole other continent—no doubt cold, but still. It could be mountainous, or flat, or forested.

Surprisingly, the North Pole and the Garden of Eden had a lot in common. For one thing, both had tantalized explorers by being always, seemingly, just out of reach—and not for lack of trying. The search for Eden had been going on for centuries—without much to show for itself in the way of flag-planting territory. By the end of the nineteenth century, it was thought that fanciful locations for Eden, in exotic locales like Sri Lanka and the Orinoco, were a thing of the past. This was a newer, wiser age. Besides, so much was known about the world that there was no remote area in which to uncover an earthly paradise. We had reached the ends of the Earth. Or almost.

A race for the Pole had been going on since the 1820s—but at a glacial pace and at exorbitant financial and human costs. The Arctic region was treacherous enough even if westerners knew what they were doing, and for much of the early nineteenth century, they did not. British explorers continued to wear British wool, even though it absorbed sweat, which then froze and lost any insulating ability. Scurvy is easily avoided by eating raw meat, as the Eskimos do, but it took European explorers decades to figure this out. In the meantime, they suffered. Scurvy not only weakens the muscles but also messes with the mind, leaving early explorers convinced that they could accomplish more than was humanly possible. Yet for every failed expedition, with its loss of lives to scurvy and starvation, there seemed to be a dozen more soldiers or sailors ready to sign up as reinforcements. The Pole was magnetic in more than a geologic sense. It drew hundreds of men into its circular orbit.

The great Arctic explorer Elisha Kent Kane set a new record for reaching "farthest north," in an expedition of 1851; he also set a new standard for Arctic survival. After an eighty-three-day march across the ice, only one of his crew froze to death. Kane returned home to front-page *New York Times* fanfare, and his two-volume *Arctic Explorations* sold 69,000 copies and made him a rich man. He died in Havana (where he'd gone to recover from the effects of scurvy) in 1857, and his monthlong funeral procession—from Cuba to New Orleans, up the Mississippi to Cincinnati, by train to Philadelphia, stopped at every stage by throngs of mourners—was said to be the most spectacular of the nineteenth century, excluding that of Lincoln.

William Warren rode this great wave of public Polar imagination. He stepped out of his Boston University classroom and tested his theory behind other podiums in Boston, New York, and Chicago. Everywhere he went, he enthralled audiences with his rapturous descriptions of the northern lights, the aurora borealis, or as he called it, "diluted lightning."

"Sometimes these electric discharges not only fill the whole heaven with palpitating draperies, but also tip the hills with lambent flame, and cause the very soil on which one stands to prickle with a kind of life." Imbued with still-mysterious electrical power, Warren's North Pole seemed to pulsate expectantly, as if about to give birth to a new world, and that's exactly what Warren believed had happened.

In his lectures, and in his 1882 pamphlet "The True Key to Ancient Cosmology," Warren detailed over and over again his theory of just how the world began. He was well aware of the scholarly disagreement surrounding the Eden question—as he liked to say, "The modern Babel is worse than the first!" And he was there to swoop in like a benevolent God, to provide one language that everyone could understand.

All these petty geographical disputes, Warren thought, had kept centuries of theologians from seeing the one, simple, symmetrical, northern solution. These disputes were easily overcome. He told his audiences to take a closer look at the names of those four rivers. Start with the one that is not disputed by anyone, in any Biblical translation, the one river everyone thinks he knows: the Euphrates.

According to Warren, "Euphrates" is the Greek translation of an original Hebrew name "Phrath"—a general term meaning "the Broad" or "the Deep." "The Deep" could of course apply to more than one river "just as Broad Brook is the name of many an American stream." Possibly then, the "Phrath" of Mesopotamia could have been named for some older, beloved river from the pre-Flood world, wherever that was. "That it was so," he wrote, "is the firm belief of various learned writers," whom he then went on to cite at length.

Once Warren dismantled the idea of a Middle Eastern Euphrates, he could begin building his idea of a northern Eden, starting with the original "one river that watered the Garden." According to Warren it wasn't really a river at all, but simply rain. Not having seen rain before, the "First People" believed it to be part of a "finer and more celestial stream whose headsprings were in the sky." In the center of the hypothetical "circumpolar land" there was an elevated area, a Polar mountain. If Adam and Eve stood on top of this mountain, they'd be standing in the center of the compass rose. Looking down, they'd find four separate streams flowing symmetrically in opposite directions "toward all the cardinal points of the horizon."

Such a well-watered place would obviously be extremely fertile. Warren populated his Eden with numerous species of trees—beeches, oaks, planes, poplars, walnuts, limes; even a magnolia or two—and especially, a species of giant pine closely related to the *Sequoia gigantea* of California. Some of these red-bark evergreens grew 400 feet tall, and had been found to be almost 2,000 years old. Uncannily straight, and stunningly out of scale with the rest of the landscape, the last surviving sequoias are "witnesses [of] a far-off world, witnesses whose testimony [even] the most incredulous must accept." If these individual primeval trees could struggle against unfavorable biological conditions to survive for two millennia, "who shall declare it impossible that the men of the time and place of the origination of the *Sequoia gigantea* should have averaged more than six feet in stature, or attained an age quite surpassing our threescore years and ten?"

That's right—here in the Polar paradise, under the electric skies and alongside gigantic trees, there were people. Giant people. Adam and Eve—or "hyperborean Eocene man," as Warren called his first race—must have been "of giant stature."

Warren stated this theory over and over again. At first he was cautious. The idea of giant, long-lived people was "by no means scientifically incredible." Then he became a little bolder. So what if the oldest human skeletons known by paleontologists had been of only ordinary size, if not smaller? None of them, Warren pointed out in his own defense, had been found in Arctic regions. Darwin himself once said, "Plants and shells of the Arctic region are eminently variable." So why not humans?

Warren dismissed as small-minded anyone who was *not* inclined to believe in prehistoric giant Polar men. We hadn't been there; we were in no position to judge. We were like "a man who in all his life had never seen any other specimen of journalism than the *North British Wool-growers Monthly Bulletin.*

He reminded those provincial wool-growers who had never seen a giant man that even in 1885, and even in warmer latitudes, there was great variability in human height. Occasionally, he wrote, men appeared who were four or five times the height of the smallest adult dwarf. With that rate of variability, who knows what might have existed at the dawn of the world? "If we were to assume two and one half feet as the minimum adult stature in Polar Regions in primeval times, the still-prevailing range of variation would give us some men from seven and one half to twelve and one half feet in height." Assuming a minimum adult stature of two and a half feet must have been comforting to a man of five feet six: according to the "still-prevailing range of variation" he was not short, only average.

The physical stature of hyperborean Eocene man was matched only by his religious prowess. In the glorious early years, man was monotheistic, and in "instant personal" communication with his Creator. Humans were perfect moral creatures, living in the world's "first theocracy." They knew how to live in harmony with the land and with each other, so they lived for a long time. "Threescore and ten," that is, seventy—the traditional human life span mentioned in the Bible and taken up by Shakespeare—was just a bare minimum for hyperborean Eocene man.

These men were also strong and muscular. And it was inevitable, according to Warren, that "such a lusty race" would be restless. Not realizing what they had, hyperborean Eocene men instead "coveted experimental knowledge of evil as well as of good." Warren had learned his second language well: even the Fall of Man, the mysterious temptation at the heart of the Eden story, came out sounding like science.

What exactly did Adam and Eve "experiment" with? Debate about the symbolism of Eden's forbidden fruit could (and did) fill many libraries. But most of the interpretations have to do with sex. Before they ate the fruit, Adam and Eve were naked and unashamed; afterward, they had to cover up, and they had children: Cain and Abel. Whole medieval libraries are devoted to the question of whether or not Adam and Eve could have sex in Eden before the Fall. Some say of course they could; otherwise, how would it be paradise? Others say no, the first people had no need of such depravity. The age-old debate on sex in Eden was often connected with the debate on the species of fruit. The apple is only a late, Victorian afterthought. More sensual traditions held that Eve ate a pomegranate—blood-colored, grows in warm climates, full of seeds—or maybe a fig, softer and more fertile.

Warren stepped daintily around the question of how exactly his Adam and Eve had sinned. But there may be a clue in his ideas about the Tree of Knowledge, the Tree on which the forbidden fruit grew. If Warren's Tree was a sequoia, the forbidden knowledge probably didn't involve sex. The sequoia doesn't even have fruit; it has just small winged seedpods. Usually, the trees reproduce asexually, regenerating new sequoias out of the roots of old sequoias.

Still, whatever Adam and Eve's experiment with evil was, it must have been bad, because God immediately sent down a tsunami of wrath, drowning the Polar Paradise for eternity. Perhaps it's worth noting that sequoias are famously flood-resistant.

Not so the giant humans. Those few survivors fled, traumatized, southward toward dryer lands. Meanwhile, as the earth gradually cooled, the floodwaters froze, locking the Polar Paradise under miles of ice. There was something geometrically satisfying about humanity's peopling the Earth gradually from the north, as if God had cracked an egg on the top of the Earth, and then, slowly, the yolk ran down on all sides in wide, equal streams.

This took a long time. At first, the people's ears rang and they were disoriented. They wanted to stick together, but they were widely scattered by the deluge. In paradise, they'd had everything. They knew how to build carriages for transportation out of the abundant natural iron and brass. Now in the post-Flood tumult, all their scientific knowledge became confused. They had to use whatever they could find, which wasn't much. They had to walk. And because they were isolated, they began to lose the traditions and special knowledge they'd had before the flood. On the positive side, for a while at least, there were no wars: the survivors were too eager for companionship to turn against each other. But soon, things started to fall apart.

In the post-Flood world, man—who had been seven to twelve feet tall—became four to seven feet tall. Monotheism devolved into polytheism. Perfect friendship unraveled into bitter ethnic rivalries. Different ancient peoples degenerated in direct proportion to their noncompliance with God's laws. The more you sinned, the more savage and undeveloped you became. The closer you stayed to God's law, the more you'd be rewarded with steps toward regaining modernity—fire, the wheel, the steam engine, and finally the Bible.

Warren wasn't interested in finding the birthplace of man simply for its own sake. In the 1880s, all kinds of thinkers were trying to sort out the ethnic ancestry of the human race. Why was there such wide variation? Did one race evolve from another, or were the races created separately? A geographic location of Eden could also provide answers to much-discussed theological, ethnic, and scientific questions of the day. As Warren put it, "The problem of the original home of the human race is not [only] a question of Hebrew exegesis—it is a race-problem."

Warren's cracked-egg vision of the peopling of the world from the north left these different "races" scattered and isolated. He organized all the descendants of hyperborean Eocene man—Hindus, Persians, Greeks, Egyptians—into a hierarchy of worthiness based on the similarity of their present-day religious beliefs to those of Christianity. Belief in one God was a must. Prohibitions against idolatry, faith in salvation, and other Christian characteristics followed closely behind. Sometimes these rankings were surprising: the Chickasaw of Mississippi rated unexpectedly high on the civilization scale because they still retained a belief in one "Great Spirit" that was superior to their numerous other deities.

Other rankings followed a more traditional Anglocentric viewpoint. In an 1883 debate at Chautauqua, then a Methodist retreat center in northern New York, Warren and a colleague discussed the relative level of civilization of various peoples. As tersely reported in the *Washington Post*, "The vast antiquity of China was pronounced imaginary. The Anglo-Saxons were declared to be as ancient as any people." Warren's human-family tree had everyone descending from one universal ancestor, hardly a common assumption in the 1880s. The topic of his Chautauqua lecture was "The Unity of Man." Man *had* to come from one common, Christian ancestor. How could a Methodist missionary justify spreading the Word of Christ around the world without believing that he was reintroducing the natives of foreign lands to their ancestral faith?

Warren wanted to build a universal belief system based on Christian values or, as he would put it in the title of his 1892 book, *The Religions of the World and the World-Religion.* All the religions of the world could join, but everyone had to acknowledge the superior world-religion of Christianity, and the foundation of the world-religion had to be the Polar Eden. In 1885, after three years of spreading the word across the country, Warren published his masterwork: *Paradise Found! The Cradle of the Human Race at the North Pole.* It opens with a carefully redrawn world map: all the continents arrayed around the Arctic Circle, making the North Pole look like the bull's-eye in a giant world-target.

By the time *Paradise Found!* was released, there had been so many disastrous explorations, botched rescues, and inter-Army power squabbles over the seemingly futile search for the northernmost point on the globe that Congress, under the direction of Secretary of War Robert Todd Lincoln, was reluctant to fund any more trips there. It was time to sober up. Americans and Europeans agreed: it wasn't about planting a flag at the top of the world; it was about careful measurements and soundings and samplings. Out of their eminent reasonableness was born the International Polar Year: eleven nations pledged to build fifteen research stations above the Arctic Circle; the northernmost station was assigned to America. For this job Lincoln drafted Adolphus Greely, a tall, stoic Civil War vet who seemed least likely to become hotheaded at the prospect of national pride: he banned gambling, foul language, and Sunday frivolity from his ships. Greely and his twenty-five men had set off in 1881 for a two-year mission to the high Arctic. All of this had happened while *Paradise Found!* was still but a spark in Warren's brain. Now, as his masterwork was finally released to the public, no one had heard from the Greely party.

Unperturbed, Warren readied himself for the reviews. He knew his Polar theory would be ridiculed. And it was. "On the whole," mused an editorial in the *New York Times*, "if the Garden is at the North Pole it would not be worth while to find it." In fact, the discovery would be a net *loss* for humanity, because we would doubtless have to erect a monument to Adam in the center of the Garden, and committees would, for the next two centuries, solicit the public for building funds.

But Warren didn't care. Audacity was part of his point; it was right there in his preface. "Of late," he wrote, "it has required no small degree of courage to enable an intelligent man to stand up in the face of his generation and avow his personal faith in the early existence of men of gigantic stature and of almost millenarian longevity."

For those who weren't convinced by this brave personal testament of faith, Warren prepared a battery of facts. *Paradise Found!* positively reeked with academic authority. There were long passages in French, German, and ancient Greek in the footnotes. The index of "authors referred to or quoted" lists 580 sources—for 495 pages of text. Right next to Darwin is Ignatius Donnelly, who claimed that the lost island of Atlantis was real; it was destroyed by the near-collision of the Earth with a comet. His 1882 book *Atlantis* was wildly popular. (Donnelly had another theory—that Shakespeare's plays might actually have been written by Francis Bacon—but at the time that was considered too ridiculous to be taken seriously.) Some reviewers felt that the wanton citations did Warren's argument no favors, but many readers didn't seem to make such distinctions.

The second printing of *Paradise Found!* was released only a few months after the first, and Warren peppered it with numerous testimonials from people who agreed with his account. One was Mr. Alexander Skelton, a machinist and blacksmith of Paterson, New Jersey. As Warren wrote proudly, this "plain unschooled Bible student" had written an unsolicited testimonial in which he came up with his own argument for an Eden at the North Pole—and a "remarkably comprehensive and cogent" argument at that. And there was Professor Heer, a famous and haughty Swiss paleontologist who claimed Warren was plagiarizing *him*. Warren was especially proud of an endorsement from the British archaeologist Archibald Henry Sayce, who also happened to be an Anglican priest. At least, it was an endorsement of sorts: "Provisionally, I may say that your view seems to me eminently reasonable." (Sayce's words actually referred to an earlier work of Warren's, a comparative mythology text putting forward a new theory on the cosmology of Homer's *Iliad*. But they received prominent placement anyway.) Warren's theory was "rapidly superseding every earlier hypothesis" on both sides of the Atlantic—if Warren did say so himself.

So it was a matter of continuing frustration for him that other Eden theories continued to appear, as they had for centuries. A German archaeologist, Von Moritz Engel of Leipzig, had the gall to publish *The Solution to the Paradise Question* simultaneously with *Paradise Found!* Engel's Eden was an oasis in the desert outside Damascus. His four rivers were flood torrents that disappear in the dry season, come May or June. What was wrong with this? Well, for one thing, Warren sniffed, it was *ugly*. It was as if Mr. Engel had never even read Genesis, with its picture of abundance and plenty!

Engel's Eden was ethnocentric and narrow-minded. It was as if he had never even noticed that there were "myths of the Happy Garden" found in dozens of other ancient traditions! Worst of all, Engel's Eden was unscientific. Engel made no effort to incorporate "the facts and theories of ethnologists and zoologists as to the beginnings of human life."

According to a bemused Warren, Engel behaved as if the Eden story had "as little weight toward settling the question as to the primitive seat of the human race as the *Rime of the Ancient Mariner* might have in settling the question of the first discoverer of the Pacific Ocean." Ridiculous! Warren, on the other hand, knew the Bible's Eden to be an authoritative source of information about the origins of humanity—because God wrote it.

Warren found Engel's theory strange and entertaining. Ever the optimist, he was sure such reductive theories could never have the importance of his, which was universal, ecumenical, big-tent. "All attempts to solve the problem in this isolated and micro-topographical method are predestined to perpetual failure. The time for studies of such narrowness as this is past."

Meanwhile it had been four years since the Greely party set off, and still no word. Congress had sent a rescue mission, which couldn't make it through the Arctic ice and had to turn back before it could leave even a stash of food for Greely's men. Then Congress sent a second rescue mission, this time with two ships. One of them sank after colliding with Polar ice, and its surviving crew finally reunited with the second ship after a month of near misses in foggy harbors. By that time, it was too late in the season for the rescuers to make their way north to Greely. They, too, turned home, to face a congressional inquiry.

Finally, in the summer of 1884, Congress sent a third rescue mission, which managed to find what was left of the Greely expedition. Out of the twenty-five men in the original group, there were only six survivors, including Greely. For months, they'd been frozen into a sleeping bag in a collapsed tent on a windswept Arctic island, subsisting on shoe leather and, possibly, human flesh. They still hadn't reached the Pole. Congress decided it would not fund any more attempts to do so.

There was likewise a very good reason not to attempt a trip to Eden. In the third chapter of the Book of Genesis, God drives man out of Eden in no uncertain terms, and He bars any return: "He drove out the man; and at the east of the garden of Eden he placed the cherubim, and a sword flaming and turning to guard the way to the tree of life."

Some Eden seekers knew this. Columbus, like other Catholics, believed that there was no going back to an earthly paradise. He never ventured upriver to survey his Venezualan Eden. Instead he reported sadly to Ferdinand and Isabella that he could not claim Eden for Spain, because "no one can go [to the earthly Paradise] but by God's permission." Adam and Eve's defiance of God's order not to eat from the Tree of Knowledge of Good and Evil—original sin—could be redeemed, but only by selection as one of God's elect. If anyone happened to find the Garden of Eden, it would be highly presumptuous, if not dangerous, to walk right in.

For Protestants like Warren, however, the door to the Garden might be open a crack. Christ is sometimes referred to as a "second Adam," given to humanity by God specifically in order to undo Adam and Eve's transgression. If Adam's original sin can be undone by Christ's sacrifice, wouldn't the cherubim at the gates of Eden have to lower their swords and allow Christian believers back into the Garden?

Warren's enthusiasm for the North Pole was undiminished. The *New York Times, Atlantic Monthly, Washington Post*, and *Atlanta Constitution* all wrote dutifully detailed reviews of *Paradise Found!* And with every bit of notice the book received, Warren enhanced his status as a go-to expert on the North Pole. As the *Atlanta-Constitution* put it, Warren had "pre-empted a right to northern affairs."

Thus, for Warren, the existence of Eden became connected to the possibility of salvation. Because humanity was still imperfect, Eden had to be somewhere far away. Exactly *how* far away Eden was depended on your theology.

In order to be worth anything, salvation had to be difficult. Warren hailed the brave survivors of the Greely expedition in an appendix, calling their failed voyage "the grandest and most beneficent enterprise in which the Christian nations have for centuries, if indeed ever, engaged." Congress had given up on the North Pole, but Warren's readers hadn't. Houghton Mifflin reprinted *Paradise Found!* eight times in 1885 alone.

Salvation had to be possible, in order to give Christians hope. In 1888, Warren wrote an essay in the *Boston University Year Book* calling for the establishment of a permanent scientific research station at the northern magnetic pole—then thought to be a point on the globe of seventy-five degrees north, still on the North American continent. The United States should take up this great mission, wrote Warren, in honor of the four-hundredth anniversary of Columbus's discovery of the New World.

Columbus, the hapless explorer in awe of the supernaturally large rivers of South America, was Warren's hero, and "the sole supremely fitting commemoration of this hero's immortal explorations is to finish them." Such a station would be outfitted by a permanent congressional commission of scientific experts, including military and civil engineers.

Though Warren based his public argument about the North Pole strictly on science, some of his "unity of man" theology still sneaked through. The research station would represent "the unification of all existing seacoast lighting, weather reporting, high-sea survey-ing, ephemeris construction and the like, in one comprehensive international system, working everywhere in uniform methods." Warren clearly expected not a patch of ice, but a magical, electrical world still throbbing with the original life of the planet. He called for an electric generator, which could measure mysterious "polar pulses that predetermine storm and calm, and affect for good or ill whatever lies in earth or sea." It could report these pulses "daily, or, if necessary, hourly." And there might still be some relics of early man at seventy-five degrees north. The investigations, he wrote, "are almost certain to give us facts of inestimable value both to natural science and to archaeology." By 1891, a profile of Warren ("A Man You Ought to Know!") in the *Boston Tribune* claimed that "thousands" believed his North Pole theory.

Some gave Warren credit for a kind of liberalism—"a charming spirit of open-minded, frank inquiry." At least he was willing to *consider* evidence for theological matters outside the literal words of the Bible. For this, thought the *Atlantic Monthly*, "The naturalist will be glad to welcome the author as a man of science, however much he may question his use of the methods of the art." Mid-western reporters gave him grudging credit for being from Bos-ton, but not *of* Boston—that is, not as uptight as his Puritan city's reputation would have painted him. He *was* practically radical in his insistence that "primitive man" was actually more advanced than today's human race.

But actually, Warren was making a boldly medieval move back-ward. The phrase "hyperborean Eocene man" may sound like

science—one pictures an apelike Adam strolling through his sequoia garden on all fours, giving everything Latin names. But the
term is actually oxymoronic. The "hyperboreans" were ancestors
of the ancient Greeks, recorded in their myths, who came from a
realm "beyond the north wind." And "Eocene" is a geologic epoch,
part of the Cenozoic era, when major new mammals appeared.
Unfortunately for Warren, however, the first apes didn't appear on
earth until about 30 million years *after* the Eocene epoch. So there
were no Eocene men, hyperborean or not.

And the Adam and Eve of giant stature? This, too, was a much-
rehearsed idea in the Middle Ages. It explained how Adam and
Eve were able to step over oceans and mountain ranges on their
way down from Eden—in heaven—to Europe. Their legs were as
long as continents and their heads touched the sky. After all, if God
made Adam in his image, wouldn't Adam have to be as big as God?
Other theologians were more down-to-earth. Since Jesus Christ
was meant to be a "second Adam" sent to redeem us from original
sin, Adam would have to be only as tall as Jesus—about six feet.
Eve would be proportionally shorter, to match the height of the
Virgin Mary, about four feet six inches. In A.D. 900, the bishop of
Baghdad called all these theories "ridiculous."

None of this dissuaded Warren. He retired from the presidency
of Boston University and went back to teaching theology full-time,
but always with his eye on the Polar prize. With the government
out of the Polar exploration game, the private sector had had to
step in. In 1908, Commander Robert Peary set off toward the
Pole on his second expedition. The stakes were high: he had failed
once before and was running low on funds. He did receive many
offers of financial support—including two-cent royalties on film
footage, sponsorship of chocolate-dipped Triscuits, and a $4,000
advance on the story from the *New York Times*—but they were all
contingent on Peary's actually reaching the Pole.

The expedition began in typical style. Peary, whose feet had
long ago been frozen and amputated, strapped tin-can lids to the

stumps on the end of his legs to keep them from sticking to the dogsled on which he would remain for the entirety of the expedition. Then he and his party took off across treacherous terrain. They had to stop many times a day to hack their way through pressure ridges—cracks in the polar ice which, due to repeated heating and cooling, could build up to the height of a two-story house—or navigate "open leads," spaces of water that could appear and disappear unpredictably in the explorers' path.

Peary dropped off the rest of his twenty-three-man crew and continued northward with his black manservant, Matthew Henson, and several Inuit guides, and reached the North Pole, according to his accounts, on April 6, 1909. Upon his return to the United States, Peary found unexpectedly that he would have to defend his claim against that of another American explorer, Frederick Albert Cook. Since neither Cook nor Peary had thought he'd have to support his claim, both had kept spotty records. Peary's travel speeds logged after leaving the crew were three times that of the speeds they'd logged beforehand, and there's no reason to believe that those two-story pressure ridges or ever-shifting Arctic waterways they'd encountered earlier would have disappeared closer to the Pole. Nevertheless, Peary's lobbying efforts with, among others, the National Geographic Society, proved more successful than Cook's, and he was officially certified to have "attained" the North Pole.

Maybe it was the unseemly dispute over such claims, or maybe it was the fact that both Peary's and Cook's descriptions of the supposed Pole were completely unexciting, but Polar fever seemed to have died down. A 1912 editorial in the *Washington Post* cried anticlimax. Both poles had been found to be surrounded by ice—indistinguishable from all the other ice the many dozens of previous explorers had had to cross to get there. "The poles are tiresome spots ... and now that they are found it would be no great loss if they were to be lost again." No great loss, except, the editorial writer admits, for the supply of myths that could be smashed—a supply, he notes, that is "really seriously lessened" by the polar discoveries. No open sea, no land, no fossils, no magical world-mountain. Just ice.

Warren himself didn't actually think the Eocene garden would be found when explorers reached the North Pole. But one had to read 433 pages of *Paradise Found!* to realize this. On the last page before the numerous appendixes, Warren writes, "Long-lost Eden is found, but its gates are barred against us. Now, as at the beginning of our exile, a sword turns every way to keep the Way of the Tree of Life. Sadder yet, it is Eden no longer. Even could some new Columbus penetrate to the secret centre of this Wonderland of the Ages, he could but hurriedly kneel amid a frozen desolation and, dumb with a nameless awe, let fall a few hot tears above the buried and desolated hearthstone of Humanity's earliest and loveliest home."

The only comfort that could dry poor Columbus's tears was the closing chapter of the Book of Revelation, in which we are shown a glimpse of the paradise that is available to us if we accept the sacrifice of Christ. "Blessed are they that do his commandments, that they may have right to the tree of life." Follow Jesus in life, and in death you can walk right past the cherubim with their flaming swords.

But a dead Eden and the promise of a more perfect afterlife did not satisfy the itch for a living paradise. For those thousands who believed in a Polar Eden, and for others, future salvation did not fill in the map. An invisible paradise after death was too remote to be believed. And so, despite his best efforts to be the last word on the matter, Warren had actually inspired another generation of Eden seekers. Just as he had cited many other sources and experts, these new seekers cited Warren as authoritative backup for the other Eden claims, claims that continued to pop up, undeterred.

Dr. George C. Allen, a Boston University philologist, took his colleague Warren's word for it that Eden was at the North Pole. But he made one important modification. He claimed that the North Pole moves entirely around the world every 25,000 years, so "careful mathematical computations bring the original paradise where Ohio now is."

A three-part newspaper editorial, "Garden of Eden: Its Position on the Globe Has Been Definitely Located," explained that California's Santa Clara Valley had all the characteristics of Eden—pristine condition, perfect climate, and the giant sequoia. If Warren was so enthusiastic about the sequoia, the writer notes, why didn't he choose California? "In coming so near the truth it seems strange that the able scientific writer did not receive the true light as to the location of the original home of man."

Warren can't have been happy to find his work praised by Wyoming novelist Willis George Emerson, in the preface to his 1908 science fiction novel *The Smoky God*. The book claimed to be the true account of a Norwegian fisherman who in 1829 had fallen through a hole at the North Pole into the interior of the "Hollow Earth"—where the Garden of Eden was reachable by monorail. "In his carefully prepared volume, Mr. Warren almost stubbed his toe against the real truth, but missed it seemingly by only a hair's breadth." The idea of a "Hollow Earth" had been popularized in the 1840s by John Cleves Symmes, who believed one could gain access to the "inner Earth" through openings in the Earth's crust at the north and south poles. Warren, like most people, thought Symmes was crazy.

Even Warren's own Methodist colleagues seemed willing to give up on his vision of the perfect Polar paradise. They were content to stay in upstate New York. Said Reverend E. D. Ledyard in front of an audience of 5,000, after explaining that God could make a new Eden even more glorious than the first, "In Chautauqua we see one place where Edenic privileges have been restored. Christ is the central figure here. Through the second Adam paradise is being regained."

But Warren himself never gave up his original theory. He remained utterly, evangelically convinced of its veracity and universal utility. "Not one of its multitudinous converging lines of proof has been successfully assaulted. It has shed a blaze of light into some of the obscurest recesses in the history of human thought. It has solved some of the most hopeless riddles of well-nigh forgotten mythologies. It has shown itself the supreme and inevitable generalization from all the facts of modern knowledge respecting man and the world. It has harmonized the oldest traditions of religion and the latest achievements of science."

Thus it is perhaps no surprise that, on his passport application from 1903—he was taking his wife and daughters on a trip to Germany to celebrate his retirement—Warren's own height, noted as five feet six by the *Boston Tribune* in 1891, was unaccountably listed as six feet ten.

And during his paid retirement after thirty years as Boston University's president, Warren continued to try to win converts. In 1909, as Peary and Cook fought over a patch of ice, Warren sent a copy of the eleventh printing of *Paradise Found!* to a colleague at Union Theological Seminary with a note: "It rejoices me to learn that you take interest in ancient cosmology, for it is a study which has been unaccountably neglected. Last Thursday I started a new graduate class in the subject. Ought not your Seminary to have one?"

2

The Great Divide

IN THE BEGINNING, when the heavens had not been named,
and likewise the firm ground below, the primordial waters of
Tiamat mingled as a single body. So begins the *Enuma Elish,* the
creation myth of the Babylonians, first written down in southern
Mesopotamia nearly three millennia before the Bible. Does it
sound familiar? Friedrich Delitzsch thought so.

"May I lift the veil?" Delitzsch asked his audience. The trim fifty-
three-year-old scholar wore a carefully tailored suit with a broadly
striped tie. His hair was thinning, but he sported a large mustache.
It was January 1903, and Delitzsch was professor of Assyriology at
Berlin University, and a founding member of the German Oriental Society. He stood onstage at the Singakademie, the most
prestigious concert hall in Berlin, on Unter den Linden between
the Brandenburg Gate and the palace of Germany's redoubtable
emperor—Kaiser Wilhelm the Second.

The high-powered location was no accident. Delitzsch, sick of
analyzing the finds of French, English, and American explorers,
had been lobbying for Germany to "arouse herself and secure a
share" of the vast archaeological treasures available in Mesopotamia.
Finally he'd caught the ear of the kaiser, ruler of Germany—and
a major proponent of the bald-and-mustachioed look. The kaiser
had personally secured government funding for a 1902 expedition
to southern Iraq, exactly as Delitzsch had wanted. The expedition
had returned triumphantly just a few months before his lecture.
Among other miraculous relics, it had delivered to the kaiser pieces
of the Ishtar Gate, the forty-seven-foot-high entryway to the

city of Babylon, built for King Nebuchadnezzar of blue glazed tile—Nebuchadnezzar who was both a real Babylonian king and a central figure in the Old Testament. Appropriately, then, the kaiser had commissioned Professor Delitzsch to give three lectures on the topic "Babel and Bible," that is, the comparison of the words of the Christian holy book with the ancient Middle Eastern literature of Babylon, in southern Iraq.

The lecture at the Singakademie was the second of the three. The kaiser had responded so enthusiastically to Delitzsch's first lecture—given only for his Highness and a few selected friends— that he even stepped in to help the professor change the slides in the stereograph machine. For the second lecture, the kaiser sat far above the stage in the royal box, with his wife, Empress Augusta Viktoria; his personal chaplain; the minister of culture; the minister of public worship; and several other important Lutheran clergymen. He was eager to see what they—and his 400 subjects seated below him in the orchestra—thought of his new pet project.

Mesopotamian archaeology was hardly an idle hobby on the part of the kaiser. In 1903 the Ottoman Empire, which had controlled Mesopotamia for centuries, was crumbling, and European powers positioned themselves for maximum economic gain when the "sick man of Europe" should finally expire. And Berlin wanted in. The kaiser was already working with the Ottomans on a railroad line from Constantinople all the way to the southern port city of Basra, giving Berlin priceless Persian Gulf access. Anything that enhanced the public's interest in this part of the world—including this lecture—could only work in his political favor. At least, that's how the kaiser saw things.

Delitzsch, however, was delivering the "Babel and Bible" lectures for personal as much as political reasons. The son of a revered religious scholar, Delitzsch had chosen to go into the obscure discipline of Assyriology, and he had plenty to prove. He had radical ideas and a burning desire to get them out into the world. But until January 1903, no one had been listening. This lecture was his chance to show the public that many of their beloved Bible stories originated in the literature of the Babylonians, a "polytheistic cult" from "primitive" Mesopotamia.

The stage at the Singakademie was lit with limelight, an astoundingly bright white glow produced when a small cylinder of limestone was subjected to very hot flame.

"May I show you something?" Delitzsch asked. All over the nearly 5,000 acres of Mesopotamian swamps north of Basra, between the Tigris and Euphrates, stones about the size and shape of wine corks were turning up. Called cylinder seals, they were small enough to put in your pocket. Incised with images of Babylonian gods and heroes, they were designed to make an impression on wet Mesopotamian clay. Almost 5,000 years later, they still could. Delitzsch had rolled one across a slab of plaster, photographed the image it left, and enlarged this photograph so that it could be seen all the way to the back row of the Singakademie. That night, when the limelight was lit, he must have heard gasps from the balcony.

The audience saw two figures in profile, sitting facing each other: a figure with horns, presumably male, on the right, and a female figure on the left. Between them was a thin palm tree with three fronds on one side and four on the other, and then, a short way down the bare trunk, two symmetrical shapes that appeared to be dangling fruit. Both figures reached one hand downward, toward the fruit. And just behind the left elbow of the horned figure, stretching vertically in one dimension, was a snake.

Delitzsch didn't need to explain to his largely Lutheran audience that these shadowy figures resembled Adam and Eve, the Tree of Knowledge, and the serpent. He just let them look at the image for a moment and waited for the gasps to subside.

"Is it not the very *acme of likelihood* that there is some connection between this old Babylonian picture and the Biblical tale of the Fall of Man?"

Babylonian sources like the "Adam and Eve" tablet and the *Enuma Elish* had existed since approximately 3000 B.C. Scholars today generally agree that the earliest parts of the Bible were compiled from sources written down around 1,000 B.C, and that the Babylonian relics were 2,000 years older than the oldest version of the Bible. In 1903 Berlin, the seniority of Babel over Bible would have seemed even more dramatic. Before the discovery of the Dead Sea Scrolls in 1947, the oldest known copies of the Bible dated only back to A.D. 900.

The connections between Babel and Bible run deep. In 1835 English scholars first decoded the wedge-shaped hash marks covering thousands of clay slabs found in Mesopotamian digs. This alphabet, called cuneiform, is the world's oldest, shared for millennia by the Babylonians and their predecessors: the Assyrians and the Sumerians.

By 1903 museums in London, Paris, and Berlin held hundreds of clay tablets that quietly related uncanny parallels between Babylonian mythology and the Old Testament, or Hebrew Bible. In the *Epic of Gilgamesh,* the story of the flood takes up an entire chapter, and it's told with the intimate detail befitting people who lived between the two exceedingly flood-prone rivers of Mesopotamia. God decides (or rather, several gods decide) to flood the world, but one man—Ziusudra—survives, in a boat, with family and animals. After a while he sends out several birds, and when they don't come back, he knows the flood is over.

The Biblical Tower of Babel exactly echoes the spiral-shaped Babylonian temples called ziggurats, the tallest obstructions on the flat Mesopotamian skyline, built to honor the goddess Innanna. The legend of Moses's birth—and his rescue from a basket in the river—was told about the Mesopotamian king Sargon, who ruled 1,000 years before Moses was supposed to have been born. In the law codes of the Babylonian king Hammurabi, echoes of the Ten Commandments and other Biblical laws are rampant: Babylonians were also forbidden to commit murder, adultery, and theft. In fact, according to Delitzsch, the Babylonians prohibited these universal evils "in precisely the same order as they are given in the Fifth, Sixth, and Seventh Commandments of the Old Testament."

Scholars had known all this for decades. But until Delitzsch, no one was willing to tackle the religious implications of the connections between Babel and Bible, especially not in public. What did it mean that such similarities could be found in material centuries older than the earliest known copies of the Bible? For Delitzsch, there was only one answer: the Bible was not the Word of God.

"Who would dream of asserting that the laws of Babylon were of Divine origin? Just as the Babylonian laws are of human origin, so are those of Moses."

This was a problem. Many people in Delitzsch's audience believed that the Bible was the revealed Word of God, transmitted directly from Him to Moses. Every word of it came directly from God to his people—the Jews, and later, Christians. And God most certainly did *not* get His material from the primitive, polytheist Babylonians.

Delitzsch was impatient with anyone who still believed in the revealed Word of God or, as he called it, "the greatest mistake of the human mind." According to him, science had long ago demonstrated that the Bible evolved over time through "constant reconstruction and adaptation of entirely heterogeneous literary elements." That is, the Bible was a product of human history. It was time for Christians to modernize and move on.

"The walls that formed the impenetrable background to the scenes of the Old Testament have suddenly fallen and a keen invigorating air and a flood of light from the Orient pervades and irradiates the hoary book." But here Delitzsch hit a wall. German Christians did not want their Old Testament to be pervaded by Oriental light. They didn't want to wrap their canon of Bible characters around the unfamiliar consonants of Marduk, Ziusudra, and Gilgamesh. And they fought back.

The day after Delitzsch's lecture, the press had a field day: "Book of Moses Held Plagiarism! Story of Nebuchadnezzar Is Declared a Myth! Kaiser, by Patronizing Radical Views, Shocks Church People." A cartoon showed Delitzsch on the witness stand in a courtroom, facing off against Moses. With his right hand he points to a line on the stone tablets from Mount Sinai, with his left he points to the corresponding line in a Babylonian book in front of him. The expression under his mustache is calm, even stoic, and he's shrugging his shoulders. Moses—a giant stone statue who bore, it must be said, a striking resemblance to Poseidon—looks personally offended. Moses's clergyman counsel points a finger straight up overhead and rails, "I'd like to call a witness from above!"

A Jewish organization threatened to protest—this was their holy scripture, too. But that didn't seem to matter. In another cartoon two elderly Jewish men, distinguishable by their long beards and sidelocks, trudge through the snow carrying parcels on their backs. One says to the other, "Hey, Joel, did you hear what the Kaiser said about the Babel-Bible controversy? He said it wouldn't hurt God's Chosen People, because most of our holy traditions have disappeared already."

Delitzsch's clay picture of Adam and Eve seemed to his audience like a crude rip-off of the image of Eden they already had impressed on their imagination, an image like Albrecht Dürer's beloved 1504 engraving *Adam and Eve (The Fall of Man)*. In Dürer's image, too, there's a tree in the center, with dangling fruit. Again, Adam stands to the right of the tree, Eve to the left. (Women were always on the left, the side of evil.)

But that's where the similarity ends. Whereas the Babylonian Adam and Eve are flat, isolated figures against a blank background, Dürer's engraving—a new art form created by etching thousands of tiny lines in a steel plate—is remarkable for its abundant European detail. Adam and Eve stand symmetrically in familiar classical positions: weight shifted to one side, opposite knee slightly bent, arms reaching up and out heroically. Their pale, gently muscled flesh makes them seem to leap forward out of the dense foliage of the Garden behind them. Their heads, covered in flowing, curly hair, are one-eighth of their total height. This proportion was based on the Renaissance sculpture Dürer had studied in Italy the year before, which in turn was based on idealized forms from ancient Greece and Rome. Adam as Apollo and Eve as Venus. Between them is the Tree of Knowledge, a spindly fig tree laden with fruit.

Twined around the tree is the serpent, about to drop the fig in his jaws into Eve's outstretched hand. (She's already got one fig hidden behind her back.) Adam also has one hand outstretched, but there is a confused look on his perfectly proportioned face. With his other hand he grasps a branch of the Tree of Life—a mountain ash, which grows only in the colder parts of the northern hemisphere.

Arrayed around Adam's and Eve's feet are four animals representing the medieval idea of the four humors. As legend goes, before Adam and Eve ate from the fig of knowledge, these four essential human qualities were held in balance. After original sin, everything fell apart. Dürer has captured the moment right before the Fall: the choleric cat prepares to attack a mouse; the sanguine rabbit stares down the phlegmatic ox; the melancholic elk lurks in the undergrowth behind the fig tree.

In order for the Christian idea of original sin to mean anything, the punishment—being kicked out of the Garden of Eden—has to be a huge loss. Eden must be perfection, plenty, paradise; it has to contain "every tree that is good for food and pleasant to the eye." And paradise is always on the brink of destruction: one false step, one sin, and everything goes to hell. This was the foundation of the world that Germany's orthodox Lutherans lived in, a world held together by the fear of sin.

The ancient Babylonians had very different ideas of sin. In their precursor to the story of the Flood, the gods flooded the world not because of some major moral failing on man's part, but simply because man was making too much noise for the gods to get their sleep. In the Babylonian tablet, the serpent—the instigator of the Fall, the most potent of all the symbols in the Eden story—exists simply as a vertical squiggly line.

In Dürer's engraving, you can see the pattern of the snake's scales, the evil expression on its tiny face, and the four mysterious spikes coming out of its head. These spikes are said to represent the four nails used to crucify Christ—planting the seeds of the New Testament in the Old. Even as humans are being offered the temptation of sin, their redemption is in store through the sacrifice of Christ, the second Adam. Without original sin, what is Christ's sacrifice for? And without Christ's sacrifice, where's the hope for human redemption? Without the Old Testament, the New Testament would just be so many empty words.

You can't see any of this temptation, redemption, or sacrifice in a squiggly line sketched in primitive clay. All this was playing itself out in the minds of Delitzsch's audience. *Those primitives didn't even believe in the one true God, let alone the New Testament, so how could their moral fabric be cut from the same cloth as Christianity?* How could Delitzsch remove all that was sacred about this story and still call it the Bible? Behind the indignation there was an even more alarming question—what if Delitzsch was right? If the story of the Fall wasn't original, how could it be sacred? If Adam and Eve were just products of human history, what was the point of Christian living?

But Delitzsch didn't care about the religious sensitivity of his audience. He had confidence in his conclusions; he had the backing of the emperor—why should he worry about what anyone thought? Indignant Lutherans found the wunderkind Assyriologist unapologetic, so they turned on his sponsor, the kaiser, who was already known to be susceptible to unfortunate influences, and somewhat inept. (According to legend, after admiring the ball gown of a visiting European dignitary, the emperor tried his hand at designing his own. When he presented his sketches to Empress Augusta, she pointed out that he had neglected to provide a way into or out of the dress.) The week after the lecture, another cartoon showed the kaiser rushing down his royal stairs past a confused butler, who asks, "Hey, sir, what's the hurry?"

"Don't bother me—I have urgent official business. I have to send a telegram."

"To who?"

"To King Nebuchadnezzar in Babylon. To thank him for his help writing the Five Books of Moses!"

A member of Parliament railed against Kaiser Wilhelm for throwing his support behind an "advanced thinker" instead of Lutheran orthodoxy. Others reminded the kaiser that, as the monarch, he was also Supreme Bishop of the National Protestant Church. What right did Delitzsch have to the limelight, when representatives of the Orthodox party complained to the *New York Times* Berlin correspondent that they received erratic favor "like the flashlight of a signal lamp"?

Delitzsch didn't pay much attention to the controversy at first. He had the public exactly where he wanted it. The veil between Babel and Bible had finally been lifted. And, maybe most important, he had finally stepped out of his father's shadow. This was the moment he'd been waiting for most of his life.

Delitzsch's father, Franz, whom the *New York Times* called "one of the most famous Professors of Hebrew in the world," taught in the department of Semitic studies at the University of Leipzig. His professional warmth was legendary; his opinions were prized. Born to impoverished Jewish parents, Franz Delitzsch studied Hebrew and Jewish literature, but a friend converted him to Lutheranism in his youth, and he had put his all into the new faith. His son Friedrich, born in 1850, received an orthodox religious Lutheran education, with all the zeal of his father's enthusiastic new Christianity.

And it was good—until young Friedrich went to university. In a course on the Biblical Book of Deuteronomy, one of his professors expressed what was then a radical view: that Deuteronomy was not actually written by Moses, but by a whole group of writers in the sixth century B.C. Stunned, young Delitzsch blurted out, "Then Deuteronomy is a falsification!" Said the poor professor: "For God's sake! That may be true, but one must not say such a thing." At that time, professors could still be charged with heresy, so even the more progressive Biblical scholars had to tiptoe around certain big issues. Delitzsch kept quiet for a while, trying to behave like a dutiful scholar and son. He received a doctorate in Sanskrit, and, at the young age of twenty-seven, became a full professor in the same department as his father—Semitic studies at the University of Leipzig.

But next to his father, there was no room for Friedrich to shine. Franz Delitzsch was known as the "Christian Talmudist"; Franz's translation of the New Testament from German *into* Hebrew was the unquestioned standard (it still is, a century later). So Friedrich lit out for new territory in which to prove his worth: Assyriology—a brand-new discipline combining archaeology, history, and the ancient languages of Assyria, Sumer, and Babylon. Assyriology was so new, in fact, that William Warren, who relied on all kinds of little-known lore to prove that Eden had existed at the North Pole, found the discipline and its translations "obscure" and unreliable.

At age thirty-one, in 1881, Friedrich Delitzsch published his first book: *Where Was Paradise?* Note the past tense: this is not a here-and-now question. Strictly of historical interest, strictly distanced, strictly scientific. By 1881, the problem of Eden's location had been solved so often and so variously by reputable scholars that the topic exasperated critics and readers alike, including Delitzsch's father, Franz.

Franz Delitzsch was on the record with his opinion about Eden. He thought Eden could not be found on Earth; the closest we could get would be Josephus's vague medieval idea of the Four Great Rivers—which put Eden precisely nowhere. Friedrich Delitzsch wasn't deterred by such nonsense. He'd show Dad. He'd address the classic theological problem using the new science. And Delitzsch didn't go halfway. He dove right into the thick of the most contested and confused area of study: Mesopotamia.

Eden seekers of all stripes had, especially since Calvin, looked to this region, for the obvious reason that the Bible mentions the Tigris and the Euphrates—the two rivers that give Mesopotamia its Greek name, meaning "land between the rivers." (Delitzsch liked to use the particularly descriptive German term "Zwillingstromland" instead.) But two rivers were not enough. Scholars scrutinizing the map of Mesopotamia for the geography of Genesis always got stuck on the other pair of rivers: the ever-mysterious Pishon and Gihon.

Delitzsch approached the centuries-old problem in a sauntering, mock-casual tone. "It seems appropriate . . . that we at least passably remove this bone of contention. This does not appear difficult." All those laboring religious scholars could be put out of business by rational, modern Assyriology.

"Why must Pishon and Gihon be rivers in the manner of the Tigris and the Euphrates?" In German, like English, there is a word for "river" and one for "canal." But in Babylonian and Hebrew, the word "nahar" stands for both, and ancient canals were being discovered all over the place in Mesopotamia. The parting of the stream of Paradise into four branches obviously refers to irrigation. Obviously. The Pishon and the Gihon must be *man-made irrigation canals*. Here Delitzsch briefly lost his cool; the phrase is printed in bold type. But that's it. Whereas William Warren was flamboyant, making his North Pole Eden a declaration of personal faith, Delitzsch preferred simplicity, logic, and evidence.

Delitzsch said he could prove that the rivers of paradise were actually canals, particularly with his translation of a 4,000-year-old list of rivers, which actually included several canals. And there was another example of a river-canal in the Bible. The Hebrew prophet Ezekiel had his vision on the banks of the "Chebar canal" while he was exiled in Babylon.

In Genesis, the river Pishon "is the one that flows around the whole land of Havilah, where there is gold." Delitzsch identified the Pishon with a canal that had for millennia run west of the Euphrates, past the ancient city of Babylon (about eighty-five miles south of Baghdad), and south into the Persian Gulf. "Havilah" corresponded to a region of desert whose Arabic name meant "land of dunes," which was close enough to the meaning of "Havilah" in Hebrew, "the sandy." According to cuneiform inscriptions, gold was found just northeast of this desert.

The Gihon, according to Delitzsch, was just another canal that ran east of the Euphrates, parallel to the Pishon canal. The Bible says the Gihon is "the one that flows around the whole land of Cush." Medieval scholars had identified it with Ethiopia, but Delitzsch insisted it matched the borders of the land of "Kassu," a central Mesopotamian kingdom mentioned in ancient inscriptions.

The one river that watered Eden was the middle branch of the Euphrates, as it flowed south. All of these Babylonian connections and conjectures transformed the four rivers of Paradise into one river, a river branch, and two canals. And Paradise was the rectangular district of land between Babylon and Baghdad, from the Tigris to the Euphrates.

Delitzsch admitted that this swath of marshy lowland was no longer anything special. In 1881, Eden was technically just an impoverished province of the Ottoman Empire, though European treasure hunters and archaeologists were everywhere making deals with Ottoman and Persian authorities to dig up the mounds of sandstone that rose "weatherbeaten, grave, and silent . . . from the lonely and lifeless desert."

But it wasn't always so; the Mesopotamian swamps used to be beautiful. At least, the Babylonians who called them home thought so. Like all his conclusions, Delitzsch's assessment of Eden's beauty is somewhat underwhelming, based as it is on translations of ancient cuneiform texts. According to Delitzsch, the Babylonians called this region "Kar-Dunias," meaning "the grove of the god Dunias." And the Hebrew word "Eden," speculated Delitzsch, might be a "phonetic imitation" of the Babylonian word "edin," which means not "paradise" but "plain"—the geographic term applied to the flatland between the rivers.

There was one large problem with Delitzsch's theory: canals are man-made. And how could he claim that something man-made had been in existence before God made man? Before God kicked Adam and Eve out of Eden, there was no labor at all, let alone the kind of complex engineering necessary to design and build a major irrigation system. Besides, if Eden was the oldest thing in the world, how could canals pre-exist it?

To answer this seemingly harmless question, Delitzsch took a radical leap. His conclusion: Eden *wasn't* the oldest place in the world, and it wasn't made by God. It was just a place in the middle of the desert that had once, millennia ago, inspired a Babylonian to tell a story. Twenty years before he stood onstage at the Singakademie and declared the entire Bible to be human, not divine, he had said the same thing about the Four Rivers of Paradise.

In 1881, excited by the magnitude—and newness—of this theory, Delitzsch set about trying to conquer every objection that stood in his way, to separate the geographic from the theological. First he stripped out all the later Christian lore. Eden had not been destroyed by Noah's Flood: the Flood was a myth, not history. Eden was not guarded by two angels wielding swords, and you didn't need God's permission to get back in, as Columbus seemed to think. No apples grew anywhere near Eden. Apples came from Central Asia, thousands of miles east of Babylon. Any special fertility or abundance that might have been attached to Eden by the Babylonians was only relative: compared with the desolate desert surrounding Babylonia, the swampy area between the rivers might have appeared to be a lush garden.

Delitzsch tackled this project as if it was the solution to all the problems of Assyriology. He added more and more of Eden to the "Babel" category, until almost nothing was left in the "Bible" category. One can almost hear Delitzsch's old professor in Leipzig shushing him, in vain.

The Babylonians, Delitzsch wrote, even had a Tree of Life and a Tree of Knowledge of Good and Evil. And they were two different species of trees. The holy Tree of Life appeared on cylinder seals and temple walls; the species is not entirely clear—it may be a pine or a cypress, but it's definitely an evergreen, since it's often depicted with needles and seed cones.

But the Tree of Knowledge, as shown on the famous "Adam and Eve" cylinder seal, was certainly not evergreen, since it had fruit large enough for the male and female figures on either side of it to reach for. (The tablet caused so much trouble onstage at the Singakademie that it might seem safe to assume this was a new discovery in 1903. Actually, the tiny clay tablet had been languishing in the British Museum in 1881, safely out of reach of the German religious public.) This Tree of Knowledge was clearly some kind of palm tree, which to Delitzsch made much more sense than the traditional fig tree of Dürer's Eden.

Delitzsch dismissed the fig tree of knowledge out of hand. Anyone who's ever seen a fig tree, he wrote, knows that the leaves are far too small to sew together to cover oneself, as legend has it Adam and Eve did after the Fall. No, if they were smart, and of course we hope that they were, the Babylonian Adam and Eve would have selected leaves like those of the banana tree, which can be up to ten feet long. Delitzsch didn't go so far as to say the fruit of temptation was a banana, only that it must have been something growing on a long-leaved palm—possibly a date palm, which grew everywhere along the shores of the Tigris and the Euphrates.

Delitzsch's Eden was an anticlimactic collage: two people might have eaten fruit from a palm tree in a well-watered spot in lower Mesopotamia between the Tigris and Euphrates, and they didn't eat from the pine tree. This Eden was fairly plain.

But that was OK with Delitzsch; in fact, that was the point. He had tried to divorce a Christian Paradise from a Babylonian Eden—to publicly sever the Babylonian idea of a garden near the Tigris and Euphrates from the Christian ideas of perfection and original sin. He felt that the world needed to be set straight before it could move on to its bright, modern future.

But in 1881, Delitzsch failed. It was a radical surgery, and it didn't take. Everywhere he looked, religion and reality remained all tangled up together. He was expecting a thunderous ripping sound, and he heard only silence—or even worse, denial. Religious scholars actually liked his Bible-blasting book! In 1882 in a review of *Where Was Paradise?* in the *Chicago Daily Tribune,* Reverend Charles H. H. Wright—an American—declared, "The geographical correctness of the writer of Genesis has been clearly demonstrated." How could this be? Sure, Wright knew that Delitzsch believed two of the rivers of paradise are canals, but this didn't trouble the man of the cloth. For him, the four rivers of paradise were "large water-courses, afterward transformed into canals, but which seem originally to have been natural arms of the Euphrates." Wright would put heaven and earth back together: rivers, canals—same thing.

The urge to keep the Bible special, pure, and unaccountable to scientific rules was not limited to clergymen. In a long and diligent summary of Delitzsch's book published in the *Nation,* the author, believed to be the distinguished older German scholar Theodor Nöldeke, presented a barrage of questions that "militate too strongly against Professor Delitzsch's solution." "Why, if the streams of Eden be the middle Euphrates, is it left unnamed in the narrative, though it is certain that the Hebrews were perfectly familiar both with the middle and the upper course of that river?"

The reviewer neglected to realize that if the Hebrews were getting their Eden geography from older tales of the Babylonians, as Delitzsch had attempted to prove, it didn't matter whether or not the Hebrews themselves knew about the whole course of the Euphrates. Quarreling with the geography of an adapted legend would be like insisting that Santa Claus can't live at the North Pole, because he is not an Inuit. It's beside the point. But the reviewer kept going along these lines.

"Why, if the Pishon and Gihon designate canals, are they said in the Bible to flow 'all around' lands which Delitzsch's canals only passed straight through?" Again, requiring all four rivers or canals to actually *circle* the whole land they are associated with, something that no river in this part of the world does, stems from a misunderstanding of Delitzsch's whole point. No one wanted to buy Delitzsch's idea that much of the Old Testament was based on Babylonian myth. Critics preferred to keep refuting his arguments on their old terms, and ignoring his new ones.

Sure that he had taken down Delitzsch's argument, Nöldeke ended with a backhanded compliment: "We have no hesitation in saying that his dissertation is . . . probably the most brilliant production in all Biblico-Assyriological literature." Better luck next time, Junior.

Even William Warren—advocate of prehistoric giant men at the North Pole, collector of obscure Hindu and Celtic mythology, believer in Atlantis and in the Sequoia of Knowledge—thought

Friedrich Delitzsch was full of hot air. We might say *especially* William Warren. In *Paradise Found: The Cradle of the Human Race,* Warren did pause briefly to pay his respects to Delitzsch, among his hundreds of other sources, probably out of respect for Delitzsch's theologian father. Delitzsch's Eden theory, wrote Warren, was "advanced with great confidence and supported with remarkable acuteness and learning." Then Warren dismissed young Delitzsch's carefully supported theory as not credible. "Despite the conceded ability of the plea, there seems at present little prospect that it will secure acceptance among scholars." (Ironically, he was right. Delitzsch wasn't securing acceptance anywhere.)

Warren didn't stop to notice that this was not a simple geographic debate: North Pole or Mesopotamia? It wasn't even a theological debate: Eden as paradise lost or Eden as paradise never had? It was a fundamental disagreement about the nature of the world. Warren took for granted that the "Paradise" of the Bible would turn out to be the same place as the actual, biological "cradle of the human race." The creation myth from Genesis and the scientific story of the origin of the Earth were the same. Delitzsch knew the two had to be separated.

The Old Testament, said Delitzsch, was magisterial, inspiring, essential, but it was *not* science, or history. The Babylonians had both literature and science—including an advanced astronomical system—and they kept the two separate. They treated the science as fact, and the stories as myth, revising, editing, and retelling them over many centuries. If the originators of the stories could tell the difference between science and mythology, we who inherited these stories millennia later had to accept that the Bible could not possibly be used as a guide to the real world. All attempts to "harmonize" the creation story with the results of natural science "are and will forever remain absolutely futile." Alas, even with Assyriology at his command, Delitzsch was apparently powerless to stop this gross misunderstanding. He couldn't keep Warren or anyone else from harmonizing and mingling, denying both religion and science their separate due.

Perhaps the most blatant example of this confusion of biological origins with Biblical events was the strange case of the anthropologist Henry W. Seton-Karr. In 1896, Seton-Karr found, scattered across the Somali desert, a cache of stone tools that he believed to be from the very oldest humans. According to a colleague in the peer-reviewed *Journal of the Anthropological Institute of Great Britain*, the stone implements were certainly of a "very great antiquity." Maybe that's what inspired Seton-Karr to make an ill-advised announcement the following spring. This serious anthropologist claimed publicly that his finds were "from the original Garden of Eden."

But the idea that "the Garden of Eden" could be in Africa was considered ridiculous. The *New York Times* called upon Harvard professor D. G. Lyon for a professional rebuttal. Lyon, as the *Times* put it, "was much inclined to treat the subject jocosely." The eminent scholar remarked, "I shall not think that Adam ever used those bludgeons unless he can show a photograph of Eve knocking the apple down with one of them." But the professor wasn't ridiculing the very idea of finding evidence of Eden.

No—after he stopped laughing jocosely, Lyon offered his considered opinion on the *real* location of the Garden. "If any one will read the first ten chapters of Genesis, I think the idea will be fixed that Eden must have been in Western Asia. . . . There ought to be some grand discoveries some time in Palestine and the vicinity of the Holy Land." It would be difficult to say who was more confused. Seton-Karr assumed that the Garden of Eden was a legitimate description of human origins. And D. G. Lyon thought that science could exhume Eden—just not in Africa. (Seton-Karr, possibly disappointed that he could be dismissed so easily from archaeology, went back to his other favorite African pastime: hunting big game. The 1974 discovery of the *Australopithecus* skeleton known as "Lucy" in Ethiopia, only a couple of hundred miles to the west of Seton-Karr's Somali stone tools, came too late to vindicate him.)

Delitzsch, unlike Seton-Karr, was far too stubborn to give up his insistence on separating religion and science in the face of public dismissal. So, what was a revolutionary to do? He took on a figurative partner, allying himself with another German Biblical movement called higher criticism. Its founder, Julius Wellhausen, argued that the part of the Old Testament known as the "Five Books of Moses" was actually compiled from four independent texts. He created a system for identifying and dating these original pieces, which he called J, E, D, and P after the different Hebrew names of God found in each of them. Wellhausen's method is still highly influential in modern literary studies of the Bible.

He proceeded to slice the Bible into smaller and smaller pieces, enraging the previous generation of critics, not to mention religious believers and clergymen, including Delitzsch's father, Franz. But Friedrich was not enraged; he immediately recognized a kindred spirit. He called Wellhausen's new science a "branch of inquiry which seeks to increase and clarify our knowledge of the many diversified sources of which the five books of Moses are composed." Like Delitzsch, the higher critics believed in treating the Bible as a product of human history, in radical contrast with the treatment of the Bible as the infallible Word of God. But their argument was sharper. Reading Wellhausen, Delitzsch realized that he had been too polite, too cautious in *Where Was Paradise?*.

By the time of his 1903 lectures, though, Delitzsch had his country's ear, his emperor's support, and vast Mesopotamian wealth amassed for Germany's treasury—*now* he could make the case he had started in 1881 in his first book. He stood in the limelight, took hold of the knife, and dissected the Bible in terms of Babel. This time, it worked. Delitzsch got the kind of incensed reaction he'd expected twenty years earlier after *Where Was Paradise?*.

The first two lectures on "Babel and Bible" were quickly translated into English, and published in London, Chicago, and New York to great hubbub. Doctor T. W. Goodspeed of the University of Chicago called Delitzsch a "representative of the extreme school of deconstructive critics," and his ideas, nonsense. "It is all bosh, and it is strange that any man who considers himself well-educated should say that the ancient Assyrians had higher ideals of morality than the people of Israel." This was a slight mischaracterization of Delitzsch's argument. He wouldn't have called Assyrian morality "higher," but he did believe that the ancient Israelites got many of their concepts from the earlier civilization. Nevertheless, Dr. Goodspeed's disapproval stuck.

A Professor Koeberle claimed that "notwithstanding a certain external agreement" between the Babylonian and Old Testament accounts of the creation and flood, the Old Testament actually contradicts the Babylonian narrative. "The Bible is not only independent of Babel but goes beyond Babel and antagonizes Babel." Delitzsch, Koeberle declared, "stands almost alone in many of his conclusions." The more the world pushed back at Delitzsch, the more solid he became in response. His Babylonian tablets were "facts which from the point of view of science are as immutable as rock, however stubbornly people on both sides of the Atlantic may close their eyes to them."

Delitzsch had planned an American lecture tour, but three weeks after his calamitous appearance at the Singakademie, he announced that he would not take his show on the road, "owing to ill health." (He did eventually make it to New York several years later, where he lectured to sold-out crowds at the Academy of Medicine and the Horace Mann School on 120th Street and Broadway. The sponsors had to turn away 200 latecomers eager to see the professor who'd given the German emperor such headaches. The fact that Delitzsch gave lectures only in German seemed to make his presentation all the more novel.)

A month after the Singakademie lecture, on February 19, 1903, the chaos already christened the "Babel-Bible controversy" was raging. Delitzsch was still commissioned to give a third lecture in Berlin, but no one knew when that would happen. The kaiser was under mounting pressure to divorce himself from Delitzsch's ideas. When he did so, he didn't go halfway. In a letter to the president of the German Oriental Society, enthusiastically republished in Berlin newspapers, he urgently advised Delitzsch to proceed cautiously. He accused his former friend of knowingly destroying the "innermost, holiest possession" of his audiences—their faith. Hereafter, proclaimed the kaiser, Delitzsch was to "ventilate his theses" only among his university colleagues. "Spare us laymen and above all the Oriental Society from hearing of them!" Stick to the excavations and the science, please.

And in case there was any doubt: he the Emperor believed in God, and believed that human beings needed the Bible as a form to teach His existence, "especially for our children." But he was not going to stand in the way of progress. "The present version of [the Bible] will be possibly and substantially modified under the influence of research through inscriptions and excavations. *That does not matter.* Religion has never been the result of science, but the pouring out of the heart and being of man from intercourse with God." The kaiser was so taken with his own letter that three weeks later he presented copies of it to both the Catholic and the Protestant chaplains of the navy.

Delitzsch must have been puzzled. Of course he agreed with the kaiser that religion was *not* the result of science; his lecture at the Singakademie was the culmination of a long struggle to separate the two. But he was also angry; he did not want to ventilate his theses among his university colleagues. He wanted to "burst the barriers of the scholar's study and enter the broad path of life." Assyriology was the field of the future: the Bible investigated with cold hard facts on the ground.

At first, Delitzsch had seemed willing to wait for the public to come around to his perspective. He reminded his readers, and himself, that great minds (even Luther) had "contemptuously rejected" the Copernican system of astronomy when it was introduced in 1543. (Luther wrote of Copernicus: "The fool wants to turn the whole art of astronomy upside-down. However, as Holy Scripture tells us, so did Joshua bid the sun to stand still and not the Earth.")

43

It took at least a century for the Earth to lose its place at the center of the universe. So, Delitzsch reasoned, it would take a long time for the public to recognize that the Bible is a product of human history, to separate the heavens from the Earth.

But after the release of the kaiser's letter to newspapers across Germany, Delitzsch was reportedly "smarting" under his former patron's criticism. He lost his patience, and went on the defensive. He told the newspapers: "His Majesty, like myself, is not an orthodox Christian. His views are almost the same as mine. To his statement that I should not have discussed religion before the laity, my reply is that my audience consisted of intellectual, highly cultured men. The educated people of the whole world are now fully prepared for new scientific knowledge when it is presented to them in proper form." And, no, Delitzsch said wearily, he was not an atheist.

To make matters worse, a fellow Berlin Assyriologist, Delitzsch's own former student Dr. Hilprecht, came out publicly in favor of the kaiser's point of view. According to the *New York Times,* he said "that the Semitic religion never came from the decaying polytheistic culture of the Babylonians." Delitzsch was infuriated by this personal betrayal, and sought to ruin Hilprecht's reputation among his colleagues in Berlin.

He had not intended to give his final "Babel–Bible" lecture, in Berlin, until the fall, but in February, reported the *Chicago Tribune,* Delitzsch had "resolved to deliver another lecture [in Berlin] as soon as possible, with the intention of making it a counterblast to the emperor's remarkable attack."

He may have been preparing a "counterblast" in public, but in person, Delitzsch seems to have realized that attacks would get him nowhere against such a powerful enemy. Instead, he tried to extend an olive branch. Delitzsch attended a dinner given by Chancellor von Bülow. The kaiser was also in attendance, and he approached the renegade scholar. "My dear professor, we have broken a lance with each other." The newspapers reported Delitzsch's witty response. "Only one lance, your Majesty." That is to say: I may have fallen out of *your* favor, Kaiser, but you never fell out of mine.

Delitzsch's position was heavy with irony: in order to make his radical separation of religion and science, he had to stick close by the person in power. Without the kaiser's protection, it was lonely being out on a limb.

There was only one sure way to win back the attention of the famously fickle monarch. As expressed by Rabbi Kohler, president of Hebrew Union College in Cincinnati, in the summer of 1903, "It is the characteristic sign of the times that any professor or writer in Germany that craves popularity to-day needs but to blow the horn of anti-Semitism to receive the favor of high and low."

Delitzsch participated in the zeitgeist all too enthusiastically. He made it his mission to take the "Hebrew" out of "Hebrew Bible" and to baptize the Babylonians as Germany's true ancestors. Never mind that he was the son of the greatest Hebrew scholar Germany had produced; never mind that he himself had Jewish blood; the kaiser's patronage was more important. Fortunately Delitzsch's father, the Hebrew expert, was not alive to see this last regrettable development. In another of his efforts to upgrade and modernize everything that his father stood for, Friedrich Delitzsch took his own anti-Semitism on the fast track. Delitzsch began to use the new science of archaeology to show that Germans—blond, blue-eyed Germans—were the most advanced civilization on Earth. In the faded gray of the clay tablets, Delitzsch divined that a certain figure "was apparently a princess of Aryan blood with blond hair." Few would see it so.

He believed not only that the Babylonians were the originators of the Bible, but also that Babylonian literature was "purer" than the Bible itself because it hadn't yet been corrupted by anything Semitic, Hebrew, Israelitish—in short, anything Jewish.

According to Rabbi Kohler, theoretical anti-Semitism like this had actual consequences. He laid the blame for the bloody anti-Jewish riots in Kishinev in May 1903—in which local authorities promised Jews protection and then allowed the massacre to occur anyway—directly at the feet of Delitzsch, the "ultra-conservative . . . despiser and mocker" of the Old Testament, and his "sham utterances."

And Rabbi Kohler saw only the beginning of Delitzsch's down-fall; in preposterously provocative later works such as *The Great Deception* (a collection of the Bible's mistakes) and *Whose Son Is Christ?* Delitzsch attempts to prove, among other things, that Jesus was not a Jew but a misplaced Aryan directly descended from the Babylonian forefathers.

Delitzsch believed Germans should look to Babylon—not to other European nations—as a model for becoming the great civilization Germany was always meant to be. "Certainly not Paris, and at most Rome, can bear comparison with Babylon in the extent of influence which it exercised upon the world for 2,000 years." His ideas fed into a short-lived movement called pan-Babylonianism, which aimed to simultaneously erase the cultural history of the Jews and justify Germany's colonial hand in the Middle East.

Delitzsch himself would never have claimed outright hatred of Germany's present-day Jews. When in 1912 vicious rumors spread that a Russian Jew had murdered a young boy in order to drink his blood for religious reasons—the ancient "blood libel" against Jews—Delitzsch was one of a number of prominent Germans who signed a protest letter: "Not even a shadow of a proof has ever been brought forward in justification of this superstition." He would have said that his anti-Jewish sentiments were strictly historical, strictly scientific, and had no bearing on present-day politics. Maybe that's what he had to tell himself. But it's pretty clear that Delitzsch gave up all semblance of scientific objectivity for the kaiser's favor and for misguided German patriotism. Once, he would have questioned whether the Babylonian Eden had anything to do with perfection at all, let alone paradise or politics. Now, Delitzsch thought his Babel-Bible connections could "help establish the recognition that it was high time for Germany to pitch her tent on the palm-crowned banks of the streams of Paradise!" Presumably, he meant this literally.

Yet, try as he might, he never could get back into the kaiser's good graces. It was a full year and a half after his Berlin performance when he finally delivered his third "Babel and Bible" lecture, in

October 1904. This time, he traded the Singakademie for a much humbler whistle-stop tour through the German countryside. No bright lights, no indignant press, just friendly local literary societies in the smaller cities of Barmen and Köln, 300 miles west of Berlin. There, he explained, among other things, about the consequences of sin, and how Christian ideals really were vastly superior to those of the Babylonians. But, once again, no one was listening.

Though of course he'd never want to admit it, Delitzsch himself embodied the story of the Garden of Eden. He had enjoyed perfect harmony with the powers that be. But he went too far, and as punishment he was sent into permanent exile. Fear of sin had done its job. In order to maintain the pretty, integrated picture of Dürer's Garden of Eden, the unified German Christian world had to expel the heretic.

Delitzsch had been right about one thing: the Bible was a product of human history, subject to both human strength and human weakness. Unfortunately, he never learned that he was, too.

3

The Serpent Lesson

IN THE BEGINNING, the Lord God created man in Adams County, Ohio, just north of Peebles and south of Chillicothe.

On the westernmost edge of the Appalachians, in the craggy countryside of southern Ohio, the three branches of a small river called Brush Creek converge in a valley lined with pitch pine and chestnut oak trees. A steep rocky bluff rises 100 feet above the riverbed. And on top of this bluff lies an ancient mound of soil, waist high, built in the shape of a serpent. The snake's head—120 feet long and sixty feet wide—faces the north end of the bluff, overlooking the river. From there, the snake's body stretches southward 1,300 feet in loose waves, and ends in a tightly curled triple spiral.

Serpent Mound, one of the largest Native American earthworks in North America, was opened up to the public in 1901. At the time, archaeologists knew it was the work of an ancient tribe. They called this tribe the Mound Builders, but no one could say for sure who the Mound Builders were, what they believed, or why they built a 1300-foot serpent on a cliff overlooking a river. There were many theories, but only one that involved fruit, temptation, and sin.

The Reverend Edmund Landon West, who had been born and raised in Adams County, believed Serpent Mound marked the actual site of the Garden of Eden, and in 1901 he began to spread the word.

"There is now, yet to be seen on the Earth's Surface, and near Lovett's Post office, in Adams County, Ohio, the figured lesson of a large Serpent, which gives wonderfully clear and faithful testimony to the facts given by Moses." The facts as West saw them: Adam and Eve were given eternal life, but the serpent of sin tempted

Eve, they ate of the forbidden fruit, and as punishment, God took away human immortality. Since then, we have been cursed with death—not to mention war, slavery, and all the other sins. West believed the snake was created "either by God himself or by man inspired by Him" in the early days of Creation—not on the first day, but soon thereafter—as a "mighty object lesson" in the dangers of sin. Let all humanity, for all ages, know that the wages of sin are death: it happened here first.

The whole story was right there in the shape of the mound itself. According to West, the triangle shape emerging out of the snake's long neck were its open jaws, and the soil oval just north of the jaws had to be the "fruit of deception," which the snake was in the process of eating.

For if God was going to use an image of the serpent to symbolize the Fall of Man, as a warning that it should not happen again, how better to represent the "one sad event" than to show the serpent "in the act of itself eating fruit, *when it is well known that serpents do not eat fruit?*" The three coils at the end of the serpent's tail represent "the writhings and twistings of the body" in the painful throes of its inevitable demise.

Though the mark of Eden was now plain as day to West, it had taken him years to recognize the serpent lesson. He was born in 1841 and grew up "attending school and Sunday School . . . within one mile and in sight of the Serpent." Both sides of his family had been farming in the Brush Creek valley for two generations. And yet, as a boy, he had heard very little about this unusual local landmark near the post office. Its mysteries, he assumed, were "sealed thoughts intended for others." He went about his life, scraping out a living on the hilly Appalachian farmland. The serpent's meaning wouldn't be revealed to West for decades, and the eventual revelation would happen through a unique collaboration of science and religion.

In 1861, when West was twenty, he attended school in nearby New Vienna, Ohio. This was the New Vienna Academy, founded by James Quinter, a preacher in the German Baptist Brethren Church, which traced its roots directly back to eight religious dissidents in Schwarzenau, Germany, in 1708. The New Vienna Academy was the first German Baptist school in existence. The German Baptists were against anything that made their church more worldly, including, as they saw it, a paid ministry, missionary work, religious education, and even Sunday school. The Brethren believed in simplicity. They needed no other creed, no other text, no education other than the Bible itself. They wanted only to follow the life of Jesus, as expressed in the New Testament, word for word.

The so-called Schwarzenau Brethren had first split from the predominant German Lutheran church over the sacrament of baptism—who should receive it, and how it should be performed. Brethren believed the Bible prescribed baptism only for adults able to make a conscious choice—not infants. And because in Romans 6:1–4 it is written "we are baptized into [Christ's] death," and because at the moment of his death, Jesus's head fell forward, the Brethren baptized believers by immersing them in water in a forward direction—not backward, as was traditional. These practices made the Brethren outcasts subject to persecution, and in the early eighteenth century much of the Brethren community immigrated to the United States, where they formed close-knit religious communities in Pennsylvania.

But by the late nineteenth century, the Brethren, like seemingly everyone else in America, were moving westward, and James Quinter saw a need for more formal religious training and wider communication. He would spend thirty years as editor of the major Brethren newspaper, the *Gospel Messenger*. His school in New Vienna lasted only three years; in 1864 church pressures and the strain of the Civil War forced him to close its doors. But Quinter's school had made an impression on West.

Perhaps he was attracted to the simplicity of the Brethren way of life. No complex theology was needed; deeds were more important than words. The Brethren of southern Ohio, unlike other Christian denominations, wore their faith on the outside, in their everyday life and practice. Women kept their heads covered. Men had beards, trimmed square, starting farther down on the cheeks so that believers could exchange the traditional cheek kiss known as the "kiss of peace." German Baptists did not wear mustaches alone, because in ancestral Germany only the military wore mustaches—and the German Baptists were pacifists: along with the Mennonites and Quakers, they are one of the historic "peace churches" that have categorically condemned war, in all cases, as sin.

Still, during the Civil War, some Brethren felt that the sin of slavery outweighed the sin of war. Some enlisted but refused to kill. Landon West made another compromise. At age twenty he was stricken with typhoid fever, which kept him bedridden for months and left him too weak to join the Union Army. However, he did pay for a substitute to take his place. Several months later, twenty-one and recovered, West was baptized into the German Baptist Brethren Church. He dove into his new religious life with conviction and tremendous energy. His friend John Garman had overseen the building of a new German Baptist meetinghouse in the Brush Creek valley, and West was the first person elected to the ministry in the new church. He also married John's daughter Salome, mother to his first three children, and with his father-in-law he traveled around the area every Sunday, preaching humility, denouncing evil, and urging a return to the basic truths of the Bible. As he would write later, "The Bible is our main witness, the faithful and the true one, and is always good and always sure. It tells nothing, promises nothing, and proves nothing but what is both good and sure." We need all of it, and we need not a word more "to insure to us the favor of Heaven's King."

In an early photograph, West's scraggly beard crawls up his cheeks, and he does wear a faint mustache, which accentuates his pronounced frown. His heavy-lidded eyes bore into the camera as if scrutinizing its soul and finding it severely wanting. This was a man who'd survived typhoid fever and who would suffer for years from arterial sclerosis and bacterial skin disease. He came by his unblinking intensity honestly, and it served the hard work of building churches in farm villages.

West described himself as a "Minister of the Gospell," but the Brethren did not have a paid clergy—they feared that paid ministers would become "merchants" of God's Word, beholden to their consumers rather than to God Himself. Since Brethren congregations in Ohio villages were tiny, and pastors had to make a living outside the church, it was normal for both congregations and ministers to join forces with other local churches on Sundays, creating a larger, circulating congregation. West helped establish new churches at Strait Creek, Marble Furnace, and May Hill, and they all joined his Sunday rotation. At one point he had six congregations to visit every week. His wife Salome died young in 1873, and West regrouped, bringing his three children to live with his brother.

In 1877 he was inducted into the second level of the ministry, which allowed him to administer baptisms and the twice-a-year ritual replication of Jesus's Last Supper called the "love feast," where believers washed one another's feet, ate together, and received communion. Soon West became an elder, responsible for his congregations' spiritual health, and for representing them at the churchwide annual conference in Elgin, Illinois, where rulings on theological and practical issues were hammered out in discussions to reach a consensus.

In the 1880s however, consensus was getting harder to achieve. Aside from the long-standing debates over Sunday schools and the paid ministry, the Brethren had to reckon with the many modern innovations that some perceived to be encroaching on their hard-won, sacred simplicity. What was to be made of carpeting or credit unions? Did the installation of a lightning rod in a farmhouse imply simple practicality or a lack of trust in God's providence? This last question acted as a figurative lightning rod, causing days of impassioned—and sometimes tearful—debate.

During this tumultuous period, certain factions of West's church began to lobby for opening the sacred "love feast" and its attendant communion to nonmembers of the German Baptist church. They thought this might give outsiders a better impression of the practices they knew looked bizarre from the outside. And besides, if there was only "one faith," the faith of Christ, then all men should be one, whether church members or not.

West struggled with these issues, and eventually came down on the side of keeping the ceremony private. He did believe there was only one true faith, but he knew that even within a small community like the farming towns of southern Ohio, friends and neighbors could hold wildly differing religious views. As he wrote in his 1880 pamphlet *Close Communion*, "One need not go to China, or to Salt Lake City, to find extremes in doctrine, for these can be found *here*." So, while an open communion might be an agreeable idea, we'll never know, because "We cannot know the tree but by its fruits."

The only fruits the German Baptists could trust were those of their own tree. Church members adhered to a rigorous moral code; they held themselves upright above "the evildoers who abound everywhere." What if the nonmember attending communion had, unbeknownst to the German Baptists, committed adultery, or some other sin? Allowing such criminals in the eyes of God to participate in the love feast would be the end of the church altogether. No, concluded West with determination, "We must know who is in and who is out to have a church at all."

His words were sadly prescient. Soon enough the German Baptist Brethren *would* know who was in and who was out. In 1881, the year after *Close Communion* was published, the church formally split into three groups. A conservative leader frustrated by the refusal of the annual conference to condemn liberalism left the church and created the Old German Baptist Brethren. At the same time, a liberal church leader was "disfellowshipped" from the main church and formed his own denomination, the Brethren Church.

The four German Baptist churches in Adams County, which had shared congregations and pastors, became divided. Landon West found himself pulled in two directions. He was conservative—he opposed open communion and paid ministers. He was progressive —a stalwart advocate of Sunday school and of opening the faith to the "colored" people who had endured the horrors of slavery.

So he stayed put with the middle-ground group of Brethren, still the largest division of the three. Since many of the best pastors in Adams County had gone with the new progressive church, West took on preaching duties at even more congregations.

During this active period in the aftermath of the split, West met and married Barbara Landis, daughter of two prominent German Baptist families from Miami County, about 100 miles northwest of Adams County. In 1882 they moved with his three children to a farm near Barbara's family, where they had five more children—Mary, Martha, Susie, Samuel, and Daniel.

Around this time, Serpent Mound began to get renewed attention. It had been surveyed and documented in accounts of Native American culture long before, but in 1885 Frederic Ward Putnam, professor of American archaeology and anthropology at Harvard's famous Peabody Museum, passed through Brush Creek Township on a field mission. He marveled at the size of the remarkable earthwork, which was then suffering "the effects of age and neglect" on the property of Mr. Lovett—owner, presumably, of Lovett's Post Office. On his return to Boston, Putnam drafted a letter to the *Boston Herald* setting forth the mound's value as a Native American artifact. The letter, widely republished, came to the attention of Miss Alice Fletcher, described by an Ohio historian as "a noted Indian enthusiast."

Miss Fletcher brought the matter of the mound's preservation up for discussion at a lunch party in Newport, Rhode Island, with some of Boston's leading ladies, who promptly printed a circular and raised $6,000 for the restoration of the site, which was in turn promptly undertaken by the Peabody Museum. Serpent Mound—which had been damaged by a tornado in the 1880s, and neglected by Lovett—was returned to "a most excellent and attractive condition."

As the mound was restored, West's health was failing. In his late forties, he was forced to give up his duties as presiding elder at Twin Valley and Circleville. His presence in church was no longer an everyday occurrence but a special occasion. He preached the first services at Cassel's Run in 1887, and organized another new church in 1888. In 1890 he conducted a revival in New Carlisle along with Pastor Hixson, one of the progressives who had left the Adams County Brethren church years earlier. Perhaps, in West's worsening physical condition, church divisions started to seem less important to him.

In the meantime, Professor Putnam had visited Columbus, Ohio, for a meeting of the American Association for the Advancement of Science, where he met Mr. E. O. Randall, secretary of the Ohio Historical and Archaeological Society. They struck up a conversation about Serpent Mound. Putnam offered Randall a deal: if the Society could agree to "accept, repair and suitably preserve and guard the property," Harvard would turn the ownership of the property over to it. Randall and the Society got to work on their end of the deal.

At some point near February 1900, West's preaching activity slowed down again, as he and Barbara and their eight children moved back to her hometown, Pleasant Hill. He still attended the annual conference, and he was part of a special delegation to Canada to advocate for missionary work, but gone were the days of circulating between six hill-country congregations every Sunday. Barbara West purchased from her brothers a fifty-acre parcel of her family's land just north of town, less than a mile from the Pleasant Hill German Baptist Church. West could preach, farm, and live all within a twenty-minute horse-and-buggy ride. With his physical radius thus reduced, West's mental energies began to roam, and his thoughts turned to Serpent Mound.

Though he no longer lived in Adams County, he had been paying attention to the news from Serpent Mound in the intervening years. That first fall in Pleasant Hill, in 1901, West started talking to newspaper reporters about Eden.

He had heard various theories about the purpose and origins of the mound, but he didn't believe them. It could not have been a large gathering place—there was not enough room on either side of the mound for large crowds to gather without falling off the cliff. He had heard that the snake might be a made-up symbol; he wasn't having it. The serpent's jaws, he said, were in realistic proportion to the rest of the body. How did he know this? He went out and "measured living serpents." A daunting task, but one that proved to West that this snake wasn't just a figurative rendering; it was meant to represent the "real" snake of the Garden of Eden.

West even incorporated Professor Putnam's research into his own. Putnam had tested the soil of Serpent Mound to determine its age, and he discovered that this soil was much older than the soil nurturing the trees and farms in the surrounding area. Therefore, according to West, the snake must have existed before Noah's Flood, which would have washed away all the rest of the topsoil around, leaving only the "Mark of Eden."

Native Americans could not have built it. No, the "noble dimensions and perfect proportions of this majestic figure" suggested to West "the hand and intelligence of a divine creator with limitless resources." This left West in a quandary, since even by the late nineteenth century it was well known that Serpent Mound *had* been created by Native Americans, and "fairly intelligent" ones at that, as the *New York Times* put it in 1894, when it reported a local foxhunter's discovery of Native grave sites near the mound.

West neatly solved this problem by agreeing with the scientists: the Mound Builders, not the Native Americans, had built Serpent Mound. Of course the scientists believed that the Mound Builders *were* Native Americans, but West saw things differently. He believed that the Mound Builders were America's first people: Christian people who "most assuredly" knew something of the Bible events recorded in Serpent Mound.

And because of those burial sites discovered nearby, we could tell for sure that the Mound Builders "had wars, and burials, thus showing that they were of the one human family," the family that began with Adam and Eve. They were just like us: they died because they had sinned in the eyes of God. They made their mark, and then, like Warren's hyperborean Eocene men, they were swept away by Noah's flood. The Indians—the ones who "yet dwelt" in parts of America in 1901—didn't show up until after the Flood. (West didn't say so, but it was implied that these "red men" were *not* like us.)

West wasn't the first to draw a line between imagined ancient Americans and the present-day Indians who "yet dwelt" in America; nor would he be the last. It was a useful divide. If America was a land unspoiled by human contact—a renewed Eden—what were the settlers to make of the Native Americans who were already here? Were they an idyllic race representing a pre-Fall Paradise? Or were they a troubling reminder that the land was not in fact laid out by God for Europeans? Splitting Native American history in two—pre-Flood and post-Flood, as West would put it—allowed West to have it both ways.

And now, with the arrival of the "Pilgrims" from Europe, the American Eden had yet another new beginning in store. Ohio's population was starting to expand, bringing in not just German Baptists from Pennsylvania but others "in various tongues and colors" in search of an independent way of life. These new immigrants had found "a free and peaceful home in the wilderness of America." And hadn't the prophet Isaiah foretold that in the last days, all of Earth's "wilderness should be made like Eden"?

Ohio's new network of canals helped make the expansion possible, providing new routes for trade and transportation. Ohio had Eden's requisite abundance: hills, valleys, rivers, forests. There is an unexpectedly wide variety of trees near Serpent Mound: chestnut, pine, sourwood, red cedar, yellow oak, maple, willow, sycamore, elm, cork elm, cottonwood, and the Ohio buckeye. That's almost "every tree that is pleasant to the eye and good for food."

West even had an Ohioan solution to the problem of the four rivers of paradise. One mile north of the serpent, he said, the three main streams of the Brush Creek all come together and flow southward, where they join the fourth branch of the creek near the snake's head: "Thus giving four streams of water, as Moses names, to form a Union of one stream, at the very head of the serpent, which here marks the land of Eden."

West believed in the literal truth of every word of the Bible. But he also paid careful attention to what the Bible *didn't* say. When reporters asked him how he could go against the commonly held belief that Eden was somewhere in "the East," in Asia, West noted, accurately, that nowhere in the Bible does Moses actually *write* that Eden was in Asia.

According to West, people assume that the Garden of Eden was in Asia only because the Bible says that Noah's Ark landed on top of Mount Ararat, and there is a Mount Ararat in what's now Armenia. But that didn't mean Noah had to *start out* on Mount Ararat. God created Adam in Ohio, and all the generations between Adam and Noah lived there. Then came the Flood, which lasted five months. Noah built his Ark on the Mississippi River and was "given a floating" downriver with the help of the prevailing currents, which were doubtless strong during such calamitous rainfall. For the sake of argument, West assumed an average speed "of only two miles per hour." Then, Noah could travel forty-eight miles a day, so 7,500 miles in five months—the distance between the Gulf of Mexico and Armenia—was hardly a stretch.

Once you start to take the Bible at its word, you can get into trouble. Strictly speaking, the Bible doesn't say "Armenia" either. It says the Ark settled in "the mountains of Ararat," which some scholars think is actually an ancient typo. If you accept the premise that the Bible's Eden story originated with the Babylonians—and most scholars would—the geography doesn't fit neatly. The mountains of Armenia were outside the known world of the ancient Babylonians. On the other hand, the mountains of "Urartu," in the northern part of what's now Iraq, were not. Hebrew words consist only of consonants, and in translation, sometimes the wrong vowels get assigned. That's what likely happened with Noah's arrival point. The mountain now known as Ararat was probably named *after* the Biblical typo; Armenians nearby still refer to it as Mount Massis.

But wherever the Ark landed, said West, from the time of the Flood to the time of Plymouth Rock, people had had to rely on oral tradition to perpetuate the story of Eden. This was unfortunate, because for all those years Serpent Mound, "this perfect illustration of thought and of history," was right here in Ohio. "For people to now say there was no such land as Eden is no honor to them, to our race, or to our Creator, who has been so careful of it as to locate it, to name it, to describe it, to mark it and preserve it even until now."

The Columbus correspondent for the *St. Louis Republic* wrote a lengthy article expounding West's theory: "Preacher Says Ohio Was Garden of Eden, Holds That the Famous Serpent Mound Marks the Exact Home of Adam and Eve." The story was picked up in Chicago, in Omaha, and even as far away as New York. The *Elyria (Ohio) Reporter* ran a story from the *Chicago Record-Herald* in which West's theory was considered "certainly ingenious if not always convincing." Still, the reporter recommended keeping an open mind.

"It certainly cannot be maintained by any good American that there are insurmountable reasons why the Garden of Eden should have been located in some Turkish province rather than in the grand old State of Ohio. Let us not, therefore, be too ready to cry down the theory of the Reverend Mr. West." Had the *Elyria Reporter* known of Dr. George C. Allen's nineteenth-century theory that the Garden of Eden had begun at the North Pole and then rotated around the world and landed under Cincinnati, he doubtless would have considered it to be corroborating evidence.

The good-humored secretary of the Ohio Historical Society, E. O. Randall, played a large role in propagating West's theory. First he printed the *Herald's* article in the quarterly journal of the Ohio Historical Society. Then he reprinted the theory—or as he called it, a "fancy"—in the annual anthology of the journal the next April in 1902, with a caveat:

> The following article is not exactly archaeology nor history though it contains something of each. It is, however, so unique and entertaining that we reproduce it as it has been given to the public in the daily press. Here is food for the "higher critics," the Egyptologists, archaeologists and the Biblical students of all classes.

West was proud that his theory had reached people outside the church. He kept several copies of the Historical Society publications. The entry for Landon West in the *Brethren Encyclopedia* notes that he received "wide recognition" for his "carefully presented" theory. At a time when European critics and archaeologists were getting worldwide attention for shaking up our ideas about the Bible, and attaching them to the faraway banks of the Euphrates, in some Turkish province, this German Baptist preacher had come up with a homegrown solution. And who wouldn't rather have Eden nearby?

A sixty-mile state road had just been built, passing right over Brush Creek. You could drive right up to Serpent Mound, through the new gateway, and onto the grassy lawn, "where the serpent picture lies for all to see."

In October 1907, Randall published the second edition of a 128-page booklet—"an attempt to present in popular form all that is worthy of publication" about Serpent Mound, "the origin and purpose of which was still a mystery." It was a popular mystery; the first 1,000-copy edition of the booklet had apparently sold out, and visitors were clamoring for more. On page 93, under the heading "Curious Theories," Randall again reprinted West's Garden of Eden fancy. Randall called West's idea "amusing," "ridiculous," "curious," and "fantastic." But he still published it. He was willing to do anything to bring more people and more attention to the mound.

Early in 1908, Randall successfully lobbied the Ohio general assembly for the then lavish sum of $500 to build an observation tower overlooking the earthwork. The Columbus Wire and Iron Works Company won the contract, and the 6,000-pound tower—twenty-five-feet tall with an eight-square-foot platform on top—was transported south to Adams County, and erected near the serpent's tail.

Finally, reported Randall, "from the platform the observer may see and carefully study the entire length of the serpent which heretofore could not be viewed entire from any one point, owing to the irregular convolutions of the Serpent." This development wasn't lost on West. He took the new visibility as his opportunity to finally broadcast his theory himself. He had an eighteen-page pamphlet, entitled *Eden's Land and Garden with Their Marks Yet to Be Seen,* printed for him by a friend in nearby Troy (one copy by mail: six cents). He printed this pamphlet because he hoped that people *would* see the marks. And now they could.

West didn't want others to make the mistake he had made as a boy, of assuming the "serpent lesson" was "sealed," or "intended for others." West had given up trying to keep communion closed. His lesson was intended for everybody, German Baptist or not. His pamphlet reads more as a sermon than a theory. It repeats itself. There are lots of exclamation marks. Rules of evidence do not apply. Because West used the word "fruit" for "sin" and the word "death" for "losing our immortality" it is easy to misread his pamphlet as a treatise against the consumption of poisonous fruit. Like a sermon, West's theory is original and deeply felt. And like sermons, the Eden theories of Bible believers like West are only as convincing as the person behind them. West believed that the Bible is the Word of God, and that Moses was a "writer of history." Given these beliefs, when confronted by an unexplained 1,000-foot-long snake, what was the preacher supposed to think? The way he saw it, he hadn't gone out in search of Eden. Eden had come to find *him.*

Serpent Mound, this majestic symbol of ancient history, needed a spokesperson. "It has not sought to court or please the opinions of people but to teach and give faith to all people." Now that Eden had been "definitely located," what did West want to happen next? According to him, all of mankind, whether they were church members or not, Bible readers or not, had a tremendous opportunity to learn the "object lesson" of Serpent Mound. The lesson was simple: sin no more, and stick together. It was the same message that William Warren had seen in his North Polar Eden: once, humanity had been unified, and we could be again. In the chaos at the turn of the century, the need for stability was strong. Friedrich Delitzsch had pushed against unity and suffered the consequences. When West was a boy, the whole of Adams County had consisted of just a few farming families, many of whom had belonged to the four united German Baptist churches. Now there were "over 500 styles of religion" in the world, and fifteen houses of worship in Brush Creek Township alone. In fact, Brush Creek Township didn't even exist anymore; now it was called Peebles. In 1908, West's church had agreed to change its name from "German Baptist Brethren" to the "Church of the Brethren" to avoid confusion with either Germans or Baptists. Everything seemed to be changing at all times. His country, his family, and his church had all split and re-formed themselves in his lifetime. Even God's Word did not mean what it used to. But Serpent Mound hadn't changed; it hadn't crumbled, split, or been washed away. Indeed, it had been restored to its past glory, and had become more and more prominent. This gigantic mark, universally readable, had clearly survived for aeons, "through floods and flames."

And now, finally, its day had come. The earthbound illustration had "even more power than is now shown in the Bible." Much as it must have saddened him to say so, West now realized that "the Bible cannot unite the people on any one thing."

If the Bible wasn't universal and transparent, that left the serpent lesson as "the only mark of unity that our world, with its nations, races, and religions, now has." What was the message of the traditional symbol of original sin? "This great serpent lesson shows the mark to unite all humanity in one line of descent that goes back to creation, showing things in common to all people."

One might have expected a message along the lines of "Repent, ye sinners, or burn in hell!" But by 1908, Reverend Landon West was sixty-seven years old. He would live for eight more years, but his constant poor health may have made every day feel like his last. His daughters had married; his sons were seeking education elsewhere. He had once been full of hellfire and brimstone, but it had all been preached out of him. He just wanted humanity to have a second chance to follow the rules. "Had Eden's tempted ones stood united in loyalty to God's law, their peace, their liberty and happiness would have continued." And as long as humanity refused to give up sin, the serpent lesson would stand.

PART II

Civilization

4

The Salt River

IN THE BEGINNING, all that Babylonian stuff happened—the tree, the garden, the serpent—but it didn't happen the way the Babylonians told it; it took one genius Hebrew scribe to get it right.

When Friedrich Delitzsch first met Archibald Henry Sayce back in the 1870s, he thought there must be some mistake. The German scholar had expected Sayce, the Oxford scholar who had written the first and only grammar of the ancient Assyrian language, to be a venerable gentleman with a white beard.

But Sayce looked just like Delitzsch. He was in his early thirties, trying to make his way in Assyriology. For months after their first meeting, Sayce and Delitzsch sat elbow to elbow in a back room of the British Museum in London, silently hunched over tiny un-cataloged pieces of ancient clay, brushing the dirt off inscriptions that had not been read since 612 B.C.

Sayce and Delitzsch agreed on much, including the location of the Garden of Eden. For Sayce as well as Delitzsch, Eden was a Babylonian story, so the Garden had to be located where the Babylonians said it was: southern Mesopotamia, the low-lying floodplain between the Tigris and the Euphrates, just north of the Persian Gulf.

And yet, by 1903, when Delitzsch's infamous Bible-bashing lecture was reported in the London newspapers, Sayce had, for twenty years, been assuring the public that archaeology *confirmed* the historical truth of the Bible. How did two friends looking at exactly the same sources, with the same Eden, come up with such irreconcilable, opposite conclusions?

There had always been a good-natured divide between English and German "Orientalists." At a public dinner celebrating the end of the 1881 Oriental Congress in Berlin, the Anglo-French minority watched from their end of the table as the champagne flowed freely, the German members became more and more noisy, and a distinguished gray-haired scholar danced a reel on the table. Finally the British secretary of the Society of Biblical Archaeology took a fork and drew it across the table between their group and their uncouth German hosts. "Here," said the secretary, "ends civilization."

In Germany, the Orthodox party of the government had successfully suppressed the results of the new archaeology—presumed to be dangerous to religious belief—preventing them from leaking to the public. Their caution gave Delitzsch a chance to make a sensation. In England, Sayce had been touting Middle Eastern archaeology as *proof* of the Bible, in broad daylight, for decades. And he found an eager audience. The British public was already caught up in the debate over science versus religion that had been cycling through newspapers and lecture halls since Darwin burst on the scene in 1859.

The public had to reconcile the new discoveries with their schoolchild memories of the Bible. With archaeological finds from cities like Nineveh, in southern Mesopotamia, Sayce wrote, "we find ourselves face to face with Sennacherib, with Nebuchadnezzar, whose names have been familiar to us from childhood." The conservative clergy needed help navigating the mass of archaeological discovery and linguistic translation coming out of the Middle East, not to mention the more literary "higher criticism" coming out of the scholarly centers of Germany.

Sayce was just the man to act as ambassador between European faith and Middle Eastern fact. As a specialist in ancient languages, he understood the need for progress. But he also had a strong attachment to the Biblical fantasy world of British childhood.

Tuberculosis had kept him in bed and out of school for his first seven years; there was no point in teaching a small boy doomed to die how to read and write. So he took refuge in listening to stories. "In my early days the Book of Genesis was like a story in *The Arabian Nights,* perfectly possible in a world, different, it is true, from that in which I usually lived, but not from that into which my dreams, whether waking or sleeping, might transport me." It was difficult for a child to distinguish whether the worlds of *The Arabian Nights* or the Bible were in fact figments of the imagination, or just very far away.

In either case, the key to both dreamworlds was language. Once his parents realized young Archibald was not going to die, they tried to make up for lost time, teaching him to read by making him memorize and recite two pages of the dictionary every day. By age ten, Sayce claimed, he could "read and write almost anything," including Homer in the original Greek, and the Bible in the original Hebrew.

"Strange characters had a particular fascination for me, and my chief delight was in a Hebrew Bible, the verses of which I copied over and over again. Naturally I wanted to know what the characters meant, the result being that I knew the Hebrew alphabet before I had learnt my own." The more strange characters he learned, the further he could be transported into the Book of Genesis.

Throughout Sayce's life, this pattern of nearly fatal illness and language learning would continue. As a teenager he contracted typhoid fever, and spent "the pleasantest hours of my convalescence in dreaming that I was floating on a raft down the Tigris past Nineveh and Assur with great bulls inscribed with arrow-headed script." By the time he was well enough to go back to school, he had learned how to pronounce "a good many" of those arrowheaded cuneiform signs. With such an early start, it was no wonder he'd composed the world's first Assyrian grammar by the time he was twenty-seven, in 1872. By the time he was sixty, Sayce had suffered typhoid fever (again), a hemorrhage, blood poisoning, sciatica, a septic injury, a nearly fatal snakebite, and several attacks of temporary blindness. He had also learned Hebrew, modern Persian, classical Arabic, Egyptian hieroglyphs, Sanskrit, Japanese, and Basque.

Sayce's constant illness instilled in him a deep resignation to powers beyond his control. "I knew, as I knew nothing else, that everything is determined before hand, and that whatever happens . . . is in accordance with the decree of an inexorable and passionless fate." He had no fear of death, having faced it so many times at such a young age. For Sayce, belief in fate was the seed of a deep religious faith that stood with him throughout what would be a surprisingly long life. But it took him some years to find out what shape that seed would grow into.

Sayce's father was an Anglican priest, in the High Church tradition, which was closest to Catholicism in its ritual and practice. Its detractors called it "bells and smells" for its heavy use of chimes and incense. As soon as he was old enough, his family decided, Sayce would go to Oxford and take holy orders, like his father. And he did, albeit unwillingly. Sayce sat squirming through his own ordination ceremony, performed by the bishop of Oxford, a friend of his father's and a man, Sayce wrote, who was "unfortunately lacking in humor." Why an Oxford bishop should be expected to display a sense of humor during an ordination ceremony is an open question.

Dissatisfied with "bells and smells," Sayce turned briefly to the other end of the Anglican spectrum: the Low Church. Inadvertently, he went on a school holiday with a group of earnest Evangelicals, as they called themselves. They were far too serious for him. They had no sense of the decent separation between church and life. "At the breakfast table I was obliged to start acrostics and anagrams by way of preventing conversations about the conversion of souls."

Next Sayce turned toward the Broad Church, a loose affiliation of liberal Anglicans interested in neither ritual nor soul-saving. They were interested in politics. They advocated for women's suffrage; they became socialists; they lobbied for "native" rights in colonial Africa. One of these Broader churchmen was the Anglican bishop in Natal, South Africa, John Colenso. When one of Colenso's young Zulu parishioners asked him, point-blank, if Noah's Flood was "true," the bishop was thrown into a crisis of faith. He began to examine the Bible's description of the flood, finding it highly unrealistic, and this slowly led him to believe that the rest of the Old Testament was not a literal account of historical events as written by Moses. He would eventually publish *The Pentateuch Examined,* a seven-part critique of literalism, each volume of which caused widespread controversy when released in England. Religious authorities declared that the book was "spued out of hell"; some say the Anglican High Church found Colenso's critiques—coming as they did from a dedicated religious missionary—much more dangerous to orthodoxy than Charles Darwin's *On the Origin of Species,* which had been published at around the same time.

Sayce not only publicly supported Colenso but also helped the bishop's sixth volume of Biblical criticism make it to the press after the controversy, and entertained Colenso's son Robert at Oxford dinner parties. All this was much too radical for the Oxford establishment, High Church ordination or no. Sayce had been offered a job as chair of the Hebrew department. Before the existence of Israel, Hebrew at Oxford was studied not as a modern language but as a tool for Biblical study, as it had been also for both Franz and Friedrich Delitzsch in Berlin. So after the higher-ups learned of Sayce's support for Colenso, they withdrew the offer at the last minute and gave the chair in Hebrew to Samuel R. Driver, who could be counted on to toe the theological line.

Sayce continued in his lesser post at Oxford, forming lifelong friendships with scholars and politicians of various stripes. Though he was physically a slight man with a narrow face, birdlike nose, and pale, delicate complexion, Sayce liked to characterize himself as "Keltic," by which he meant someone more gregarious, more hospitable, more of a dreamer than the Kelt's age-old rival the Anglo-Saxon. He certainly was generous with his knowledge: he wrote prefaces, introductions, and editorial notes for seemingly everyone who asked, including William Warren. For his part, Warren knew Sayce's reputation among serious scholars and always gave his testimonials a prominent place in new editions of *Paradise Found!*

Sayce also traveled wherever his curiosity led him, including, once, to a serpent-shaped mound on the banks of a Scottish lake that was supposed to be "similar to the famous serpent-mounds of America." He was disappointed to learn that although the serpent's head had been made by Neolithic humans, the supposed body of the serpent was actually just a natural formation. Geology did not have the same magic as mysterious ancient people.

In the 1870s, Sayce became enchanted by Heinrich Schliemann's reputed discovery of the city of Troy at an archaeological site in Turkey. Schliemann was a man after Sayce's own heart. The prevailing scientific wisdom of the day held that Homer's *Iliad*—and even Homer himself—was completely mythological, and that to seek in myth for grains of history would be as useless as "to seek in the sunshine for grains of gold." But Schliemann had refused to keep myth and history separate, and his discoveries, for Sayce, had proved the truism false. Seeking in myths for grains of truth was exactly what Sayce had been in training to do from a young age. It was no longer necessary to believe in the myth to believe in the history. It wasn't necessary to believe that "gods fought with men on the plains of Troy" to believe that there *was* a Troy. And if there was any book close to the Bible in British consciousness, it was the *Iliad*. If it were possible to see the real city of Troy, in the flesh, what would happen if we could look at the Bible up close?

Schliemann's adventures in Troy were not universally admired. He was an untrained archaeologist whose only qualifications for finding Troy were a passion for Homeric Greece, and a vast fortune. He destroyed several layers of his dig in his anxious efforts to get to the bottom, which he assumed to be Troy. He found an unlikely cache of gold he called "Priam's treasure," a few fish bones that he supposed were the "hair pins of Helen," and various other dubious relics. In a sarcastic 1876 editorial, the *New York Times* suggested that since Schliemann was having such luck at Troy, he might want to "exercise his remarkable genius" in other, more interesting searches. He was just the man, for example, to find the Garden of Eden.

Schliemann would have no trouble, the *Times* said. All he would have to do "would be to visit the Plain of Mesopotamia; to pick out a good-sized garden plot, and to announce that he had fixed the exact position of the Garden." Then, he could go about finding items of personal property belonging to Adam and Eve, which they of course left behind in the suddenness of their departure. "He would soon lay bare the asphalt paths over which Adam was accustomed to walk, and would find his lawn-roller and sickle in a rusty but still easily recognizable condition." Schliemann's map of Eden would show, of course, the position of the fateful apple tree, and not only that. There would also be "Adam's Swimming Pool," "The Croquet Ground," the "Sartorial Fig-Tree," and a dotted line labeled "Probable route of the Serpent on entering and retiring from the garden."

Sayce felt it to be his duty to protect Schliemann from such abuse. He wrote a preface to Schliemann's magnum opus *Troja,* and publicly defended his finds. Magnanimous himself, Sayce seemed to inspire generosity in others: he and Schliemann became such close friends that the older man wanted to include Sayce in his will. Sayce, ever the gentleman, refused. He had already received something else of value from Schliemann: inspiration to look again at the Bible from his professional standpoint as an Assyriologist. He knew where the Garden of Eden was, and knew he could make it sound much less ridiculous than the *New York Times* had.

So when in 1882 the Religious Tract Society, an evangelical publisher in London, wanted Sayce to write something for a popular audience about archaeology and the Bible, he didn't hesitate—despite his previous disdain for the Low Church. In three weeks, he wrote a 156-page "little book," *Fresh Light from the Ancient Monuments: A Sketch of the Most Striking Confirmations of the Bible from Recent Discoveries in Egypt, Assyria, Palestine, Babylonia, Asia Minor.* The Religious Tract Society paid Sayce what he considered an exorbitant fee for the book, but he thought so little of its prospects that he didn't bother to retain the copyright, which meant he wouldn't receive royalties.

The society printed *Fresh Light* in an affordable, perfectly palm-size edition, bound in lavish bright red cloth, with the title stamped in gold foil and endpapers decorated with advertisements for other titles in the publisher's series "By-Paths of Bible Knowledge." In Britain, the facts about Babel weren't seen as a challenge to the Bible; they enhanced it: dangerous Assyriology was rendered fit for Sunday school. Inside this gem of a book, among other things, Sayce laid out his plan for Eden in southern Mesopotamia. Although he agreed with Delitzsch on the Babylonian shape of Eden, somehow when Sayce said the Garden was in Mesopotamia, it didn't sound revolutionary. It sounded entirely reasonable, maybe because he expressed it with such confidence—not the puffed-up confidence of Delitzsch, the young man racing headlong against his father, but the sincere assurance of someone already perfectly confident of his place in the world. Yes, there'd been a lot of debate on the location of Eden, and the identification of the mysterious rivers Pishon and Gihon, but all that has been "cleared up" now by the fresh light from cuneiform tablets.

Though it had been Sayce's childhood dream to go by raft down the Tigris, he had actually never traveled to Mesopotamia, which was not considered safe enough for a man of his ill health. Instead, Sayce used only the Babylonian cuneiform tablets in the British Museum, and his prodigal powers of translation.

The word "Eden" itself, Sayce agreed with Delitzsch, comes from "Edinu," the ancient Babylonian word for "plain." But unlike Delitzsch, Sayce maintained that in Hebrew, the word "Eden" came to mean "delight." Delitzsch's Eden is plain; Sayce's delightful. And Sayce didn't stop there: There's an ancient Babylonian city called "Eridu," which means "the good," right at the southern edge of the marshes, before the rivers merge into the Gulf. Near this City of Good, then, the Babylonians built a Garden of Delight—or almost. Sayce's description, while not as severe as Delitzsch's, did display a certain British understatement and reserve. Eden wasn't really so much a garden as "what we should now call a plantation, mainly of fruit trees." In the center of the paradise plantation grew a particularly special tree, a shrine to the Babylonian god Irnin, a prototype of the Tree of Life. Sayce had looked over Delitzsch's shoulder at the "Adam and Eve" tablet in the British museum, and he, too, proclaimed that the Tree of Life must be a pine tree, and the Tree of Knowledge some sort of palm.

Delitzsch had traced Bible stories to Babylonian authors in order to discredit them. Sayce, counterintuitively, believed that the more Biblical details he could credit to Babylonian mythology, the more likely the Bible was to be true. He simply chose to look at the bright side: an echo of the Bible was an endorsement of the Bible. So what if the Babylonians came first? The time line of history would simply have to be rearranged in order to fit the theology. To do this, Sayce relied on the Hebrews, giving them back their historic role as inheritors of the Old Testament from the Babylonian sources, the role that Delitzsch had tried to obliterate. In fact, wrote Sayce, the Babylonians and the Jews were related. Adam and Eve were really Adamu and Ivar, ancient Semitic words for "Man" and "breath," respectively. They refer to a tribe of Babylonians who were the "first people"—if not biologically, then culturally. Sayce believed that civilization spread from Babylon, via the Persian Gulf, to Asia and to Europe.

Both Sayce and Delitzsch clearly had their favorite parts of the Eden story. Delitzsch was charmed by the Babylonian snake. Sayce was partial to the cherubs, those two angels with the flaming swords that the Bible says God placed at the gates of Eden to keep Adam and Eve from returning. He pointed out, somewhat gleefully, that the Babylonian word "kharibi" referred to a winged mythical creature with the body of a lion and the head of a human, or the body of a human and the head of an eagle. These fearsome creatures often appeared in pairs, carved in stone on either side of gates and doorways, and sometimes, in Assyrian sculpture, on either side of the Tree of Life.

The flaming sword was the same flaming sword that the Babylonian god Marduk used to slay primordial Tiamat. It was important for Sayce to prove that *every single* aspect of the Genesis verses describing Eden could be traced to ancient Babylon. Though all these Babylonian elements had yet to be found on one single piece of the ancient record, Sayce was nevertheless "fairly certain" that they would be.

Sayce accepted his old friend Delitzsch's theory that the Pishon and Gihon must have been ancient man-made canals, which flowed parallel to the Tigris and the Euphrates, and which were named on ancient lists of "rivers." Just like the reviewers of Delitzsch's early work, Sayce could reassure himself that the man-made canals had been God-made rivers first.

The only hint of conflict between Sayce and Delitzsch was their gentlemanly disagreement about the translation of the word "Gihon," the most mysterious of the four rivers of paradise. They conducted this debate for years in the pages of their books and in academic journals, always with the utmost deference to each other. Sayce had started it way back in 1872, in the journals of the Society of Biblical Archaeology.

Nine years later, in *Where Was Paradise?*, Delitzsch cautiously debunked Sayce's translations, calling them "a stretch." He then begged "with reservations" to suggest an alternative reading of the word.

Some weeks later, in the journal *The Academy,* Sayce praised Delitzsch's book—which he said had been eagerly awaited by scholars in the field for three or four years. Delitzsch, "with a self-denial . . . rare in these days," had refused to publish his re-sults until they were thoroughly vetted, and Sayce appreciated his conscientiousness.

He found Delitzsch's analysis of the word "Pishon" "ingenious." But his old friend's "Gihon" was still a sticking point. Delitzsch's alternative reading was "as little satisfactory as my own." Sayce was willing to leave it at that. "It is out of the question, in the space at my disposal, even to glance at the many new things of which Dr. Delitzsch's book is full." After years of debate, he declared, "it is questionable whether the names of the Pishon and the Gihon have hitherto been detected on the cuneiform monuments." That was not to say they would *never* be detected. Just not yet.

While he waited for such a definitive discovery, Sayce couldn't resist adding his own flourish to Delitzsch's solution for Pishon and Gihon, in the spirit of friendly English-German competition. He believed he could identify the "one river that watered Eden," the one that Genesis said split into four. Sayce worked backward: Eden had to be where the Babylonians said it was, in southern Mesopotamia. The four rivers of paradise were the Tigris, the Euphrates, and two other, smaller river-canals nearby, yet to be determined. And Eden had to be near the shrine city of Eridu.

The only body of water that could possibly connect all four was the Persian Gulf, to the south of Eden. Delitzsch had speculated that the "one river" was a branch of the Euphrates, to the north of Eden. Sayce had inverted Eden. The Tigris and Euphrates *end* in the Persian Gulf; and the Bible seems to indicate that the "one river" was the beginning of its four branches. Must the world turn upside down? Not at all, argued Sayce with his usual panache.

The Persian Gulf is of course a body of salt water. According to Sayce, the Babylonians, unfamiliar with the open ocean, called the Gulf "bitter river" or "salt river." And salt water was of course subject to tides. In a rising tide, water from the four rivers poured into the Gulf. In a falling tide, the water would have seemed to Babylonian observers to be spewing back *out* of the Gulf into the rivers.

Sayce claimed that the Persian Gulf flowed upward into the Tigris and Euphrates, delivering salt water into the river flow, making the four great rivers of paradise—somewhat disappointingly—brackish, and making the famously freshwater Mesopotamian marshes salty. Salt tides could reverse north and south, and make four rivers flowing into the ocean into one "salt river" giving birth to four. Before centuries of silt built the land of southern Mesopotamia, Eridu, city of good, the ruins of which now sat sixty miles inland from the Gulf, had been right on the "salt river." And the four rivers of paradise emptied directly into it.

Fresh Light sold like hotcakes; it was reprinted eight times in ten years, and translated into numerous languages. So Sayce wrote more: *Assyria: Its Princes, Priests and People; Life and Times of Isaiah as Illustrated by Contemporary Monuments; Historical Evidences of the Old Testament; Races of the Old Testament; Egypt of the Hebrews and Herodotus; Patriarchal Palestine; Joseph and the Land of Egypt; First Book of Moses Called Genesis (edited by A.H. Sayce); Book of Daniel Unlocked;* and *Only Key to Daniel's Prophecies.*

He had become a missionary of Middle Eastern archaeology, a veritable Saint Paul. Like the salt river he posited for Eden, Sayce's own career had dramatically switched course: from liberal professor to orthodox Reverend. He didn't see it that way: he hadn't changed. He never claimed to be a theologian. In fact, he claimed that those who read his books because they were written by an Anglican deacon were in for a surprise. But the holy orders his father had forced him to receive did allow him to use the title "Reverend" on his books for the Tract Society, not to mention those for the Society to Promote Christian Knowledge, which in turn allowed the more orthodox elements in British society to claim him as their own.

Sure, some of his former colleagues called the Reverend Professor Archibald Henry Sayce a "vulgarizer," and claimed that he stretched scientific truth for religious gain. But Sayce didn't mind. The more injuries he survived—whether physical or professional—the tougher he seemed to get. And after all, the storm of criticism coming out of London was nothing compared with the dangerous bite of an Egyptian horned asp that he'd suffered in the winter of 1888. It spit so much venom into his right ankle that "the muscle seemed to give way," and his leg had swollen up to the knee. Sayce knew firsthand the evil snakes were capable of! He somehow managed to make it to the kitchen area of the Nile riverboat on which he found himself, grab the cook's red-hot tongs, and cauterize his own leg twice, "burning the wound down to the bone." Sayce's bold move had saved his own life, but he expressed it with typical humility. "I was of course lame from the effects of the cauterization for many weeks afterwards, but the dry warm air of Upper Egypt has a healing virtue."

After his father's death in 1890, he had both the psychological freedom and the money to do whatever he wanted. And what he wanted to do was cut the last of his ties to Oxford. His lungs started to bother him again; his doctor told him his days were numbered, but that he might increase that number by wintering abroad. So he took off for Cairo, planning to "spend the residue of my days under the warm skies of the Nile." But Oxford didn't want to lose him completely to Egypt and the Religious Tract Society. While he had been writing *Historical Evidences of the Old Testament* for the Religious Tract Society, he had also been writing *Introduction to the Science of Language, Principles of Comparative Philology,* and *Aramaic Papyri* for Macmillan. Oxford offered him a compromise position: nonresident Professor of Assyriology.

Sayce gladly accepted, and held the job, such as it was, for the next thirty years. "Nonresident" was the operative word. Sayce had bought himself a *dahabiya,* a low-slung Egyptian houseboat designed to sail up and down the Nile, and that's exactly what he did. His boat, the *Ishtar,* was one of the largest on the river, and required a crew of nineteen—plus Sayce's personal servant, Mustafa.

In those last years of the nineteenth century there were no bridges or dams across the Nile to block the passage of these ancient watercraft. The invasion of the steamship had only just begun. With a good wind, the *Ishtar* could sail; without wind, the crew rowed. But always the houseboat crawled right along the shoreline, so that Professor Sayce could stop at whatever Egyptian scenery caught his fancy. He was partial to wide, rolling cotton fields and deserts. This was the life. He would take a book from his 2,000-volume library in the salon on one end of the *Ishtar* out onto a covered balcony, sit and read for a while, then climb the stairs to his drawing room abovedecks, where he might entertain other "Nilotics"—fellow Europeans who wanted to escape the European way of life. Sayce never married. He spent June through October lecturing at Oxford, and October through May on the

Ishtar. This was as close as he could get to his childhood dream of floating down the Tigris on a raft.

All was not entirely peace, sunshine, and royalty checks, however. There was an episode of blood poisoning in 1898, when a surgeon threatened to amputate his right arm. Sayce forbade the surgery; he said he'd rather die than lose the ability to write. He survived, and became more and more assured. Archaeology, not higher criticism, could prove the Bible was true history.

At first Sayce was genial enough toward his rival German critics. He insisted he was all for progress, all for looking at the Bible scientifically, but higher criticism was simply the wrong scientific method. German scholars holed up in their studies could never match the strong, clear, fresh, English light from the ancient monuments. Why waste time dissecting later Hebrew and Greek versions of the Bible for answers when the "problem could be solved forthwith" with a little digging? "Light is poured in upon it from outside, and the ineffectual attempts to light it from within have been superseded." The Bible didn't need the surgical knife that Delitzsch had borrowed from the higher critics; it just needed a spade.

But Sayce wasn't just about advocating archaeology. He actively believed that the German higher critics—the same people his friend Delitzsch had recently aligned himself with—were wrong about nearly everything. They claimed that the book of Genesis was written by two early Hebrew scribes, whom they called J and E, writing many centuries after the events the Bible described. Since J and E were supposed to have existed long after the Babylonians, their account could not possibly be historically accurate. That's why the higher critics could find mistakes in the Bible—redundancies, anachronisms, even spelling errors.

Sayce was having none of this. He was a modern man, a scientist, and he was not going to claim that God had dictated the Bible to Moses. But he *did* believe that Moses had existed. He believed Moses was a Hebrew scribe who copied down Babylonian stories. But it did *not* follow, for Sayce, that those stories were wrong. Sayce believed that the Eden story was a true event, just as Noah's Flood was a real account of a "great catastrophe which had once swept over the civilized earth."

If Delitzsch had put Moses on trial for plagiarism, Sayce dropped the charges. Then he issued a pardon for the great Hebrew scribe: Moses did the most important part. He edited the Babylonian accounts to reflect the Hebrews' new monotheistic morals. In the Babylonian flood story, for example, the gods punish Ziusudra and the rest of humanity because they made too much noise and disturbed the gods' sleep. In the Babylonian creation story, the world is formed from the many-headed dragon goddess named Tiamat. Moses rescued the Bible from all that.

He neatly removed the primitive, polytheist paganism from the holy book. This wasn't a stylistic choice on Moses's part; it was simply the practical way to go. Like Sayce himself, Moses was a man of progress. After he came down from Mount Sinai with the Ten Commandments and read number three, "You shall worship no other God but me, for the Lord is a jealous God," he knew the Babylonian canon needed some serious revision. (Never mind that, according to Delitzsch, three of those Commandments—against murder, adultery, and theft—came straight from the polytheist Babylonian king Hammurabi.)

The Old Testament reflected a higher, more developed form of religion than its Babylonian predecessors. It was *not* made up; it was just edited for Jewish—and then Christian—consumption. There were still, according to Sayce, "no theological fairy tales, but accounts of events which are alleged to have taken place in this work-a-day world." Delitzsch had tried to separate the heavenly theology from earthly history, Sayce tried to put them back together.

Not everybody was going for it. Samuel R. Driver, the Christian company man who had been granted Sayce's promised Hebrew post at Oxford, immediately and publicly opposed his colleague. Sayce's argument that the Book of Genesis comes directly from Babylonian history via one Moses-like Hebrew scribe "could not be taken seriously." There was a difference, Driver insisted, between an *illustration* of the Bible and a *confirmation* of the Bible.

Driver brushed aside all of Sayce's connections between archaeology and Biblical truth. Sayce's claim that the story of Joseph was historically accurate was "illusional," his discovery of the Biblical priest Melchizedek in the Amarna tablets "destitute of solid foundation," and his theory that Biblical patriarchs like Abraham lived directly under the law of the Babylonian king Hammurabi "too slight to merit any attention"—any scholarly attention, that is. But Sayce was getting a lot of attention outside of academia.

The rest of the British archaeology community—those not busy trying to connect every word of cuneiform to the Bible—knew that they did not have the public's ear the way Sayce did, and this worried them. Sayce's optimism had upstaged Delitzsch's creative destruction. Instead of one sudden blast of light quickly shut down, Sayce's performances were widespread, almost franchised. In London theaters during the nineteenth century, pro-Bible "arguments by monument" became a staple form of entertainment, along with the constant stream of travelogues from the Middle East and the expansion of public museums. The public was far more prepared to listen to the findings of archaeologists than to those of the "higher critics."

In short, argued Driver, "our popular literature on the Old Testament is becoming an obstacle to progress." As Driver put it, "[Sayce] constantly popularizes his results without indicating whether they are peculiar to himself or not, and through the attractiveness of his style and the concessions to Biblical orthodoxy, these results have obtained such a currency in the English-speaking countries as to be practically incontrovertible."

And it didn't help matters that Sayce was such a nice guy. Even a few of his scholarly friends were willing to forgive Sayce his trespasses. As a fellow Assyriologist wrote in the journal *Biblical World*, "I pardon his wild tilts against Old Testament criticism because of his immense services to learning elsewhere, and because of his wonderful qualities as a gentleman, a Christian gentleman, and a friend."

There were, however, holes in Sayce's stylish and attractive argument. First, how was it possible to argue both that the Bible was accurate down to the historical letter and yet that it did not come directly from Moses? How could Babylonian borrowing and Hebrew editing make for something as accurate as a newspaper? Was the Bible human history or divine providence? And what about Delitzsch's contention that the Babylonians kept their myth and their science separate? If that was true, how could their myths be real history?

Sayce slid past these difficulties with charming ease, using a brilliant reliance on scientific uncertainty. Just as he had refused to sign on to any one translation of the words "Pishon" and "Gihon," he refused to posit a date when the Babylonian stories would have been copied and adapted for monotheism by the Hebrew Moses—not yet; not until the definitive tablets had been discovered. And that one note of caution preserved his scientific credibility in a late-Victorian world hungry for both scientific advance and religious reassurance.

Beware, he said to them: higher criticism may seem to be "in accordance with the scientific requirements of the day," and we don't want to throw out science—quite the contrary. But science doesn't know everything. And in that void, the incomplete ancient record, the contested translations and dubious dictionaries, Sayce made room for the hope that the old beloved traditions would be borne out, or at least maintained, when the records were found.

There were also holes in Sayce's charming personality. His tilts against German criticism grew wilder and wilder. It's as if that meeting of the Oriental Congress in 1881 had played out again, but the line between the Germans and British had been drawn not with a fork, but a sword. The Germans were in love with their "subjective fantasies" and ignorance. They "ruthlessly" assigned one Bible story after another to the realm of permanent myth, not caring whom they hurt or what precious beliefs they destroyed in the process. It was a good thing archaeology had come along when it did! "At the very moment when the assailants of Scripture had adopted new methods of attack which could no longer be met by the old modes of defense, God was raising up unexpected testimonies to the truth of Biblical history."

For Sayce, all the "heaps of controversy and abuse" placed on him by his colleagues were worth it. The events of the Old Testament must be proved definite, because it was to those events that Christ appealed for proof of his divinity. According to the Gospel of John, Christ directed his followers: "Search the scriptures; for . . . they are that which testify of me." So finally, despite his world travels, his liberalism, his public likability, and his advocacy of archaeology, Sayce actually had something in common with the sheltered German Christians in Delitzsch's audience at the Singakademie. The Singakademie spectators saw in the spiky head of Dürer's engraved serpent a promise for redemption from original sin through Christ. Sayce, too, believed that the Old Testament was the rock on which the New Testament was founded. And British society, as Sayce saw it, was founded on the New Testament. Like William Warren, Sayce believed it was worth all measures to maintain a Christian civil society. Modern Christians could not serve two masters. Either they believed that the messianic prophecies in the Old Testament were accurate, and that Christ was right and should be believed, or they believed, along with the critics, that the prophecies were "an illusion of the past," and threw out, along with the Old Testament, their Christian faith.

In August 1914, Germany declared war against Great Britain. The conflict between England and Germany moved out of the scholar's study and into the field of battle. Almost immediately, Sayce's academic objections to German Bible criticism became open attacks on Germans in general. In a letter to the *Times* of London that December, Sayce claimed to examine the worthiness of German contributions to Western culture in "the dry light of reason."

"As I have been seeking to show for years in the domain of Oriental archaeology," Sayce wrote, "the German can laboriously count syllables and words and pile up volumes of indices, he can appropriate other men's discoveries in the interests of culture; but beyond this, we get from him only theories which take no regard of facts."

It got worse. "[The Germans] are still what they were fifteen centuries ago, the barbarians who raided our ancestors and destroyed the civilization of the Roman Empire." On the day that war was declared, Sayce had been in meetings deciding on the program of the Oriental Congress for 1914—and, presumably, whether the reel-dancing German professor would be invited back. The next day's meeting was called off, and Oriental Congresses became "one of those things that will never happen again." With the end of civilization in the air, time could not be spared for considering its origins—certainly not with the enemy.

During the war Sayce lost contact with his former German colleagues, although he did learn that the elderly Delitzsch had completely lost his hearing. Sayce, now in his seventies, suffered another of his episodes of blindness. Even if they could have met, the two old colleagues would have had nothing to say to one another.

5

Far East of Eden

IN THE BEGINNING, when the heavens were like the white of an egg, and the Earth was like the yolk, God created Adam—or as the Chinese call him, Tien Hwang.

So wrote a forty-two-year-old businessman, Tse Tsan Tai, on Sunday evening, October 25, 1914. Outside his study on Queen's Road East in Hong Kong, thunder pealed and lightning flashed. Two months before, Germany had declared war against France and Britain, and Japan had entered into an alliance with Britain. Soon, the aging Ottoman Empire officially declared itself aligned with Germany—to the delight of Kaiser Wilhelm and the despair of Archibald Henry Sayce. The European world was falling apart. From his home 6,000 miles away along the South China Sea, Tse wondered what he could do to help put it back together.

The solution came to him, as he put it, "like a flash of light"—the Garden of Eden. The Garden of Eden was not in southern Mesopotamia near the head of the Persian Gulf, where the misguided Europeans thought it was. After all, Mesopotamia was bare and ugly. "Is it likely that Almighty God would create man and place him in such a corner of the World?" So where *was* Eden, then? In order to better focus on finding it, Tse skipped dinner and stayed up all night. By eight the following morning he had completed a draft of *The Creation, the Real Situation of Eden, and the Origin of the Chinese*. For seven days and seven nights, he rewrote and revised without eating or sleeping. Finally, he rested.

The "real situation" of Eden was in China—specifically, in a crescent-shaped oasis in the Mongolian desert known as Chinese

Turkestan. On this high plateau between two jagged mountain ranges, there were the four necessary rivers: the Kashgar (Tigris), the Aksu (Euphrates), the Kholan (Pishon), and the Yarkhand (Gihon). The four rivers flowed into one great river, Tarim, as the Bible said. The Tarim flowed eastward, as the Bible said. The Tarim river basin was well known for its precious stones, as the Bible said it would be. Though he'd never been to Chinese Turkestan himself, Tse had it on good authority that the bed of the Yarkhand was covered with multicolored jade pebbles. Mesopotamia, on the other hand, produced no precious stones or minerals, only "an abundant supply of clay and bitumen!" Tse must be forgiven for not knowing just how valuable the black, molasses-like liquid bubbling out of the ground in Mesopotamia would turn out to be.

The Creation was published by Hong Kong printers Kelly & Walsh, in English, several weeks later. Instead of a title page, the slim thirty-five-page book opened with a formal photograph of the author. Tse wore a dark suit jacket and striped tie. His short hair was perfectly parted in the English style, and his tough eyes stared confidently out at the camera. There were no angles, no shadows; nothing was hidden; and just the slightest hint of a smile beneath his pencil-thin mustache. Tse wanted to be judged on his own merits and treated without prejudice by anyone.

Tse lived an outwardly respectable Hong Kong life: he had attended high school and the university; he joined the civil service as a secretary for the public works system; then he went into the shipping business, one of bustling Hong Kong's staple industries. He lived on Queen's Road, the first thoroughfare built by the British when they colonized the island in 1842. Though it sounded grand, Queen's Road was really a narrow unpaved track designed for commerce. On either side, identical white-columned buildings pressed toward each other like precarious pigeon nests. Wise residents affixed cast-iron grilles to their windows to keep out thieves.

Hong Kong, said the British proudly, was an "object lesson" in British colonization; the lesson seems to have been in lopsided economics. Hong Kong exported luxury leisure goods to Europe—silk, tea, palm-leaf fans, ginger, rattan, and cane for cricket bats. There were thirteen preserved-ginger factories in Hong Kong alone. The best of Hong Kong's duck feathers filled European feather beds; the lesser-quality feathers became toothpicks and mulch for British farmers. In return, Hong Kong imported everything that was actually *needed* from Europe—including flour, sugar, coal, hardware, and machinery.

The British touted their success in *Present Day Impressions of the Far East*, an extravagant 1,000-page gilt-edged catalog of imperial pride. Tse's work for the shipping firm of Shewan Tomes—the industry leader in arms, rope, coal, and mortgages—earned him an entry in this colonial encyclopedia under "Hong Kong: Prominent Chinese, Professional and Industrial."

"The career of Mr. Tse Tsan Tai," gushed the writer of this entry, Chesney Duncan, "has been more remarkable than that of the vast majority of his fellow Chinese citizens."

By age forty-two Tse was so successful in business that he could afford to move himself, his wife, and his eleven children—five boys and six girls—to an estate in the less developed "New Territory" just off Hong Kong Island every summer. But business was hardly Tse's only interest. Duncan didn't seem to have enough titles for all of Tse's roles: social and political reformer, scholar, patriot, businessman, philanthropist, journalist, author, inventor of dirigibles, historian, and art collector. Tse was also known for his personal discipline: "Further, he is a staunch teetotaler and non-smoker."

By the time Tse published *The Creation, the Real Situation of Eden, and the Origin of the Chinese* in 1914, both English-speaking and Chinese-speaking readers in Hong Kong would have known who he was, and what he thought about nearly everything: Tse was always speaking his mind about politics.

Back in 1899, at age twenty-seven, he had published a political cartoon in *Chinese Punch,* an English-language satirical magazine modeled after its famous British namesake; Tse was the first actual Chinese person to do so. His cartoon, "The Situation in the Far East," was meant "to warn the people of the impending danger of the partitioning of the Empire by the Foreign Powers." Like the Ottoman Empire, China's Qing dynasty stood on the verge of collapse under its own obsolescence and corruption. No longer able to defend their vast territory against the greed and guns of the West, a succession of Qing rulers had made many embarrassing concessions to European powers, allowing their empire to be eaten away at the edges.

Tse's cartoon mapped these looming threats. From the north, a hulking black bear represented Russian encroachment out of Siberia. A chubby British bulldog sat right on top of the tiny island of Hong Kong; a smaller French frog reached out a sneaky leg toward Hong Kong's neighbor Macao; a stealthy Japanese spider bided its time to the northwest; and from the east the American eagle swooped in from the Philippines, which the United States had just conquered. China hadn't actually been partitioned yet, but this was only because the foreigners couldn't agree among themselves on how best to slice it up.

Tse was a nationalist: he wanted China to belong to its own people—all its own people. He liked to say that in Chinese politics, he had "many friends but not a single enemy." But beneath his impeccably diplomatic demeanor, the accumulated humiliations of a crumbling China weighed heavily on him, and he took the responsibility for reform personally. As everyone in Hong Kong knew, in his youth Tse had twice tried and failed to overthrow the Chinese government.

He had been groomed as both a nationalist and a Christian from a young age by his father, a player in the disastrous Taiping Rebellion—or, as its leaders called it, the "Rebellion of Great Peace"—in the 1850s. The rebels took over much of southern China and declared it an alternative nation called the "Heavenly Kingdom of Great Peace." At its height, the Heavenly Kingdom controlled 30 million people. The Taiping reformers abolished foot binding, separated the sexes, and socialized land ownership, all under the theocratic leadership of a renegade Christian convert, Hong Xiuquan, who believed himself to be the younger brother of Jesus.

They held off the emperor's forces for fourteen years, and their own armies pushed toward Beijing. The Qing ruler begged the British and French for help. Hoping to put themselves in a better trading position, the Europeans obliged. They finally put down the rebellion in 1871, but not before 20 million people—two-thirds of the citizens of the Heavenly Kingdom—had lost their lives through the fighting or through starvation, making the Rebellion of Great Peace one of the bloodiest conflicts in history.

Tse's father managed to escape this brutal fate, and fled to Sydney, Australia, where his son—Christian name: James See—was born in 1872. There was no trace of radicalism in the Sees' Christianity; James was baptized at age seven by a traditional Anglican bishop, the Right Reverend C. C. Greenway, in Sydney's Christ Church Cathedral. The See family moved to Grafton, a new settlement 400 miles north of Sydney along the eastern coast of Australia, and opened a general store on the main street, on the banks of the Clarence River. There, it was peaceful. Sugarcane farms, giant ferns, and fig trees lined the riverbanks, and many smaller creeks made perfect swimming holes. There were few other Chinese families— Tse's mother was said to be one of only a dozen Chinese women in the whole of Australia—but the store catered to Chinese miners passing through Grafton on their way to the gold and tin fields farther north. When Tse was four years old, the Clarence River overflowed its banks, flooding the main streets and trapping Tse and his baby brother, mother, and father inside their store.

Fortunately, the store adjoined the offices of the local newspaper, the *Clarence and Richmond Examiner*. Several reporters climbed up to their second-floor balcony, lowered a rope down to the front door of the Sees' one-story shop, and hoisted them all up to safety. In return, the Sees shared their stock of canned food with the reporters, and they spent the duration of the deluge holed up in the paper's offices until the floodwaters receded.

When James was a teenager, the family moved to Hong Kong: this is when James See began to go by his Chinese name, Tse Tsan Tai. At first, after wide-open Australia, the cramped houses, narrow unsanitary streets, and total absence of shade trees in urban Hong Kong made him claustrophobic. But the protected island city had its advantages. Tse was not alone in Hong Kong. There were other cosmopolitan Chinese families, not just tin miners. There were Chinese Christian churches, and secret societies that attracted revolutionaries from all over China. Tse, like his father, was determined to take down the faltering government of China's last dynasty. Tse set about planning an attack on the Qing headquarters in Canton City, almost 100 miles away on the mainland.

He couldn't tell his bosses at Shewan Tomes. The Hong Kong establishment approved of Christianity, of course, but considered the Chinese nationalist movement alternately laughable and dangerous. A few British newspapermen who championed this cause had received official reprimands from the colonial secretary: the British were on friendly terms with the Qing emperor, and inciting the Chinese to revolt against an ally of Britain's would be unseemly, to say the least.

But Tse remained resolute, and he found a willing audience among the other young educated Chinese shipping clerks in British firms. They operated furtively, right under the noses of the authorities. According to Tse, his society's revolutionary headquarters at No. 1 Pak Tze Lanc was "visited from time to time by European police detectives, who were always welcome!" To preserve proper appearances, Tse would cheerfully mingle with known spies and secret agents of the government. He claimed to enjoy the challenge of "persistently putting my head in the tiger's jaws!" He was Daniel in the lion's den, David fighting Goliath, the Hebrews under Egyptian rule. Even under observation, he managed to marshal a 2,000-man fighting force to march on Canton. But when traitors divulged their plans to the Qing authorities, hundreds of his people were arrested and several were executed.

Meanwhile, the pharoah's armies were gathering strength far away in Manchuria, a province in the northeast of China. The longhaired "Boxer" reactionaries posed a bigger threat to Tse's ideals than even the impotent empire. Downtrodden Chinese living under a feudal empire felt they were losing their Chinese identity to western religion. Christian missionary work in China had always been an immense challenge, both theologically—it took one early Protestant twelve years just to translate the Bible into Chinese—and practically: they had to make inroads into an impoverished and hostile nation. European governments began to make safe passage for their missionaries a condition of the numerous economic treaties they forced China to sign throughout the nineteenth century. By 1900, hundreds of missions dotted the mountains, rice fields, and riverbanks of rural China.

The Boxers marshaled Chinese traditions against Christianity. They believed the missions and the western-built railway lines violated the sacred principles of feng shui. The ragtag soldiers had little food and few weapons, other than wushu, Chinese martial arts that they believed could give them strength and the power of flight. (Apparently, to the British, wushu looked like boxing.) With the tacit approval of the Qing empress, the Boxers marched on Beijing and forced all the foreign diplomats then living freely in the imperial city into a garrisoned compound. Then they went after the Christians. This time the Chinese empire didn't have to beg Europe to intervene. The Alliance of Eight Nations—Austria-Hungary, France, Germany, Italy, Japan, Russia, the United Kingdom, and the United States—brought thousands of troops to the defense of their own citizens: diplomats and missionaries.

From 1900 to 1901, the Boxers murdered approximately 18,000 Chinese Catholics, 500 Chinese Protestants, and 200 Chinese Eastern Orthodox Christians. The largest missionary organization, the China Inland Mission, lost fifty-eight foreign missionaries, plus twenty-one children.

The Alliance of Eight Nations finally put down the rebellion, and then the allies' armies began their own savage campaign of destruction across China. German soldiers were said to be especially brutal in interpreting Kaiser Wilhelm's order to "Make the name 'German' remembered in China for a thousand years." But while they destroyed much of everything else, the Europeans left the Qing empire in power.

Though things looked bleak, Tse's revolutionary society was still mounting futile takeover efforts from its Hong Kong headquarters. The nonexistent Chinese Republic was real to these revolutionaries: they designed its flag—white sun on blue background—and nominated its president, Tse's best friend, Yang Quyun. After a squabble with another revolutionary leader, Dr. Sun Yat-sen, Yang decided to resign the provisional presidency rather than cause any more strife. But the imperial enemy didn't seem to get news of the change in leadership. A few months later, while Yang taught an English class in his Hong Kong home, a gunman shot him in the head in front of his students. The assassin disappeared; Yang's friends buried him in the local Protestant cemetery. Devastated, Tse immediately began planning another attack: he would blow up the Temple of Longevity in Beijing during the Chinese New Year while all the Qing officials sat inside for the festivities. It was his most ambitious plan to date, and also his most vicious. Though Tse believed military means were justified in overturning a corrupt empire, attacking people at a religious ceremony of any kind was not his style. And this plan collapsed even faster than the others: before Tse could pounce, the authorities confiscated the arms and the uniforms of the revolutionary band and arrested anyone they could find.

By 1903, Tse didn't know where to turn. His attacks had failed; he had lost his friend, and then his father. The revolution was still going on—as it would continue to do for another seven years. But Tse didn't have confidence that Sun Yat-sen could do any better, so he retired from politics and became a newspaperman. He founded and briefly ran the *South China Morning Post,* now the oldest paper in Hong Kong, as a platform for revolutionary reform; the paper didn't take off until it fired him. But elsewhere in the English- and Chinese-language press Tse kept the revolutionary flame alive, peacefully.

In 1904, he drew an update of his now famous 1899 cartoon. "The Situation in the Far East" had not improved: the British bulldog had stretched out all along southern China, its tail flapping into the South China Sea. The Russian bear still lurked; the frog, eagle, and spider still remained poised in the South China Sea. Around the edge of the map more imperial animals had assembled: an Arab camel, an Italian rabbit. But this time Tse didn't reserve his criticism for foreign powers. After the Boxer Rebellion he was just as hard on the sins of his fellow Chinese. A long-bearded opium addict sprawled across China's northern provinces; off to the West stood an official-looking figure holding up a giant gold coin: the corrupt Qing emperor. In the center, a wealthy couple dined at a fancy table, holding up their glasses in a toast to the new foreign wealth. Tse's great nation was not just fraying from the outside in; it was rotting from the inside out.

He wrote seething editorials against foot binding, slavery, the vandalization of historic relics, the opium trade that Britain had fought so hard to protect, and the "evil" practice of feng shui, used by the Boxers to justify killing Chinese Christians. Instead, he advocated religious toleration and the establishment of an independent Christian church for China, a church that would no longer have to be "of England," or the United States, or anywhere else: China for the Chinese.

He wanted the Chinese representatives serving in Hong Kong's legislative council to be elected, rather than appointed. He wanted to found a Chinese Club and Free Library analogous to the British members-only clubs. Chinese people needed to learn to take the best trappings of western civilization for themselves, without entirely merging with their colonizers. Tse dreamed of a place where this was possible.

There's no telling when exactly his dreams for a future peaceful China took up residence in the distant past, in the far reaches of the Mongolian desert. He wasn't the first to find the future in the past. The Garden of Eden has always been located both in the original past and in the idealized future.

Even so, the Mongolian desert seemed an extreme choice. Tse had never visited the "New Dominion" then known as Chinese Turkestan. Indeed, few people had. The 500,000-square-mile plateau wedged between Mongolia and Tibet had become an official province of China only recently, in 1884, after years of battling between China and the area's population of Mongol and Turkic ethnic groups; there was also the Russian threat from the north. The region's frigid temperatures and rocky terrain made it inaccessible to all but its native inhabitants, the nomadic Uighurs, who spoke a language related to Turkish, and traversed the flat desert by camel. Every year, 100 of those camels, along with some horses and 5,000 tons of grain, had to be paid to the central Chinese government. For this the Uighurs bought themselves a Chinese military governor who sat behind a fortress wall doing not much.

To the rest of China, this vast territory looked like empty space. After all, there were only 2.5 million people in a region that today makes up one-sixth of China's total acreage. (As of 2009, it was called Xinjiang and was under the semiautonomous rule of the Uighurs again.) To Tse, Chinese Turkestan looked like Paradise. If a place's mystery corresponds to its paradise potential, Chinese Turkestan was practically heaven. The American Asiatic Society sponsored a major expedition through Turkestan in 1922—eight years after Tse formulated his Eden theory—and even then, the expedition's chief geologist called the area "virtually unknown, scientifically speaking."

For Tse, the three problems in his book's title all overlapped: the creation, the real location of Eden, and the origin of the Chinese —and by extension the origin of all humanity. He tackled these enormous questions simultaneously and publicly, weaving in whatever new mysteries science discovered, in Central Asia or anywhere else. He formulated his thoughts in letters to newspapers, then republished them one by one in pamphlet form: *The Origin of the Mongolian Desert, and Its Prehistoric Fossils; The Real Mountains of Ararat; New Theory of the Universe, and Origin of Typhoons; Solution of Easter Island Mystery; The Solution of Mysterious Blank in Ancient Egyptian History; The Age of the Siberian Mammoth.*

Tse didn't bother with careful proofs: science *inspired* him to revisit the Bible. His answers came as a series of lightning bolts, like those that flashed outside his window as he put the finishing touches on his book. Tse's creation story is an electrical storm of geology, anti-Darwinism, Bible stories, Chinese folklore, and nationalist propaganda.

According to him, at the time of the creation, the world consisted of nine interconnected continents—the usual seven, plus the "Malaysian continent," and the "Polynesian continent." There were ten if you counted Atlantis, "a vast continent that once extended from China to Easter Island" but now lay submerged, underneath the Pacific Ocean.

Life in Tse's Eden took up much more space than the typical riverside garden with its population of two. During the "Eden era," Adam's twelve sons spread across this vast interconnected continent, populating the whole world—with the exception of the South Pole, which they couldn't reach. They founded the following civilizations: Easter Island, ancient China, Egypt, Greece, Chaldea (in southern Mesopotamia), Mexico, New Mexico, Peru, Switzerland, and ancient Britain. All these civilizations were to be wiped out by Noah's Flood. Unfortunately, Tse said, there were no written records of these pre-Flood civilizations. So the present natives of these lands were "quite ignorant" of their Asian origins.

That was certainly true of William Warren, who had pronounced the great age of China "imaginary"; Reverend Landon West, for whom China was so far away as to be in another world; and Archibald Henry Sayce, who insisted, like many Europeans, that civilization began in Mesopotamia and nowhere else. But Tse was appropriating a very old Chinese idea, the image of the Middle Kingdom. Everything came from China—language, religion, architecture, ceramics, horses and carriages, agriculture, mathematics, even, according to Tse, the Mesopotamian cuneiform alphabet. It only made sense that human life itself began in China, too. Still, the Garden of Eden, like salvation through Christ, can't be *too* close to home, too easy to access—if it were, how much could it be worth? Tse favored China's taking up as much space as possible: Chinese Turkestan was as far away from Hong Kong as a place could be and still be in China.

Tse did not spend a lot of time describing the landscape of his Central Asian Eden. The earliest humans lived in peace along the banks of the Tarim River, along with giant species of pre-Flood animals, such as the woolly mammoths, whose skeletons were being uncovered in Siberia as he wrote. These first civilizations existed mostly in order to be wiped out by the great Flood. Perhaps because of his early, visceral experience trapped in the flooded store, the Flood, or "the Deluge" as he called it, was the centerpiece of Tse's new world order. The flood *is* history: he uses the word "antediluvian"—before the Deluge—interchangeably with "prehistoric." Noah's Flood and the Garden of Eden always go hand in hand: one is creation from scratch, and one is re-creation. Humans take comfort from re-creation—especially in the last days of a dying empire. But Tse went farther than most.

His deluge was really a tidal wave so vast that it covered all of his proposed ten continents in water, convulsing the landmasses and splitting them apart into today's seven continents, pushing Atlantis downward and lifting up Central Asia. The great wave also caused the sudden death by freezing or drowning of all of Eden's gigantic mammals. It was important that the Deluge be sudden. The fossilized mammoths found in Siberia still had grass in their teeth. How could that be true, Tse wondered, if the Darwinians were correct, and the mammoths died out slowly over millions of years?

Chinese Turkestan turned into a vast "inland sea," with 600-year-old Noah—or as Tse claims he is named in the ancient Chinese epics, Nü Wa—floating on top. Here Tse paused for a moment to acknowledge that some people would not believe his theory: scholars of Chinese folklore, for example. They thought that Nü Wa was female. In the ancient texts, Nü Wa was usually connected to the female god Fuhi, their long snakelike tails intertwining. Sometimes Nü Wa was Fuhi's sister, sometimes her husband, sometimes her wife. There are 2,000 years' worth of stories and songs to choose from.

Tse did not have the patience for mythological variation. Chinese folklore was, according to him, simply "confused and vague." The female Nü Wa was purely a scholarly error. Fuhi, he declared, was "imaginary." Because of these mistakes, the dates for ancient Chinese history did not match up with Christian history, and the Chinese did not see the similarity of their own folklore and the Bible, of Nü Wa and Noah.

Locating the Garden of Eden in the twentieth century involved reconciling science with religion. As an English-speaking, Anglican-baptized Chinese man, Tse had spent his lifetime trying to make peace between battling cultures. He kept trying to weave together opposites—Chinese history and Christian history, English language and Chinese pride—into one story, *his* story. It was a delicate operation. The Chinese couldn't simply insert themselves into the story of Christ, as the Taiping rebels had done. They couldn't use ancient Chinese traditions against Christianity, as the Boxers did. Both ways led to disaster. Tse had had enough disaster; he wanted peace, the peace that he'd had before the river flood, back in Australia along the banks of the Clarence.

There were two important aspects of Nü Wa's Chinese character that Tse wanted to import into his Christian story. First, Nü Wa was the repairer of the universe: when the four poles of the universe collapsed into fire, flood, and plague, Nü Wa was the one who melted a special five-color stone to plug the holes in the world. And Nü Wa was a creator: According to the myths, she built people out of yellow clay because she was lonely at the beginning of the world.

In the Chinese myths, these are two separate Nü Wa stories. She creates humans out of loneliness, and then later she helps repair the world after natural disasters, including a flood. Tse merged the two: Nü Wa is the *re*-creator of people, after the disastrous flood.

He placed this new Nü Wa in his Central Asian landscape. The Bible says that after the rain stopped, Noah's Ark settled "on the mountains of Ararat." Nü Wa's boat landed on top of Mustaghata

Peak, the highest of the Tien Shan mountains. From this vantage point, Noah kept watch on the floodwaters as they slowly receded, exposing first the tops of the surrounding mountains. It was then that he started sending out doves to see if they could find any dry ground, just as the Babylonian Noah, Ziusudra, had done. Tse wasn't buying the "Armenia" theory, and not because of the typographical arguments of the Assyriologists. If Noah could see the tops of the surrounding mountains from his Ark, Tse reasoned, he must have settled on the highest point around. And the present-day Mount Ararat in Armenia is not, according to Tse, the highest point around.

After the flood subsided, Nü Wa was put in charge of building a new civilization, not an easy task in the Mongolian desert. Unlike Middle Eastern deserts, it was not sandy but full of rocks—rocks Tse believed had formed from "the action of the sun and wind on vast deposits of mud" left all over the world after Noah's diluvian tsunami. Perhaps using his masonry training from the Chinese myths, Nü Wa quarried stones and used them to repair and dam up the mouth of the Gaib gorge to stop the flood. The Russian explorer G. Grum-Grzimailo found immense fine-grained gray granite boulders in this area, fourteen to seventeen feet high and 100 feet in circumference. Tse declared these to be the stones that Nü Wa quarried.

As Nü Wa's civilization got up and running, he (or she) also found time to repopulate the world. Nü Wa had three sons: Shem, Ham, and Japheth. The descendents of Shem became the Chinese, Assyrians, Persians, Babylonians, Japanese, Samoyeds, "Esquimaux," and Burmese, and the natives of Australia and Polynesia. The descendants of Ham became the "Egyptian, Ethiopian, Hindoo, Arabian, and other kindred nations."

The sons of Japheth became the modern European nations, "whose ancestors did not become thoroughly civilized until the advent of Jesus Christ." In the meantime, the sons of Japheth became confused. In the many generations since the Deluge, they had wandered so far from China (or, as Tse said the Bible called it, Shinar), that they found themselves surrounded by vast oceans, inland seas, the frozen wilds of Siberia, and formidable mountain chains.

Because of their isolation, Tse wrote, the proto-Europeans "mistook Mesopotamia and the surrounding country to be the whole World." The ancient historians of the West took all the events that happened in the first eleven chapters of Genesis and crowded them into this flat empty corner of western Asia. This, Tse felt, was a singular shame: "Could they have made a greater mistake?" Western history even claimed that the Chinese *themselves* came from the West, from the Sumerians of Babylon. But, Tse wrote, "This theory is contrary to all the known facts." Tse could sympathize with the sons of Japheth, but he could no longer tolerate their error.

The world had originated in China, and the Chinese had originated in Chinese Turkestan, and it was time the truth be known. The idea of Mesopotamia had gone entirely too far: "It is this mistake, which has confused and confounded the church and the Thinking World for close on four thousand years." And at the moment, the "Thinking World" was engaged in tearing itself apart in its first World War.

When Tse finished writing *The Creation, the Garden of Eden, and the Origin of the Chinese* in October 1914, the war in Europe had just begun. In 1916 he reprinted the book with an additional appendix, "The War as Punishment":

> This terrible fratricidal war, which is convulsing and devastating Europe, is not due to trade rivalry, mutual fear of aggression, or the ambition of Kings and Emperors to become supreme in this world. It is the punishment of God for the crimes of Europe.

God was punishing Europe for its colonial ambitions, for lying, for stealing, and for coveting its neighbors' houses. It was not the Chinese who were a savage, uncivilized people; it was the Europeans. The Chinese were the source of all life, and the source of Christianity: "If the Christian nations of Europe believe in the

Bible, they must acknowledge that Militarism is a crime against God."

Tse had seen militarism up close, and he knew it would not work; that is to say, it would not bring forward real revolution. What did all the European powers encroaching on China share? Militarism. What had the failed Taiping and Boxer rebellions had in common? Militarism. Even the idealists closest to Tse's heart fell victim to militarism. When the Qing empire finally did collapse in 1911, and Tse's former revolutionary colleague Sun Yat-sen took control of the first Chinese Republic, Tse watched sadly from the sidelines as his former colleagues descended into hopeless infight-ing. Without the unity he had worked for, the fragile republic fell apart, and China entered a time that became officially known as the "Warlord Era."

No; in order to create the real Kingdom of Heavenly Peace, European colonizers must acknowledge that they were no better than those "savage" races they were trying to conquer. Their tech-nology, their language, and above all their Christianity did not set them above the Chinese. Tse had done his part, by showing how the "Ancient Chinese Record of the Creation and the Deluge" is "the same as Genesis."

And he hoped that once this news reached those in power, "the whole human race will soon learn to believe in The Bible, and that, henceforth, men will love and treat each other as brothers." He urged everyone who agreed with him to work toward four goals: universal disarmament; universal peace; the protection and civilization of all the weak and savage races of the world; and the brotherhood of man. Once these goals had been accomplished, and "the nations and Governments of the World have reached a state fit to be Federated," wrote Tse, China should turn the Garden of Eden into an international state, and establish the Parliament of Nations there.

"Then will there be Peace on Earth."

6

Practically Paradise

IN THE BEGINNING, William Willcocks had wanted to be a missionary, but instead he became the foremost British irrigation engineer of his time, and God saw that it was good.

In 1902 Willcocks designed the Aswan Dam—then the world's tallest, at 131 feet—across the Nile. More than a mile wide, the dam was an engineering marvel, a triumph of empire that allowed British cotton-mill owners to get rich off the newly irrigated fields. Two years later Willcocks was knighted for his work reconstructing the waterways of South Africa after the Boer War. With such a résumé, it was not surprising that Willcocks developed a reputation for megalomania. After observing him at work, the British archaeologist, writer, and sometime intelligence agent Gertrude Bell—no wilting flower herself—wrote: "Sir William is a 20th century Don Quixote, erratic, maddening—and entirely loveable; a streak of genius, a good slab of unreasonableness. . . . Good luck go with him, and may I never have to work with him." Willcocks, tall and lanky, always wore a slight scowl, and he spoke and wrote with a blunt honesty that unsettled his well-mannered English colleagues.

Whether one found him lovable or maddening, Willcocks undoubtedly approached his scientific work with evangelical zeal. He carried his Bible everywhere, although he'd memorized it long ago, a chapter a day. So when in 1908 the Ottoman Empire invited the decorated fifty-six-year-old scientist to survey the Tigris and Euphrates rivers and suggest irrigation projects for Turkish-controlled Mesopotamia, Willcocks accepted immediately. He went wherever his services were needed, British territory or not: "Politics I have nothing to do with. My ambition is to see ten blades of grass growing where there are none today."

Mesopotamia was the perfect challenge for his talents, and he'd been waiting to get his hands on it for years, calling it "the dream of my life." New development was sorely needed: without working irrigation, the Tigris and Euphrates rivers were too dry for agriculture nine months out of the year and too flooded for the other three. The drought seasons turned the southern plains into a dusty desert wasteland where no grass could grow, killing off the sheep and goats that nomadic tribes depended on for food. Yet every flood season, people had to pack up and migrate out of their settlements, leaving behind homes and crops. Small farmers could scrape out a living raising date palms or cotton, but "fertile crescent" seemed a cruel misnomer.

Willcocks could not abide this state of affairs. After all, irrigation was the world's oldest applied science. Before the Mongols destroyed Mesopotamia in 1258, the country had had the most highly developed system of dams and canals in the world. But under 400 years of Turkish rule, any improvements to the stagnant landscape had been do-it-yourself: tiny irrigation ditches through rice fields, makeshift levees of brush and bricks. In 1908, one couldn't travel anywhere in Mesopotamia without seeing ruins of the ancient waterways: canal banks rising out of dry land, long-abandoned retaining walls sitting surreally in the middle of the desert. Mostly, the canals sat empty of water, overgrown or beat up, their man-made edges dissolving into the earth from which they had once been dug. Willcocks was sure he could restore the ancient systems to general irrigated perfection and prosperity—the prosperity that must have reigned in Biblical times, in the Garden of Eden.

He left Egypt in November 1908, bound for Basra with a crew of twelve expert engineers, including his brother—who had managed to become both an engineer and an Anglican clergyman. (He led the group's regular Sunday services.) Willcocks spent a few weeks in Baghdad collecting supplies and planning routes, and installing himself in the beautiful riverside house with the shady balcony that the Turkish government had acquired for its celebrated irrigation adviser. But Willcocks was eager to be out in the field. Soon, he and his crew left comfortable Baghdad on a steamship headed south on the muddy Tigris.

Willcocks had planned to travel virtually unarmed, except for the rifles his men used to hunt ducks and partridges to supplement their food rations. But on a suggestion of friends in Baghdad he contracted a gunboat full of armed escorts to protect himself and his men from the many tribes who were continually rising against the Turks and one another. Usually, though, the other travelers they encountered were harmless. Marsh Arabs paddled by in tiny *ghurfas*, doughnut-shaped boats woven of reeds and sealed watertight with the naturally occurring petroleum called bitumen. Shia pilgrims bringing their dead for burial in the holy cities of Najaf and Karbala piled into carriages on the narrow roadway. Nomadic Bedouin on horseback led hundreds of sheep in search of greener pastures. The only real nuisance were the many informal "bridges," fleets of Turkish boats lined up to block the river and extract tolls from whoever might pass.

When the engineers reached a destination, they'd set up their tents along the shore, fill their sheepskin sacks with drinking water, and go off into the brush to hunt for dinner. The desert nights got cold: Willcocks and his men slept under sheepskin and carpets. They carried with them the latest in scientific equipment, including field telescopes and a surveying instrument called a theodolite, which could calculate the area of large swatches of land using triangulation. His crew measured the depth of the rivers at regular intervals, took soil samples, and made careful notes of all the ruined canals.

They did all this, as Willcocks liked to say, using the Bible as a guidebook. He meant this literally. On board his ship, he stood at the helm navigating with a topographic map in one hand and a Bible in the other.

He wasn't the only British official using the King James Bible as a guidebook to the Middle East. There were dozens of places in Iraq with Biblical connections. Some, like the palaces of

Nebuchadnezzar that had been discovered by Delitzsch's expedition, had been granted legitimacy by respected archaeologists. Others were pure hoax, like the shriveled swordfish in a Baghdad museum that was supposed to be the whale that swallowed Jonah. There were so many, in fact, that when bored British surveyors began naming tiny desert towns "Sodom" and "Gomorrah," as a joke, nobody seemed to notice. The names made it through numerous revisions and were not officially expunged until ten years later.

But these were all ruins. Willcocks may have been the only British official who actually thought he could *re-create*, even improve on, the Biblical world. According to the Bible, four rivers flowed out of Eden, and two of those rivers were the Tigris and the Euphrates. Delitzsch, Sayce, and many others had revealed the ancient civilizations of Mesopotamia as the source of so many important aspects of western civilization, including law, astronomy, written language—and Christianity itself. Now, the Garden of Eden was loosely affiliated with the "origins of civilization."

So it was no stretch to look for Eden in this part of the world, but where exactly? Both rivers meandered into and around obstacles, and split into separate branches or flowed into old canals. Whereas scholars such as Delitzsch and Sayce had puzzled, from a distance, over which of these other Mesopotamian rivers—or canals—could be the Biblical Pishon and Gihon, Willcocks the engineer simply measured every river or canal that came his way, dry or full. When the waterways became too narrow for his ship, he dispatched teams of men in smaller craft to follow each and every trickle of water to its end. Many of these waterways had never been mapped before. In this manner, Willcocks and his crew methodically worked their way from one end of the country to the other. They finished their preliminary survey in a remarkably short six months.

For Willcocks, Eden was not so much a matter of the exact arrangement of rivers—he could see for himself that rivers shifted course all the time in the soft clay ground of Mesopotamia. Instead, Eden was about fertility. After all, it was a Garden, and gardens need two things to thrive: fertile soil and plentiful water. According to Willcocks's measurements, the richest Mesopotamian soil was to be found along the Euphrates, in the first 250 miles of its run, where it emptied most of its precious alluvial silt from the mountains of Syria.

Willcocks was charmed by northern Mesopotamia, finding it much more beautiful and prosperous than he'd imagined, or heard from his explorer friends at London's Royal Geographic Society. In the north, Willcocks saw peace and abundance that seemed completely at odds with the abandoned chaos of the south. "Life and prosperity are before us wherever the water can reach." Here, farmers could actually make a living: from fruit trees, grapevines, cotton—and garden upon garden upon garden.

All these crops, except the cotton, wrote Willcocks, were old enough to have been "familiar to Adam." If Mesopotamia remained this luxuriant after thousands of years of neglect, just think how prosperous it would have been in Biblical times!

Willcocks knew the date palm had to be found in Eden. The date palm "even today is a tree of life to the whole Arab world." Only the date palm had leaves big enough to cover Adam and Eve's post-Fall embarrassment. And date palms appeared all over the ancient Babylonian tablets. But on this fertile upper stretch of the Euphrates most of the trees were olive.

So Willcocks pressed on. At 150 miles downstream he reached the small town of Anah—the northernmost spot where the date palm grows. The town had been praised for centuries for its exceptional date palm wine. Nearly all its houses had their own fruit gardens. This—not the deserted, flat dust bowl of the south— looked like Eden to Willcocks. Almost as an afterthought, he noted the four rivers that branched out to the south of Anah. Or rather, two rivers and two ancient canals. They were: the Euphrates, the Karbala branch of the Tigris, the Sakhlawia, and the Hindiya canal.

Willcocks agreed with Delitzsch that the missing Pishon and Gihon must have been ancient canals, though he disagreed on exactly which canals they were. He didn't cite Delitzsch, but he didn't have to. By 1908, twenty-seven years after *Where Was Paradise?*

and five years after the notorious Babel-Bible lectures, Delitzsch's original heresy—that two of the four rivers of paradise were man-made canals—was now taken as conventional wisdom. Willcocks had been following the stylish arguments of Sayce all these years, and he saw no contradiction between archaeology and belief, just as he saw no contradiction between canals made by man and rivers made by God.

Willcocks knew he needed scholarly approval of his new northern Eden. He sought it in a roundabout way. The Garden was clearly a well-watered place. Yet it had to have existed before the invention of complex irrigation techniques like waterwheels and lifting mechanisms. If the inhabitants of Eden had wanted to divert any serious volume of water in order to grow crops, they would have had to rely on naturally occurring obstructions, like rocks in the middle of the river, just as there were around Anah. Then the first people could simply build small levees of mud around the rocks. Willcocks called this kind of low-tech improvement "free-flow irrigation." Water could be gently led into the right places using nature and a little help from mankind.

There was a problem: nowhere in the Bible is free-flow irrigation mentioned. Where did that first water come from? Just before God planted the Garden in Eden, Genesis noted, "the Lord God had not caused it to rain upon the earth"; this would seem to make it difficult to grow a garden. The problem is solved in the next line, where "there went up a *mist* from the earth, and watered the whole face of the ground." But that doesn't really make sense. What was this 'mist,' and how could it go *up* from the earth? Willcocks knew he was out of his depth in the Biblical language department. That gave him a perfect excuse to reach out to the best expert in that business: Archibald Henry Sayce.

Sayce had reason to be annoyed with Willcocks. Since the Aswan Dam had been built, travel across the Nile on his beloved houseboat just wasn't the same. The waterway was crowded with steamships, so Sayce had to keep the *Ishtar* in the center of the river rather than crawling along its banks, as had been his custom. It had become "difficult to escape from the postman or telegraph boy." Everything was noisier, smellier, and more expensive. In 1908, after more than a decade wintering on his *dahabiya*, Sayce sold the *Ishtar* and returned to London. So when the dam's famous builder contacted him for help with another river project in another Biblical land, one might have expected the older man to be less than forthcoming.

But Sayce was unfailingly gracious, or maybe he just figured that Biblical queries from an engineer weren't likely to have any academic repercussions. He let Willcocks in on a little scholarly secret: that word "mist" appears only once in the Bible. It's not really Hebrew; it's Babylonian. And so, he allowed cheerfully, the word might very well mean instead what Willcocks wanted it to: water that allows "free-flow irrigation." Success! A serious scholar had approved Willcocks's work.

He became ever more determined to harmonize every detail of the Bible story with the actual landscape of Mesopotamia that he was traveling through. He looked down at his Bible, then up at his surroundings, and worked the two together. And because Willcocks was an optimist, and his Eden had a hopeful future, even the darkest parts of the ancient myth of temptation and sin came out sounding sunny. In fact, sin had been eliminated completely. Willcocks's Eden did not involve a fruit-dealing snake or a vengeful God. Traveling south on the Euphrates, Willcocks could look overboard and see through to the bottom of the river: no obstructions, no free-flow irrigation, no crops. Therefore, the Semites must have left this stretch of the upper Euphrates because of the "gradual degradation of the cataracts." So much for sin: Eden's first people had left voluntarily and gradually, and they could come back whenever they felt like it.

So, what about exile, and the "angel with a flaming sword" who, according to Genesis, was stationed at the gates of Eden to keep Adam and Eve from returning? The answer came to Willcocks while he was steaming south through deserted Babylonia. The only patches of landscape that stood out from the uniform gray-yellow clay were the jet-black steaming bitumen fields—caches of sticky tar that had bubbled up, hot, from the ground for millennia. After their anticlimactic exit from Eden, Willcocks's Adam and Eve would have paddled the same route in their reed boats, looking for more fertile lands. They, too, Willcocks surmised, "could see behind them nothing but the bitumen springs on the east of Eden, which seemed to them like flaming swords in the hands of offended seraphim."

Bitumen was a triumph of pragmatism over mythology. It certainly had its uses: hot bitumen mortar held up the walls of the ancient city of Babylon, and allowed the reed riverboats to float. Today, bitumen mixed with gravel makes asphalt. But Willcocks was no doubt the first to associate asphalt and angels. Tse Tsan Tai would have been disgusted.

Still, practical bitumen didn't take care of the theological purpose of the angel guarding Eden, which was to dissuade sinful man from ever again committing such hubris as to enter Paradise. Columbus thought explorers needed God's permission to enter Eden. William Warren was certain that even if he could enter Eden, his Polar paradise would be an icy, abandoned ruin. If Willcocks was actually standing in a pre-Fall Eden in Anah, what had happened to God's vengeance, or man's humility? Willcock, a knight of the British Empire, didn't have time for such vast theological questions. He had urgent business to take care of. This is where his megalomania came in: God had clearly granted man the ability to re-create Eden by means of science. So God must have intended Willcocks to do so.

Willcocks gave a preliminary version of his report to the Ottoman rulers in Istanbul—and he publicized it in the British press. At the heart of his plans for Mesopotamia was Anah. With its sheer abundance—of fruit, of trees, of water—the town could serve as an object lesson, a model for the rest of the country. "I do not think it possible to imagine anything more like a practical paradise than the country near Anah." If Anah could be a practical paradise, so could the rest of Mesopotamia. "Irrigation such as we propose will bring us back to the happier days of the early settlements in the marshes where the waters were comparatively free from silt and where they created for themselves gardens of Eden, whose memory has lasted so long."

Abundance was the key: what mattered was that in this Eden, like the one in Genesis, there was "every tree that is pleasant to the sight and good for food." A prosperous Eden was theologically satisfying. It dovetailed nicely with the idea of Christ as a "second Adam." If Eden was still here, still fruitful, that must be because Christ's sacrifice had made up for mankind's original sin. But, more to the point, an abundant Eden would show Willcocks's Ottoman bosses that real financial prosperity was possible where there was water.

Prosperity was not intended just for poor Mesopotamian farmers. The Turks and the British also had much to gain. Just one of the two canals Willcocks proposed for the Tigris could divert 10,000 cubic feet of water per second. This water could irrigate 750,000 new acres of cotton, which would be worth 7.5 million pounds each year.

Such miraculous results were not as far away as one might think. "We are apt to imagine that works of restoration must also take long years to bear any fruit. But in the arid regions of the Earth it is not so. There, the withdrawal of water turns a garden into a desert in a few weeks; its restoration touches the country as if with a magician's wand." It's true that water acts more dramatically in the desert than it does in temperate climates. But the reclamation of Eden depended on more than geography. It also depended on human whim.

Much as Willcocks himself may have disliked politics, his task had put him right in the center of it. As his steamer, the *Bagdad,* rounded the bend of the Tigris at Amara in the spring of 1909, it was ambushed by two different hostile Arab tribes who would not let it pass. There were only about 500 Arabs, and the *Bagdad* had received Turkish military reinforcements numbering in the thousands. Still, the fleet of boats was surrounded and shot at from both sides of the river, and could not move for weeks. Two British men died and twenty were injured in the stand-off. This kind of thing actually happened all the time, but generally not to important people like Willcocks. The crisis prompted a British colonel to lament the fact that Willcocks's irrigation plans hadn't been implemented yet. If they had, he said, control of the dams would be kept in Baghdad, so that the moment any Arab "misbehaved or refused to pay taxes . . . the water supply cuts off. The Arabs would not dare to ruin the water works as they would thereby ruin themselves."

For Willcocks, the "civilizing" benefits of irrigation were clear. According to him, the "lessons of order and method"—building blocks of civilization—"are taught so thoroughly by irrigation that it is not surprising that all the ancient civilizations of the world had their birth in the irrigated valleys of the great old-world rivers. All rivers were "rivers of paradise." Uncivilized men could live in woods, and partially civilized men in desert oases, but to survive in a country needing irrigation, "men had to be disciplined and to be amenable to laws and regulations."

British officials were worried; they needed Iraq to be stable. Willcocks had laid the groundwork for large-scale improvement, but he couldn't go ahead with any of his plans without permission from the Ottoman officials who governed Iraq. And they were the same people who had let the irrigation reach such a pathetic state to begin with. The local Turkish official in charge of Willcocks's Mesopotamian Irrigation Mission, Nazim Pasha, was himself part of the problem. The checks being paid from the Ottoman Empire to Willcocks's Mesopotamian Irrigation Mission had to be cosigned by Nazim, who therefore had all kinds of opportunity for bribery and extortion. Once, he diverted 20,000 pounds meant for Willcocks to his own coffers and used it to buy motorboats. Meanwhile, to keep up appearances, he used forced labor to build a canal that Willcocks found "completely useless and possibly harmful."

In the midst of all this political maneuvering, Willcocks took a break and returned to London to present a report on his adventures to London's Royal Geographic Society: "Mesopotamia: Past, Present and Future." The discussion afterward made clear just how much was riding on Willcocks's intelligence. In the audience was Gertrude Bell, on leave from her office in Baghdad, where she was by now Willcocks's main competition in the business of mapping Mesopotamia. Whatever her personal reservations may have been about Willcocks's methods—apparently, she had not been spared working with him—she knew that impoverished Mesopotamia needed help, and quickly. On the podium at the Geographic Society, she simply said that she "welcomed the possibilities offered by Sir William Willcocks's scheme. It is full of hope. I do not doubt it would bring back into prosperity a great province, and I more than agree with him that with prosperity would come peace and order." Whether prosperity or order came first was subject to debate, but whatever the path to civilization, it started with irrigation.

In Mesopotamia, Willcocks's title was "adviser to the Turkish government," but by November 1909, his friends in London began to call him the "Director-General of Irrigation in Mesopotamia." The Turkish empire was in disarray. In Istanbul, reformist "Young Turks" had partially overturned the old Ottoman order. In Iraq, British military and industrial pioneers began quietly putting down roots.

And Britain's most pressing needs were concentrated in the southern half of Iraq. They needed the shipping route to India through the southernmost port of Basra, on the Persian Gulf, and they needed a protective zone around the newest oil wells in Iran, just east of Basra. So Willcocks shifted his focus south, past Baghdad to lower Mesopotamia.

On a smaller boat this time, with a British colonel and an American missionary, Willcocks had an easy passage on the Euphrates all the way to Nasiriyah. There, the river's old course dissolved into the southern marshes, in which Willcocks and his friends drifted for hours before they could find their way out of the reeds. They were lucky not to drift longer: the marshes then covered millions of acres, constituting an entire ecosystem. The marsh water, Willcocks noticed, was slow-moving and impressively clear, without a particle of mud. Finally, they reached the Y-shaped junction where the two great rivers met, just north of Basra.

Willcocks would have immediately recognized that he was traveling through Sayce's Garden of Eden. He hadn't read all the Assyriological details—he didn't seem to know, for example, that Sayce had traced the word "cherub" not to bubbling bitumen springs but to Babylonian statuary. But Sayce's southern Eden had been spelled out so often—in popular books, in lectures, and in the *Hastings Dictionary of the Bible* under "Eden"—that Willcocks could not in good conscience ignore it.

Sayce likewise could not ignore Willcocks's theory of Eden—though he must have thought it ridiculous. Northern Iraq? That was 350 miles north of the floodplain that the Babylonians called "Edin" in countless cuneiform tablets. Rubbish! The entire community of Orientalists—no matter what their national origin, religious beliefs, or political affiliation—had agreed that the Garden of Eden, whatever, whenever, and however it existed, must have been in *southern* Mesopotamia, home of the Babylonians, where the twin rivers met and emptied into the Persian Gulf. Sure, they had squabbled over a few miles or river names here or there. But placing Eden north of Baghdad, closer to Syria than the Persian Gulf, was just as crazy as placing it in Ohio, or in China!

Although Willcocks was only six years younger than Sayce, they might as well have been generations apart. Sayce had grown up in the bosom of ultra-English Oxford with the exotic Orient as his escape fantasy. Willcocks had grown up *in* the Orient, in British colonial India, where he and his father were both employed by the public works department, an occupation utterly devoid of romanticism. And when times had been especially tough in Iraq, he had turned to the fantasy of *England* represented by the 1904 novel *God's Good Man*, a love story that contained rapturous descriptions of England in springtime:

> Young almond and apple boughs quivered almost visibly every moment into pink and white bloom, cowslips and bluebells raised their heads from mossy corners in the grass.

But Willcocks respected Sayce—whom he always addressed by both the religious and the academic title, "Reverend Professor." Innocently, he turned to the older man again for help in investigating his new southern territory.

Sayce, ever helpful, recommended several volumes of newly translated Sumerian tablets. This was a wise move on Sayce's part. The Sumerians are what the Greeks were to the Romans. They passed their stories on to the later Babylonians, who in turn passed them on to the Bible. Sumerian stories are some of the oldest in the world, and they include beautiful descriptions of the floods of southern Mesopotamia. They were perhaps the only historical source that could have the same enchanting effect on practical Willcocks as *God's Good Man*:

> *The storm raged high,*
> *Over the deserts the water prevailed,*
> *No man beheld his fellow.*
> *Ishtar cried like a woman in travail,*
> *Cried with loud wail the queen of the gods:*
> *"The former race is turned to clay."*

Sure enough, this time, instead of carrying a Bible on the deck of his steamship, he carried "translations of the Babylonian tablets of creation in my hand, and the plans and levels of the country before me." (His Bible, no doubt, was still close by.) Willcocks could admit that the Sumerian account of the flood "surpasses the Bible account," at least in its description of the flood itself. "The whole of the imagery of the account of the Flood is taken from the Sumerians." He couldn't in good conscience deny what Sayce had insisted all along: the Garden of Eden, Babylonian in all its details, existed in southern Mesopotamia.

But Willcocks missed his neat, tidy northern Eden in Anah. It represented—to him and to the Turkish officials—the potential for a developed Iraq. He relied on that potential. He couldn't go back on his original Eden; there was too much money and prestige riding on it, and how would that look? So he began to call his northern Eden the "Garden of Eden of the Semites," as opposed to Sayce's southern Eden, which was of course the "Garden of Eden of Sumer."

Willcocks was left in the awkward position of having to defend two Edens. He tried theology. The Sumerians, for all their highly developed mythology, did not believe in the One God. They were, as Willcocks put it, "Sons of Man." The Semites would become the Jews, the originators of monotheism and ancestors of Christianity. They were "Sons of God." For Willcocks it stood to reason that the Sons of God and the Sons of Man would require their own, separate Gardens of Eden, hundreds of miles apart. How could something sacred be the same as something profane?

Willcocks didn't know it, but if there was one thing that Eden could never be, it was double. Whoever found Eden—whether it was the place of human origins, or the site of man's original sin— would find only one. For religious thinkers like William Warren and Landon West, the whole point of Eden was to unify mankind. To have two Gardens of Eden was worse than having none at all. Even for secularists like Delitzsch, there could only be one place that the Babylonians wrote about. So one or the other of Willcocks's Edens had to fall. Would it be the fertile perfection of Anah, approved by the Turks, or the dusty ruins of Babylon, claimed by the British?

Somehow Willcocks had won from the Turks permission to begin work on what he considered the most urgent of his irrigation projects, even before he turned in his final report. The dam on the Hindiya canal would direct the Euphrates River back into its natural course and spare the surrounding lands from flood. The construction continued for six months, but it was always under siege by Nazim Pasha. Once, Willcocks was expecting a shipment of 200 camels loaded with cement coming up from Basra, and he gave the official the requisite advance notice. Days later, after the shipment didn't arrive, his men discovered the entire stock of cement abandoned on the road from Basra to Hindiya. The Turks had demanded a fine; the men who drove the camels had paid and escaped with their charges—but the cement could not pay its own fine. Later, the same thing happened with 150 donkeys carrying a shipment of iron nails.

By 1911, Willcocks was more than ready to be out of Iraq. In his frenzy to finish his assignment, he didn't have time to come to a final conclusion about the location—or locations—of the Garden of Eden. His original contract with the Turks had been for five years, but he found dealing with them so hopeless that he was leaving Mesopotamia after only two and a half. Even as he tried to finish his final report, the Turks themselves had been refusing to grant him access to sensitive stretches of the river. Finally, the British managed to get Nazim Pasha charged with corruption, arrested, and imprisoned. The good news gave Willcocks the last burst of energy he needed. He disembarked from his boat and set himself up in a temporary office—a canvas tent—on the banks of the Tigris. There, he wrote with abandon, adding new dams and canals to the list, no matter what their anticipated price tag was.

Finally back in London, Willcocks was again asked to speak to the Royal Geographic Society about the Garden of Eden. Among professional scholars, he painted himself as an amateur. "Studying these questions and pondering over them, I have formed opinions on them, but my reading is not sufficiently deep to tell me whether I am not restating what others have stated before."

Then he called the society's attention to two professionals who could have helped deepen his readings on these archaeological questions, had they wanted to: Gertrude Bell and Archibald Henry Sayce.

"Miss Bell could not be persuaded to abandon her researches into the comparative architecture of Ukhaidir." Indeed, she was still at the archaeological site of Ukhaidir, and so she could not defend herself. But of all of the British in Iraq, she spent the most time actually living in Baghdad, and in her copious correspondence and diaries she mentions Eden only once, in June 1908, and only in connection with Willcocks himself: "Willcocks spent part of the afternoon with me, dear old thing, and we discussed Mesopotamia and Eden and other sensible things." Bell preferred to stay above the Biblical history fray.

Sayce, however, did not. And he was in the audience.

Willcocks appealed to Sayce directly in his speech. "I tried to persuade the Reverend Professor Sayce to come and study the question on the spot, but Karkemish had superior attractions."

Willcocks felt that the southern location, the lack of a four-river split, and the lack of anything resembling a flaming sword to the east were weaknesses in Sayce's Eden theory. The problem bothered him.

Sayce, as a revered authority on the matter at hand, was given the chance to respond to Willcocks's speech with his own. He was perfectly satisfied to rely on his cuneiform translations, which undeniably used the word "Edin" to describe their southern Mesopotamian home—not the northern village of Anah. He was not going to let Willcocks get away with leaving two Gardens of Eden unreconciled.

First, Sayce restated his position that the Persian Gulf must have contributed salt water to the Tigris and Euphrates: the "salt river" theory that allowed him to place Babylonian Eden at the base of the Persian Gulf near the city of Eridu.

Sayce noted, politely, that Willcocks had "formerly considered that the Garden of Eden lay more to the north." (More to the north, indeed!)

Now that Willcocks had "come over to my view in regard to its southern position, I should like to ask . . . what is [your] opinion at present regarding the identification of the rivers of Paradise?"

Sayce knew that his southern Eden would need to have different rivers, and he knew Willcocks would not want to admit that.

In response, Willcocks repeated his northern rivers: the Euphrates, the Karbala branch of the Tigris, the Sakhlawia, and the Hindiya. That left the matter at a momentary standstill.

Willcocks couldn't contradict himself with regard to the rivers. But he could contradict Sayce regarding the "salt river." Here was a theory that came from the tablets but could be overturned by investigation on the spot. Sayce had never been to the place where the Tigris and Euphrates meet the Gulf; Willcocks had. And he categorically rejected the rivers' saltiness.

Not only did the waters of the Tigris and Euphrates lack salt at their southern confluence; the water was fresh all the way up to Baghdad, as Willcocks knew firsthand: "Some of the fresh-water fish of the Tigris and Euphrates are of enormous size." In Baghdad, he said to the Society, you might see a strong mule that was barely able to carry one single fish.

"If in the Babylonian or Assyrian edition of the Sumerian epic the [Persian Gulf] is called salt, it must be the handiwork of some Babylonian scribe throwing what he considered light on the subject." In other words, a fake. This was as close as Sir Willcocks would get to contradicting Reverend Professor Sayce.

The Royal Geographic Society was not going to mediate on Biblical matters. The members were more interested in praising Willcocks's undeniably revolutionary maps of Mesopotamia, which the Society published in the following issue of its journal. Willcocks had spent his two and a half years meticulously following every possible river, creek, dry river, ancient canal bed, reservoir, marsh, lake, and delta in Mesopotamia. On his map they all spider haphazardly southeast, curving into and around land features both modern and ancient, toward the Persian Gulf. Even the paths of ancient canals seem to follow this curving flow, as if man's work really were a continuation of God's. Running diagonally across the grain of this mass of rivers are all Willcocks's proposed irrigation works. They look (and sound) like steel bobby pins trying to capture unruly hair: Hindiya barrage, Basra barrage, Tigris escape, Diyal diversion, Chala regulator.

Several months after the Royal Geographic Society meeting, a reporter for the *New York Times* caught wind of the muted scholarly argument: "Were There Two Gardens of Eden or Only One?" The reporter's article never answered the question directly, but it did note sarcastically that the arguments over the location of the Garden of Eden had become "almost violent"—at least as close to violent as scholars of ancient antiquity could get.

It's not that Willcocks was too shy to fight: near the end of his life he would be convicted of libel in Cairo for accusing the current British irrigation officer of manipulating construction measurements, making a particular dam unsafe. Nearly seventy years old, he was released on his own recognizance.

But Willcocks seemed to know he couldn't push this particular issue. Sayce was an admired scholar, a fellow religious man. Sayce didn't need the northern Eden the same way Willcocks did; he did not share Willcocks's stake in the development of Iraq. He surely wanted peace to reign in the sacred lands of the Middle East, but he may not have equated peace with prosperity or prosperity with development, as even Gertrude Bell did. Sayce had still never been to Mesopotamia, though he knew all its ancient stories. But he had been to another Biblical land—Egypt—and development of the kind Willcocks had in mind had already ruined the Nile for him. The thought of technology ruining the Tigris, another of his childhood dream rivers, must have broken Sayce's heart.

But there was nothing that Sayce or anyone else who wanted to preserve the Oriental fantasy could do: real violence was about to break out. Maybe Willcocks was willing to coddle Sayce just a little bit, recognizing that the older man's ideas were soon to become obsolete.

When war was declared in 1914, the British had to fight the Germans in Europe and their allies the Ottomans in Mesopotamia. Any last semblance of cooperation between the Turks and the British dissolved. Violence spread out over the whole area that would become the country of Iraq, from the northern mountains to the southern sea. Willcocks's detailed survey maps, the first accurate maps of the country, turned out to be invaluable to the Allied armies, particularly the Inland Water Transport service, an elite corps of military riverboat captains trained on the Nile, the Amazon, and the Ganges—all rivers that had served their time as Pishons and Gihons.

British and French troops finally defeated the Turks in November 1918. The Ottoman Empire was essentially dead, and many people hoped Mesopotamia would finally settle down. In 1919, Willcocks published *From the Garden of Eden to the Crossing of the Jordan,* a soberer, much-edited version of his 1911 Royal Geographic Society lecture. Willcocks and Sayce, like the rest of Europe, seem to have come to an exhausted truce. Though Willcocks still insisted there must be two Gardens of Eden, he admitted that about their locations, "there is room for divergence of opinion."

Sayce, for his part, did agree to write a preface for the book, not that this meant much coming from a man who wrote dozens of prefaces in his time. He paid Willcocks a backhanded compliment: "He has attacked [critical theories or assumptions] with a fearless disregard of accepted conclusions."

And then, wearily, Sayce bowed to the superior power of Oriental pragmatism over Oriental fantasy. "It must be remembered," wrote Sayce, that Willcocks's theory of Eden "is written by one who has given practical illustration of his views by again turning the land of Babylonia into a Garden of Eden."

Sayce was referring to Willcocks's Hindiya barrage, finally completed, which had allowed 300,000 acres to be reclaimed for farming. This was prosperity of a sort. On those 300,000 acres, it was possible to grow almost enough food to feed the British army that would be stationed in the country for the next thirty years.

7

The Tree Is Dead, Long Live the Tree

I N THE BEGINNING, Adam and Eve got kicked out of Eden, but the tree they ate from remained, at least for a while.

Two days before Christmas 1946 the *Times* of London ran a news brief below the fold on page 3 in the "Imperial and Foreign" section:

> "Tree of Knowledge" Dead
>
> The "Tree of Knowledge," which has stood from time immemorial in the traditional site of the Garden of Eden at Qurna, at the junction of the Euphrates and Tigris, and was visited by thousands of sightseers, has withered and died.
>
> Doubtless concerned for the continuity of knowledge, the enterprising local authorities have planted a new one.

After thirty-two years of British military entanglement in Iraq—before, during, and after both world wars—*Times* readers would have been accustomed to much bloodier headlines. Perhaps the Imperial and Foreign editor thought this innocuous item by the Baghdad correspondent would be a lighthearted Christmastime novelty. The *Times* was not about to weigh in on the question of Biblical literalism—not before Christmas, anyway. "Tree of Knowledge" is safely within quotation marks. The site of the Garden of Eden is not "definite" or "absolute"; it is "traditional." Real or not, the "Tree of Knowledge" will live on, thanks to those enterprising locals.

But several retired servicemen, veterans of World War I in "Mespot," didn't find the item either reassuring or novel. They thought the story was incorrect, not to mention thirty years late. And they were in a position to know.

The next day's *Times* contained a letter from Marmaduke Tudsbery, in 1946 a noted civil engineer, beginning with "But Sir" and contradicting just about every word of the short article. Tudsbery had been to Qurna in January 1920, and back then the Tree had already been dead for a long time: it had not "withered and died" in 1946, as the article implied. And that wasn't all. In 1920, Iraqis had told Tudsbery that the dead Tree had been planted only a century before. So the Tree had certainly not been standing at the junction of the Tigris and Euphrates "from time immemorial," but only from about 1820. Tudsbery even had a problem with the story's witty last line: "Doubtless concerned for the continuity of knowledge, the enterprising local authorities have planted a new one." Since a tree had already been planted on the spot at least once, he wrote, "the enterprise of local authorities in planting a new one is not without precedent."

The *Times* had been right about one thing. The town of Qurna was indeed located "at the junction of the Euphrates and Tigris." In Arabic, the word "qurna" means "corner," and the words sound almost the same. At least, they do in theory. English-speakers called the town Kwerna; Arabic-speakers from other nations called it Kurna; Iraqis called it Gurna; the Ottoman Turks, who controlled the area, called it something else entirely.

As William Willcocks's complex maps had shown, rivers in Mesopotamia frequently change course. So no one can say for sure how long Qurna itself had been the point of confluence. On a narrow triangle of land in the center of town, there had been a man-made structure for at least 450 years—it was first noted by Italian explorers in 1563. They called the place Corno. First there was a castle, then a fort, then a customhouse. John Philip Newman, an American Episcopal clergyman passing through Iraq on a "pleasure tour" in 1876, found that there was a whole town, "with mosque and minaret . . . and huts of the poor." Standing in this town, facing south, one would be surrounded by water.

To the left was the Tigris, and fifteen miles east of that, Iran. To the right was the Euphrates. Immediately in front was the Shatt Al Arab, the long narrow channel headed straight south to Basra and out to the Persian Gulf. Behind were millions of acres of low-lying, reedy marshland.

In 1914, when the Turks became allied with Germany in World War I, the British sent military reinforcements to Basra from their colonial headquarters in India via the Persian Gulf. From Basra they made their way north toward Baghdad up the Shatt Al Arab to Qurna. Once the Shatt split in two at Qurna, the Tigris and the Euphrates rivers were too narrow to accommodate British warships. In order to make it upriver to Baghdad, the British had to disembark at Qurna and redeploy on smaller boats. In order to do this, they had to control Qurna.

In 1914, this wasn't difficult. The Ottomans had only one ship—intended to protect them against pirates—and that ancient customhouse. When the British easily overturned these defenses, the *Times* of London crowed: "This smart little affair has given us complete control of the country from the junction of the Tigris and Euphrates to the sea, and the richest part of the fertile delta."

Of course, the "affair" the British had begun would hardly end up being "smart" or "little." It was three years before they finally captured Baghdad in 1917, and they'd had to fight like hell to hold any part of the country throughout the war. But the capture of Qurna had been the first step.

The confluence of the Tigris and Euphrates was important not only geographically and militarily, but also Biblically. Qurna fell within the southern plain of Mesopotamia, roughly the same area that Delitzsch had proposed as the Garden of Eden in the 1880s, Sayce had seconded in the 1890s, and Willcocks had reluctantly endorsed in 1911. But none of these three seekers would ever have claimed that the actual Tree of Knowledge *still existed* in Eden. So, what accounted for the presence of the Tree? Everyone noticed it, on the sandy bank of the Tigris, protected by a waist-high brick wall built in geometric patterns. It was a small tree. Evidently it had once had leaves, and it certainly wasn't a date palm, although these still grew in large groves along the riverbanks. By 1920 the Tree had been dead for so long no one agreed on what kind of tree it once was. It could have been a fig, eucalyptus, pomegranate, or olive. Everyone, however, did agree that it was not an apple tree. Nonetheless, according to legend this was the Tree of the Knowledge of Good and Evil, the tree from which Adam and Eve were warned not to eat, on pain of death.

Bible translations and interpretations differ over whether it was the Tree of Knowledge or the Tree of Life that was expressly forbidden. The Tree of Life was supposed to be "in the midst" of the Garden of Eden, and this is the tree from which, Eve explains to the serpent, she and Adam are forbidden to eat. Then the serpent tells Eve that this tree in the center of the garden is also the one that would allow her to "be like God, knowing good and evil." God's express reason for kicking Adam and Eve out of the Garden is that they might now eat from the "Tree of Life" and live forever. In any case, the "thousands of sightseers" mentioned by the *Times* understood the Tree in Qurna to be the Tree from which Eve ate.

The meticulously plotted secular Eden of Delitzsch, ironically, happened to coincide with the much older religious Eden of the Protestant theologian John Calvin. Three hundred years before higher criticism, before cuneiform tablets, before topographical surveys, Calvin had determined that Eden must lie at the junction of the Tigris and Euphrates. Thanks to his map in the widely used Bishops' Bible, over time Qurna had become the quasi-official default Eden location for Calvinists.

By the late nineteenth century, when Sayce's books were popular in Britain, Qurna had double credibility as Eden for European and American travelers passing through the town on their way from Basra to Baghdad. Eden had been "discovered" in Qurna by religion, and "confirmed" by science. For once, the two streams of knowledge did not seem to be in conflict. Bishop Newman, whose "pleasure tour" eventually turned into a scouting mission for President Ulysses S. Grant, knew both the theological and the scientific histories of Qurna by the time he arrived in 1876. "By common consent, all the theories are reduced to two; and the advocates of both agree that the Garden of Eden was somewhere in the valley of the Euphrates." Newman found Qurna a place of "unsurpassed loveliness." He and his companions disembarked to read Genesis aloud and sing "the old doxology" in Qurna's date groves. "Oh, what a spot is this for paradise, at the junction of these mighty rivers, in this delightful climate, in this centre of empire!" But among the numerous written accounts, Newman's is in the distinct minority.

Most of the travelers looked at Qurna, sized it up according to Sunday school, and found it severely lacking—so unlike Eden, in fact, as to be some kind of sick joke. A wealthy British widow chastised the ghosts of Adam and Eve in her travel diaries: "Oh! Shades of one's First Parents! What blind obsession dimmed your clear vision, that you should have named the place a Garden??" "This place" was an overgrown marsh with only a few trees, and maybe fifty "miserable huts."

An American explorer who crossed the country on horseback charitably tried to put the Garden of Eden into its local context. "The few trees, and the little cultivation [Qurna] may boast, are certainly *as* a garden in the midst of a barren, black, desolated wilderness."

The British military heartily agreed with the dismal civilian assessments. Stuck in Qurna for most of the war, commanders called it the "Garden of Hell." Infantrymen claimed the swamps were full of malarial "mosquitoes as big as a bat that bite to the bone." The expert riverboat captains of the Inland Water Transport service had been trained on the great rivers of the world, and they were going stir-crazy in Eden. They had even less reverence than Willcocks for the story. If Qurna was the Garden of Eden, they decided, there was no need at all for the fearsome cherubim. "We sure didn't need a flaming sword to keep us out; whenever we had the chance we got away."

In 1919, Qurna's British troops had even more reason to want to get away. The war was over and the Turks had surrendered. The

Paris Peace Conference had ended, but Britain still had not signed an official peace treaty. Nobody knew what form the Iraqi government would take. No one knew how long his tour of duty would last. The only thing to do was wait. Even the head British officer, Civil Commissioner A. T. Wilson, was beginning to get nervous. Things were already going wrong in small, concentrated ways. Commissioner Wilson called these "storms in a teacup."

Wilson made a quick visit to Qurna by plane to gauge local support for direct British rule. Everywhere he went he was followed by Sheikh Gubashi, a member of the local council who had been a loyal supporter of the British when they first arrived. Now, Gubashi was fed up. Everybody's worried about the future, he said. Can't you British give us some sign, some kind of declaration, so we know whose side we're supposed to be on?

But Wilson's bosses in London had ordered him not to make any Iraqis any guarantees of anything until there was a treaty. In the meantime, however, Wilson was required to proceed with the huge development projects that could turn Iraq into a colonial cash cow. By February 1919, William Willcocks had decided that before he could begin work on the irrigation of southern Mesopotamia, the marshes had to be drained, or "reclaimed," as he put it. And before he would start work on the Qurna reclamation scheme, Willcocks insisted on a legal settlement with Turkey.

Until a "definite form" of government is established in Mesopotamia, wrote Willcocks, "it is idle to embark on projects of this nature." So much for irrigation as "instant civilization," turning a desert into a law-abiding oasis in a matter of weeks. The war had seriously tempered Willcocks's optimism. He dug in his heels and refused to begin work. As it turned out, he wouldn't ever get to start his massive scheme, because Iraq's government remained "indefinite" for some time.

The teacup-storm closest to Qurna arose over the military river fleet, controlled by the Inland Water Transport (IWT), that same corps of military navigators who were so eager to get out of Iraq. No one expected there would be a need for military vessels much longer, and there was money to be made by transferring valuable gear to civilian and commercial purposes. So the British decided to auction off military gear near Basra. At the auction, "rubbish" and "pots and pans" sold out immediately, but the IWT was not getting high enough prices from local merchants for the more expensive watercraft. So without telling the Iraqis or Commissioner Wilson, British colonial commanders—who ran the empire from their home base, India—decided instead to offer everything to major firms like the Euphrates and Tigris Steam Navigation Company and the Anglo-Persian Oil Company. Iraqis held mass protests in Basra. According to Wilson, who empathized with the local cause, the meetings were "full of ominous possibilities, for it was the first time that public opinion had become vocal on any issue." The profit eventually realized from the sale of riverboats amounted to more than 1 million pounds.

Despite the growing unease, London ordered Baghdad to streamline the operations—focusing manpower on places where there were known military threats, or major opportunities for profit. Qurna had neither. It was just a town of 5,000 people, most of whom were occupied with growing dates and weaving reed mats. And the British wouldn't need to send large warships up the river anymore, the war was over. So, they decided Qurna could afford to be downsized. Starting in 1920, the town would officially become a suburb of much larger Basra, sixty miles south. It would no longer have its own police station, or engineers. The British dissolved the local council, putting Sheikh Gubashi out of a job.

But they overlooked one essential function that really could not stand to be downsized any further. The Civil Hospital, a tiny mud building with uneven brick floors, could hold only four patients at a time. Yet every day, hundreds of people traveled from as far as forty miles away on foot or by boat. At the hospital, they might wait in line all day. According to the assistant surgeon, the only qualified doctor, it was almost impossible to keep the place clean. People didn't have latrines in their mud-brick huts. The British had tried to build public toilets but they were now "quite hopeless." So, mostly,

Qurna's citizens would just "deposit their excreta" anywhere, and disease spread fast. The hospital was often understaffed, since its one qualified doctor was also called on to treat plague epidemics in nearby marsh villages. In 1919, plague killed thirty-five people.

After plague and malaria, the most common complaint was blindness. People who had been slowly losing their sight for years suddenly found themselves unable to see at all, and waited patiently for the doctor, thinking he could cure them. But he couldn't make eyeglasses in his mud hut on the riverbank; and most of these patients were too far gone for glasses anyway, wrote the surgeon: "hopelessly incurable." In the rare cases where he could perform an operation, his patients either refused surgery or couldn't pay for it.

December 31, 1919—New Year's eve—was Qurna's last day as a British administrative district. That night, a group of riverboat captains—"sappers" from the IWT—tried to climb the Tree of Knowledge. No one knows why they did it. It was New Year's eve, they were drunk, and the Tree was easier to climb than those confounded date palms. To 1920! To the future! It could have been a tribute—they'd be damned if they left paradise without at least trying to see what all the fuss over good and evil was about. The military was in the midst of turning itself into a civil government, and no one knew how long his own tour of duty would last. It could have been a celebration—the men were leaving this god-forsaken marsh town! Maybe it was insurance. They could find the snake, eat the forbidden fruit, and be banished from Eden for good. Maybe they were looking for the angel. Maybe, in their festivities, the theology got confused, and they thought if they could climb this tree, they would become like God.

Had the sappers looked a little closer at the tree, in its brick enclosure on the sand, they would have noticed that it was dead already, and not likely to hold their weight. Its trunk was twisted; its bark was missing; and although it still seemed to be standing, its roots were probably already weak.

But the sappers didn't look. They hoisted themselves up to stand on the tree's pedestal. Then they gripped its trunk and started to climb. With the first footstep, the tree collapsed. The dry trunk cracked completely near its base, and the rest of the Tree of Knowledge fell sideways onto the sand.

Immediately, the sappers were surrounded. Residents of Qurna were furious—how dare they? Didn't they know this was not just any tree? These British didn't know anything—how could they be trusted? This never would have happened with the Turks. The sappers managed to escape from the crowd before they were hurt, but this storm in a teacup wasn't over. Word of the Tree's destruction spread all over the country. The local telegraph office began receiving waves of indignant telegrams from all manner of political and religious figures demanding that some reparation be made.

There were so many telegrams that the young major in charge, Cyril Blomeley of the Indian Army, started a separate folder marked "Tree of Knowledge." After four days, according to Blomeley, "it was evident there was great anger among the Arab people." Blomeley's job was to assign tasks to the appropriate military or civilian sector. It was unclear whose jurisdiction covered a broken Biblical artifact. So Blomeley sent a Works Officer into Qurna to investigate. The officer was twenty-eight-year-old Captain Marmaduke Tudsbery of the Royal Engineers. He was doubtless more accustomed to projects like building a roof for the outdoor marketplace or reinforcing the Qurna police station. But he gamely heard the grievances of everyone concerned, beginning with the British person in charge.

The assistant political officer of Qurna at the time, R. S. M. Sturges, was responsible for overseeing all aspects of British administration. He certainly did not seem very concerned about the broken tree. He knew, of course, that his assigned location was rumored to be the Garden of Eden, but he felt there was "little vestige of the Garden of Eden remaining" in this miserable district. (His own ideas about the real location of Eden had to do with a mysterious mirage island in the Persian Gulf.) Curiously, though, Sturges did claim that the Tree of Knowledge, which previous travelers had long noted was dead, "still boasted a few green leaves" when the sappers knocked it over.

Captain Tudsbery proceeded to interview other witnesses in town, and this is how he learned that the Tree had been planted within local memory. Therefore, he reported back to Blomeley that the tree "was possibly a few hundred years old and had been dead a long time." By this he meant that it was not, according to logic, reason, and science, the Tree of the Knowledge of Good and Evil. And if it was not the Tree of Knowledge, what was the problem?

Leaving aside the question whether logic, reason, and science *can* determine if something is or is not from the Bible, there is an issue of perspective. The British saw the importance of the dead tree to Qurna's residents—once it was broken, anyway. They assumed that the tree had the same importance for Qurna's Shia Muslims as it had to European Christians. The Old Testament is a sacred book for Muslims too.

But it wasn't the same. When you look for the Bible on the ground, that is what you see. But part of what gives the Bible its power is its reliance on much, much older symbols and customs. In the shadow of capital-T Traditions such as Christianity and Islam, older, lowercase, folk traditions still go on. And to see them, you have to look closely. The worship of sacred trees is one of the most common and widespread traditions in the Middle East, a practice shared by Arab Shia Muslims, Persian Shia Muslims, Arab Sunni Muslims, and Kurdish Sunni Muslims, not to mention Iraqi Christians; the Marsh Arabs; and the Kurdish, Arab, and Persian Mandeans, who practice a form of Zoroastrianism.

Although tree worship is not an organized religion, there are some basic principles to it. Sacred trees are often connected to a holy person, a local saint. Maybe he preached under the tree; maybe he is buried nearby; maybe he just leaned on it once. The tree can be any kind of tree, and it can be dead or alive. It can even be just a stump. It is often found near water. If a tree has become sacred for any reason, there will generally be a wall around it to set it apart and protect it from harm. But a sacred tree is not just to be admired from afar; it has a purpose. Usually, there will be a small door or gate built into its protective wall, so that people can come up to the tree to ask the saint to intercede on their behalf. Because the needs that people bring to the tree are important, there are also rules for how to treat a sacred tree, rules that Iraqis in Qurna and elsewhere would have learned as children. First and foremost, you cannot hurt the tree. You cannot break off a branch; you cannot even pick up a dead branch that falls to the ground near the tree; you cannot even touch the tree for any reason other than prayer. If you do, the saint—or your mother—will punish you.

Different sacred trees have different purposes, but their functions tend to be related to health. Prayers are often for fertility, or for healing, especially of mysterious or illogical ailments, like birth defects or eye disorders. Word travels from village to village, and people make special trips to visit appropriate trees. Often, people tie small pieces of cloth to the tree's branches as tokens of their particular prayers. Often, these pieces of cloth are green. Green is a sacred color in Islam, but it is older than that—it represents life.

There are also rules for what to do when a sacred tree dies of natural causes. Before it decays completely, you plant another tree nearby. If another tree is planted or grows near the first, it becomes sacred, too. There were not, however, rules for what to do if someone purposely breaks a sacred tree.

The Military Works Department was in unknown territory. All the department knew was that the Arabs were angry about this tree, and that if they were to join other Arabs who were angry about other matters elsewhere, things could get worse for the British Empire. So, whether or not this was the Tree of Knowledge, the department quickly resolved to resurrect it. Staff members repaired the broken trunk with concrete so that it stood upright again, and they reinforced the tree's mud-brick base with concrete for safekeeping. Willcocks must have been proud of their pragmatic problem-solving. Blomeley reported to headquarters in Basra that this solution "gave much satisfaction to the people," and a "troublesome little episode" had been averted. Logic, reason, and science—in the form of concrete—had prevailed over primitive superstition. But what had really been accomplished?

Qurna didn't erupt into riots like those of the Basra boat merchants, but even concrete couldn't stem the widespread anti-British rebellion. Karbala's Shia clergy, Baghdad's Sunni civil servants, and Mosul's Kurdish independents found that the one thing they had in common was a desire to get the British out of their country. By June 1920, the all-important Tigris was the only remaining north-south line of communications left, since the rebels had disrupted the kaiser's beloved Baghdad-Basra railway; and Qurna was back in the center of military action. By August 1920, the British general Aylmer Haldane would need as many troops to squelch the rebelling Iraqis as he had needed to defeat the Ottoman Turks. And by October, 426 British soldiers and approximately 8,500 Iraqis would lose their lives.

For as long as westerners had been coming to Qurna for Biblical reasons, Iraqis had been coming to the Tree of Knowledge to pray for health. In fact, it's hard to say who came first. But it is likely that in those years after World War I, when Qurna's hospitals were overflowing, the Tree received more than its usual share of visitors. If a man walked forty miles to get help because he couldn't see, and the doctor said there was nothing to be done—maybe a cataract operation, but it was risky—and then he had to *pay* the doctor: well, if there was a sacred tree nearby, he'd go and ask the saint, whoever that was, for help. With more than 100 hospital patients a day, there must have been many pieces of green cloth tied to that tree. From a distance, to the British, they would have looked like leaves.

Qurna's citizens didn't generally refer to their tree as the "Tree of Knowledge of Good and Evil." But they did attach to it the names of various holy men shared among the Abrahamic faiths. Some called it Adam's Tree; some called it Abraham's Tree. Explanations of its sacredness varied widely. It was either the place where Adam spoke to God in the Garden of Eden, or the place where Abraham stopped to pray in 2000 B.C., or where Abraham met his wife Sarah. But no matter which story the worshipper subscribed to, the ritual was always the same.

In its way, the Tree provided exactly what William Warren, Landon West, and Tse Tsan Tai all wanted for Eden, and what Friedrich Delitzsch and William Willcocks had missed: unity. The Tree brought Iraqis together. Here, religious differences were insignificant, and everyone kept his eye on the high priorities: survival, health, and human dignity. It was a lesson the British ignored at their peril. They passed by Eden on steamships, dismissing it as ugly, primitive, unbiblical. They should have looked closer.

Interlude: Survival of the Witness

WILLIAM F. WARREN's idea—that we could use science to prove the truth of the Bible—hung on for longer than one would expect. So, as it turns out, did William F. Warren. Though his enormous height was mythical, Warren did seem to possess the nearly miraculous longevity he claimed for his Arctic "hyperborean Eocene man."

He simply refused to die. On the occasion of his eighty-ninth birthday in 1922, the trustees of Boston University held a formal service in his honor in the College of Liberal Arts Building. Surely the dignitaries giving speeches assumed this was their last chance to heap honors on their founding president, nineteen years after his retirement. But no—come 1923, Warren was still alive. So the university held another ceremony, officially making Warren, age ninety, President Emeritus.

When Warren turned ninety-one in 1924, nobody threw him a party, but the *Boston Daily Globe* reported that he was "the recipient of congratulatory notes and telegrams from collaborators and educators throughout the country," and well-deserved congratulations at that.

Archibald Henry Sayce, too, was convinced that science would vindicate Biblical truths, and he, too, found himself unaccountably still alive in 1924. (He was younger than Warren, but as a survivor of snakebite and typhoid fever, he had to be grateful for every moment.) Sayce, that unorthodox ambassador of orthodoxy, was still up to his old tricks: blithely overturning previous scholarship, using his wide areas of knowledge to support whatever he happened

132

to believe at the time. Thus, the word "mist" might mean "free-flow irrigation"; why not? And the Mesopotamian marshes could be salty; why not? He did not seem to be bothered by firsthand evidence to the contrary. Everything was open to interpretation.

In 1924, Sayce finally accepted his friend Gertrude Bell's ten-year-old invitation to visit her in Mesopotamia—now renamed Iraq—a land he had never seen but knew so much about. Just then, the country was considered stable enough for an eighty-year-old man in poor health to navigate, by himself, in a motorcar.

The British had finally signed a treaty with Turkey at the Cairo Conference in 1921, and were operating the new nation of Iraq under a mandate from the recently formed League of Nations. The repaired Tree of Knowledge in Qurna was still standing. The British installed an Arab king, Faisal al-Husseini; Bell was his trusted adviser. She was also the founder of the National Museum in Baghdad, which is where Sayce surprised her one morning, having just driven down from Damascus.

Bell presented Sayce with her latest prized acquisition: a tiny clay tablet written in the world's oldest script; and she translated the first few characters for him: "one basket of dates presented to the temple."

Sayce looked skeptical. "I doubt whether that character means 'dates.' A date is round, not oblong." A couple of days later, in front of an audience Bell had invited to the museum to observe her honored guest, Sayce cheerfully declared that the supposed basket of dates might instead represent a "principal male." In a letter to her father, the principal male in her life, a bemused Bell wrote, "You never realized, did you, how easily you might be mistaken for a basket of dates." Might some Babylonian word "Edin" be just as easily mistaken for "plain"? There was no telling for sure.

An adventure by Archibald Henry Sayce would not be complete without a near-death experience: In Iraq Sayce became deathly ill with typhoid, as he had been so often in the past. The risk of having the eminent scholar expire in her newly stabilized country threw

Bell into fits of anxiety. Such an event would be both a "dreadful" political catastrophe and a personal tragedy:"Also I should be so sorry." After two weeks, though, the indefatigable Sayce had bounced back; Bell found him in the hospital "cheerful as a cricket." The Reverend Professor would live another eight years, as would his conviction that Moses really did write the Bible.

Warren dealt in certainties: science had already proved that life began at the North Pole. Sayce dealt in mystery: probably, sometime in the future, an artifact would be found that would explain everything. But both wanted the same thing: to preserve traditional Christianity, its idea of sin, and the society that went along with it. And this vision of the world was certainly getting harder and harder to maintain in the whirlwind of modernity that was the 1920s.

If—in effect—Delitzsch had put Moses on trial for plagiarism at the Babel-Bible lectures in 1903, and Sayce had dismissed the charges, then the Scopes trial of 1925 reopened the case. But this time, the charge against the Bible wasn't plagiarism; it was scientific inaccuracy. The trial was ostensibly over the right of a high school science teacher in Tennessee to teach the theory of evolution, contrary to a new state law. The ACLU drafted a star civil libertarian, Clarence Darrow, to put the law to the test of constitutionality, and Tennessee called on William Jennings Bryan, the beloved Populist preacher who had been a three-time Democratic presidential candidate and secretary of state under President Woodrow Wilson. And nearly a quarter century after the Babel-Bible controversy, Reason (in the person of Darrow) finally forced Religion (in the person of Bryan) to accept defeat.

The trial went on for six days. On the seventh day, Darrow's team called Bryan to the stand as an expert witness on the Bible. If Bryan claimed that he needed no theory of origin other than God's Word, and that God's Word could explain what science could not, well, then, by God, Darrow would make him prove it. Bryan's colleagues protested. But Bryan felt he had nothing to hide. "These gentlemen . . . did not come here to try this case. They came here to try revealed religion. I am here to defend it and they can ask me any question they please." The judge approved; the crowd applauded. Bryan took the stand, fanning himself with a palm fan.

Then followed a cross-examination that the *New York Times* would later call "the most amazing court scene in Anglo-Saxon history," a mano a mano battle of wits between Reason and Religion.

Darrow began at the beginning, with the Book of Genesis. He got Bryan to admit that the six days of creation were probably not six literal, twenty-four-hour days—because the Bible doesn't say twenty-four hours. Then Darrow continued on into Eden.

"Mr. Bryan, do you believe that the first woman was Eve?"

"Yes."

"Do you believe she was literally made out of Adam's rib?"

"I do."

"Did you ever discover where Cain got his wife?"

"No, sir. I leave the agnostics to hunt for her."

The Scopes trial was the first major trial to be broadcast live on the radio, so listeners across the country, sheltering indoors from the blistering summer heat, could follow every statement, every examination, every piece of evidence. The legendary satirist H. L. Mencken wrote disdainful dispatches from Dayton for the *Baltimore Evening Sun*. It was the original "media circus," complete with monkeys, souvenirs, and a sound track. Instead of being lit by limelight, the Scopes trial was positively ablaze with flashbulbs. And in the bright electric glow, old cherished beliefs appeared flat and childish.

Darrow asked Bryan if he believed in the story of the temptation of Eve. Bryan did.

"Do you think that is why the serpent is compelled to crawl upon its belly?"

"I believe that."

"Have you any idea how the snake went before that time?"

"No, sir."

"Do you know whether he walked on his tail or not?"

"No, sir, I have no way to know."

Bryan went on to claim that it was easy to believe Jonah had been swallowed by a whale, "if the Bible said so." By the end, Darrow had backed him into a corner, a corner from which he proclaimed, repeatedly, that man was not a mammal. Finally, the judge had to adjourn the debate. Darrow, much savvier than Bryan, had used Bryan's own methods of Biblical argument against him. Bryan, caught unprepared, was made to look like a redneck who wanted to keep people barefoot and ignorant.

Public victory thus assured, Darrow asked the jury to find Scopes guilty, so that the case would be appealed to the Tennessee supreme court; such an appeal had been the goal of the ACLU all along. The jury obliged. The judge fined Mr. Scopes $100, and the case was turned over to the Tennessee supreme court. As a side benefit to Darrow's case, this abrupt conclusion meant that Bryan could not give his much-rumored closing speech, and so the great orator was deprived of a possible redemption. The public pillorying seemed to have accomplished its goal: to stop states from enacting antievolution laws, on the grounds of freedom of speech. Of the fifteen states with antievolution legislation pending in 1925, only two (Arkansas and Mississippi) actually passed laws banning the teaching of Darwin's theory after the trial.

As if to reinforce the mythology of the event, William Jennings Bryan died suddenly just six days—six literal, twenty-four-hour days—after his embarrassment at the hands of Darrow. The cause of death, according to legend, was a broken heart, but actually it was a stomach problem. His death came so soon after his folly that he was still remembered in its bitter light, most famously by H. L. Mencken, who wrote what may be the most scathing obituary of all time: "There stood the man who had been thrice a candidate for the Presidency of the Republic ... there he stood in the glare of the world, uttering stuff that a boy of eight would laugh at! ... He seemed only a poor clod like those around him, deluded by a childish theology, full of an almost pathological hatred of all learning, all human dignity, all beauty, all fine and noble things. He was a peasant come home to the dung-pile." Without hate-filled demagogues like Bryan around, Mencken hoped, the brand of Biblical literalism Bryan embodied would die, too, freeing modern man to progress toward an inevitably enlightened future.

Though old-time religion lay dead, buried, and castigated in the press, the victory of modern science was hardly assured. A year later, the Tennessee supreme court overturned the guilty verdict—on a technicality, not on constitutional grounds—and then dismissed the case completely, with the comment: "Nothing is to be gained by prolonging the life of this bizarre case." But prolonged it certainly was, outside the courtroom.

For all its farce and fuss, the show trial was the very real genesis of the split between "fundamentalists," largely rural, impoverished, Bible-believing Christians, and "modernists," the increasingly secular, pro-science majority of the country. The traditional Christians who had been Bryan's audience and his base constituency—the ones whom Mencken insisted on calling "yokels"—certainly hadn't been converted. If the choice was between monkey grandparents and a six-day creation, they were all for the young Earth. But origin stories, if they are to be trusted, need to be universal. If we're all human, we must all come from the same place. A created world and an evolved world cannot coexist. So the Bible-believing Christians resolved to make their own world. They consciously retreated from the national stage that had been the scene of their embarrassment: they went into exile.

But in 1926, William Warren was still alive, and still in the public eye. Trying to avoid any unwarranted to-do, he spent his ninety-third birthday at his oldest daughter's home in New York City, where he still had enough vim and vigor to answer his own correspondence—on a newfangled typewriter, no less. But despite his being out of Boston, and despite his "express wish" that only family members and close friends come to pay their respects, the *New York Times* was there. Headline: "Dr. W. F. Warren now 93."

Warren lived to be ninety-six—long past the Biblical benchmark of "threescore and ten" that he'd set as a challenge for himself in

Paradise Found. To his last breath, Warren insisted that his book's premise still stood: the Garden of Eden was at the North Pole.

It might appear that the ever-increasing pace of human progress in the early twentieth century would stamp out any naive religious belief in a real Garden of Eden. It was true that the solid ground under William Warren's feet had been split in two as if by a glacier. On one side: reason, science, logic. On the other side: faith, morality, tradition. As the two ice floes drifted farther and farther apart, it required more and more complicated mental acrobatics to stand on both at once, as Eden seekers must, and avoid drowning in chaos. Though the professionals on either side—in archaeology and theology—had pretty much given up looking for Eden, there were still plenty of amateurs who had gotten caught up in the search. It seemed there was another force to be reckoned with: a peculiarly modern yearning to stare the impossible in the face and prove it wrong. Somehow, the rapid transition to a modern, secular world actually *left open* the possibility that the treasured beliefs of the past would eventually be proved true. In the wake of the vast destruction of World War I, all kinds of people—radicals, mystics, and even lawyers—embarked on their own forms of religious seeking.

In short, the search for a literal Eden did not die. It just got weirder.

The infamous Babylonian cylinder seal believed to depict an "Adam and Eve" older than the Bible.

German engraver Albrecht Durer's 1504 *Adam and Eve*, a vision of Adam and Eve most Germans were more comfortable with.

Reverend Landon
West, a member of
the German Baptist
church in rural Ohio
at the turn of the
twentieth century.

THE SERPENT MOUND, SERPENT MOUND PARK, NEAR
LOUDEN, ADAMS COUNTY, OHIO.

A drawing of the Serpent Mound, the Native American
earthwork in Reverend West's backyard.

From *The Century, a popular quarterly*, April 1890.

Archibald Henry Sayce, distinguished professor and Anglican deacon, found himself caught in the battle between archaeology and the Bible.

Library of Congress
Prints and Photographs Division

Phonetic Value (Accadian word).	Cuneiform Character.	Assyrian rendering.	Meaning.
7. bat, be ...		pagru, pitu, mutu, labiru, uduntu .	corpse, to open, to die, old, quantity
til, †badhdhu ...	"	gamaru, pagru, katu	complete, corpse, hand
us ...	"	dâmu ...	blood (offspring)
†khar ...	"		
ziz, mit, †idim	"		
...	"	nakbu, samu, captu, belu, enuva, tsêru	channel, heaven, heavy, lord, when, desert
8. lugud ...		'sarcu ...	white race
9. adama ...		adamatu ...	black (red) race
10. susru...		ussusu ...	destruction (surname of Anu)
11. gir ...		sumuk-same, padhru	vault of heaven, to strike
rum ...	"	littu, padhru	sword, point
gir ...	"	girû, zukakibu, pad-	scorpion, plough, lightning
at, adh ...		anu, birku	
12. pur, pul ...		passaru ...	to explain (?)
du, gim ...	"	edissu, sumnu	alone, fat
†mucmuc-nabi (see 107a)	"		
†usu ...	"	edisu	solitary
	"	basmu, butu, macaru, garru	sweet odour, desert (?), to sell, or exchange, expedition (?)
13. kur ...		nacru, sannu, pappu	to change, enemy, name of ch.
pap ...	"	pappu, zicaru, tarbu, natsaru, akhu	name, male, young man, to defend, brother
13a. *khal, †dili-dili-nabi ("dil twice")		muttallicu ...	passenger, sick
†gisi-u-khallacu ("joined to the sign khal")		pusku	difficult
14. utuci...		samsu	the Sun
15. zubu...		gamlu	benefit
gam ...	"	sicru...	kindness
16. taltal...		Ea ...	the god Ilea

2*

A traditional dahabeah like the one Sayce lived on in the 1890s, sailing up and down the Nile, his "river of dreams."

Library of Congress
Prints and Photographs Division

Sayce's ability to read the ancient Assyrian language allowed him access to new information about the Bible.

From *Assyrian Grammar* by A.H. Sayce.

LEFT: Hong Kong Renaissance man Tse Tsan Tai, pictured in 1914, found Eden in the midst of World War I.

From The Creation, The Real Situation of Eden, and the Origin of the Chinese

ABOVE: It was important to Tse that Eden, the origin of all life, be located in China. This detailed map came folded into the back of his 1914 book.

From The Creation, The Real Situation of Eden, and the Origin of the Chinese

LEFT: Tse's 1899 cartoon warned of foreign powers encroaching on his beloved China from all sides.

Published in Chinese *Punch* magazine, 1899.

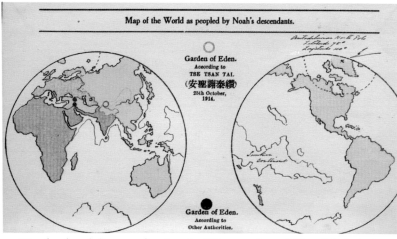

Hand-colored diagram showing the Western view of Eden (black dot), and Tse's China-centered view (red circle).

From The Creation, The Real Situation of Eden, and the Origin of the Chinese

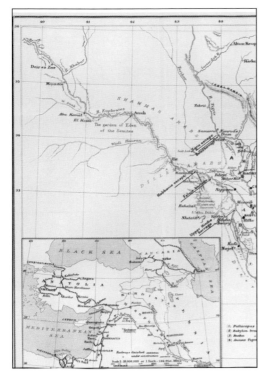

Sir William Willcocks in 1919. The maverick irrigation engineer insisted that there were actually two Gardens of Eden.

From *Sixty Years in the East*

LEFT: Willcock's minutely detailed survey of Iraq's waterways for the Royal Geographic Society.

From *The Geographical Journal*, Vol. 40, No. 2, August 1912, pp.129-145.

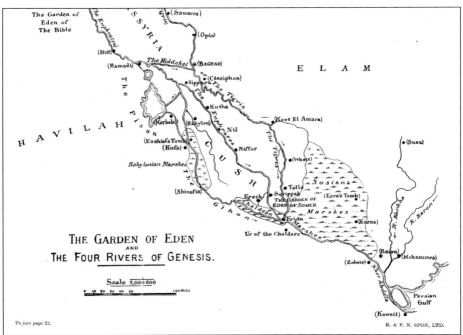

A detail of the map Willcocks drew for his popular book, *From the Garden of Eden to the Crossing of the Jordan*, showing both the Eden of the Bible and the Eden of Sumer.

From the Garden of Eden to the Crossing of the Jordan

The Hindiya Barrage, the sole outcome of Willcocks' irrigation survey of Mesopotamia, with a traditional reed-and-bitumen boat in the foreground, photographed in 1932.

A bitumen well in southern Iraq in 1932, like those that Willcocks thought looked like angels with flaming swords.

THE TREE OF KNOWLEDGE at Qurna, the traditional site of the Garden of Eden, taken in 1944. In a letter published to-day it is suggested that a garden under joint Anglo-American and Arab auspices should be re-established in this historic setting.

Norman Wright's bleak photograph of the broken "Tree of Knowledge" in Qurna, Iraq, as published in the *Times* of London, 1946.

Another 1946 photograph of Qurna, by Australian war photographer Frank Hurley, shows the Tree of Knowledge in a more complicated light. Note the British flag on the barge just off shore.

LEFT: The ordinary house on Diversey Street in Chicago where the Drs. William and Lena Sadler began to explore the alternate universe of Urantia.

Urantia Book Historical Society

BELOW: A drawing of "Government on a Neighboring Planet" made by one of the Urantia faithful.

Urantia Book Historical Society

GOVERNMENT ON A NEIGHBORING PLANET

Dr. William Sadler.

Urantia Book Historical Society

Dr. Lena Sadler.

Urantia Book Historical Society

Elvy Edison
Callaway, who
found Eden
in the Florida
Panhandle.

From *In The Beginning*

Callaway's map of
Eden, large scale.

From *In the Beginning*

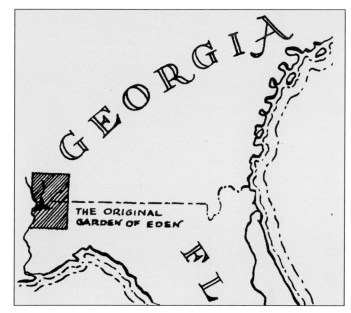

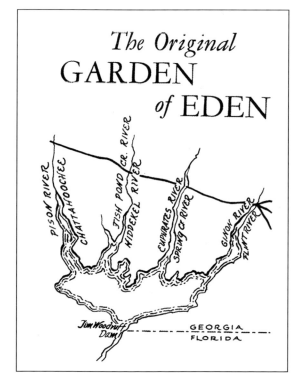

Detail of Callaway's map, showing the formation of
the four rivers of paradise.

From *In the Beginning*

The endangered Torreya yew
tree, which Callaway believed
was the tree Noah used
to build his Ark.

Torreya State Park Staff

A man and woman stand just outside the reed fence surrounding the restored Tree of Knowledge in Qurna, Iraq, sometime in the 1950s.

From *Iraq: Land of Two Rivers*, a brochure printed by King Feisal II's government in 1956.

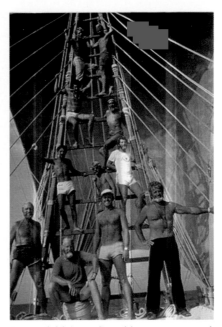

A young Thor Heyerdahl with his wife Liv in the 1930s, giving up civilization for the remote Polynesian island Fatu-Hiva.

Heyerdahl (seated) and his international crew on board his boat made entirely of Mesopotamian reeds, the *Tigris*.

The *Tigris* comes to the end of its voyage in Djibouti harbor.

A display at the Creation Museum in Petersburg, Kentucky, speaks directly to kids.

Lee Meadows, science educator, attempts to bridge the divide between evolution and creation.

At the Creation Museum's Garden of Eden, Adam names an unusual array of animals.

The Creation Museum's generic Tree of Knowledge with evil serpent.

Adam-ondi-Ahman, where Mormons believe Adam and Eve had settled peacefully after being expelled from Eden.

Joseph Smith, 1805–1844, founding prophet of the Mormon church, directed his persecuted followers to a small town in rural Missouri after they had been kicked out of Independence.

This rock at Adam-ondi-Ahman may be the one that Joseph Smith stood on to speak to his followers during the Mormon War.

A satellite photograph of the Persian Gulf. Archaeologist Juris Zarins saw the four rivers of paradise merging in the center.

Landsat imagery courtesy of NASA Goddard Space Flight Center and U.S. Geological Survey.

John Calvin's map of Biblical regions in the Middle East, the first to be included with a widely used edition of the Bible, in 1568, also finds the four rivers in Mesopotamia.

From *A History of Paradise* by Pierre Delumeau.

PART III

Progress

8

The Location Committee

IN THE BEGINNING, before they were selected by the Universal Father to usher in a utopian age on the planet Urantia, Adam and Eve were biologists. For more than 15,000 years they'd been codirectors of the division of experimental energy at the trial and testing laboratories of the central higher world.

So, of course, this Garden of Eden wasn't technically the beginning of Urantia—which we humans call Earth. According to *The Urantia Book*—a 2,000-page alternative Bible with the flavor of science fiction and the ethic of progressivism—a scouting party of supernatural beings surveyed our planet 600 million years ago, and reported favorable conditions. Then they waited 549 million years more for protoplasm to evolve into human beings. Unfortunately, after all the higher beings' patience, it took humanity only 1 million years to screw everything up. The evil human lord Caligastia, who believed in unlimited personal freedom, led a mass rebellion against the forces of good, which left Urantia devastated, and far behind the curve in terms of biological, social, and technological development. That's why Adam and Eve were brought in, as reformers, to promote cooperation, biologic uplift, and consensus building.

The Urantia Book has no official author listed on its title page. Believers credit the epic tale to a group of alien spiritual beings who descended to Earth in order to dictate their story to humanity. The book was first conceived in Chicago in the 1920s, and the circumstances of its birth are almost as strange as the unique vision of the Garden of Eden contained in its pages. Every Sunday beginning in 1924, two doctors, William and Lena Sadler, set up fifty folding chairs in the second-floor sitting room of their town house at 533 Diversey Parkway on Chicago's North Side, for tea. The house, on a modest residential street not far from Lake Michigan, was said to be the first steel-frame home in the city, and it served as both the personal residence and the professional offices of the Sadlers. The husband-and-wife team had together entered, studied at, and, in 1906, graduated from Chicago's American Medical Missionary College. Their Sunday teas were well attended by progressive friends and colleagues from the local Chicago medical community, of which the Sadlers had been members—extremely active members—for almost twenty years. No one would have imagined the Sadlers as the type to listen to the spiritual wisdom of aliens from outer space.

Lena Sadler, whom everyone called Dr. Lena, was an attending obstetrician at Columbus Hospital and Children's Memorial Hospital, specializing in the improvement of mothers and children. Her Chautauqua lectures included "How to Feed the Baby," "Piloting Modern Youth," and "The Sex Life before and after Marriage." She ministered to women who had been arrested or detained in Chicago's jails, of whom there were more and more in crime-ridden 1920s Chicago.

She served as chairman of the State of Illinois Department of Public Health and Child Welfare, and was a member of numerous medical societies including the American College of Surgeons, American Medical Association, Illinois State Medical Society, and Chicago Medical Society. In the 1920s, women in medicine had a whole parallel set of professional associations, so Lena served double duty as "doctor" and "female doctor." She was one of the founders of the American Medical Women's Association, the associate director of the Medical Women's International Association, and president of the Chicago Council of Medical Women; and she was active in the Chicago Medical Women's Club, Chicago Woman's Club, Chicago Chapter of the American Federation of Soroptimists (a women's advocacy organization), not to mention the Lakeview Women's Club.

It would seem difficult for any husband to keep up with Dr. Lena's illustrious credentials, but William S. Sadler held his own, as a professor of psychiatry at the Post-Graduate Medical School of Chicago, consulting psychiatrist at Columbus Hospital, and member of nearly as many associations as his wife—among them the American Medical, Psychiatric, and Psychopathological societies; the American College of Surgeons; and the American Association for the Advancement of Science.

William Sadler was a quick-witted orator with a ready laugh and a cherubic face, and his friends liked to claim he was the second highest-paid speaker on the Chautauqua lecture circuit, after the formidable William Jennings Bryan. (Chautauqua had long ago expanded beyond the Methodist Sunday school teachers' training center it was in Warren's time; its ecumenical lecturers traveled all over the country in what were called "tent Chautauquas.") This is not to say that Sadler and his much-more famous fellow orator would have agreed on much of anything. Sadler prided himself on his rationality and progressiveness. These were exciting times for forward thinkers, as expressed by the motto of the 1933 Chicago World's Fair: "Science Finds, Industry Applies, Man Conforms." He was a stalwart believer in evolution, and had studied with Freud in Vienna. He believed in the new disciplines of psychology, psychiatry, and psychoanalysis, and was actively engaged in disentangling them from the old discipline of religion. As the keynote speaker at a conference for university church workers, Sadler proclaimed, "I do not approve of ministers trying to be psychiatrists. They should not undertake to do things they are not trained to do or they will find themselves wading in deep water." He did believe they *could* be trained: Sadler also taught pastoral psychology at a nearby divinity school. Still, the human mind did not belong to religion; it was the domain of science.

Sadler's mission was to bring cutting-edge medical information directly to the people. At lectures, conventions, conferences, and fairs, and in classrooms, he held forth on what he liked to call "personology"—a combination of psychiatry and self-improvement. This was the era of vast prescriptions for humanity, and Dr. Will, as everyone called him, wrote more than forty-two tracts, pamphlets, and books on a wide variety of topics, from *The Cause and Cure of Colds* to *Prescription for Permanent Peace*.

In his zeal to separate the new science of the mind from the old, outmoded superstitions, Sadler made a particular case against spiritualism—people called mediums who claimed to be able to communicate, through mysterious trance states, with the dead from the great beyond. This practice usually grew popular in America after catastrophes, of which what was then called the Great War was a bewilderingly horrific example. In the first "modern" war, industry had applied what science had found, and man was forced to conform. The result? A lot of people had a lot of dead to communicate with. William Sadler carefully debunked mediums as purveyors of false comfort, and in doing so became somewhat of a respected figure of comfort himself. He listened; he took patients' grief seriously; and he dispensed the wisdom he'd learned from psychology to a growing audience at the Sunday teas.

One Sunday at Diversey Parkway, Sadler stood in front of his guests in the second-floor sitting room and gave an informal talk on psychic phenomena, a talk he had laid out in his 1929 book *The Mind at Mischief*. On the basis of his own scientific observation of people who claimed to enter semiconscious states to communicate with the dead, he wrote, "All the physical phenomena"—automatic writing, levitation, speaking in tongues, etc.—"have proved to be fraudulent." Such fraud could be easily detected by a simple physical examination. And all the psychic phenomena involved—telepathy, clairvoyance, split personalities—were "invariably explainable by the psychological laws of projection and transference": that is to say, people, especially when they are grieving or desperate, hear what they want to hear. This is not magic, Sadler insisted, but simple psychology.

At least, spiritualism could be traced back to psychology *most* of the time. In one case, however, Sadler confessed to his listeners, he was stumped. One male subject had begun to speak in his sleep, in the voices not of the dead but of alien beings who claimed to know everything about everything. This patient didn't seem to conform to any of Sadler's usual objections to spiritualism and magic. Both William and Lena Sadler had made a thorough physical examination and found the subject's sleep authentically—and unusually—profound. "So far we have never been able to awaken the subject when in this state; but the body is never rigid, and the heart action is never modified. . . . This man is utterly unconscious . . . and unless told about it subsequently, never knows that he has been used as a sort of clearing house for the coming and going of alleged extra-planetary personalities." William Sadler examined this patient using every method he could think of, and still failed to find any telltale signs that he was faking.

"Psychoanalysis, hypnotism, intensive comparison, fail to show that the written or spoken messages of this individual have origin in his own mind." William wrote that he attended at least 250 sessions with this man, over a period of eighteen years. Early on, the Sadlers enlisted the services of a stenographer to keep track of the voluminous material spewed forth by the patient they began to call the "mysterious sleeper." And this material—stories and morality tales from alien beings—had William confused. It didn't sound at all like the sleeper's own beliefs when the man was awake. (The sleeper, whose identity was never officially revealed, is assumed to be someone the Sadlers also knew in his waking hours.) In fact, the alien wisdom seemed unique.

"Its philosophy is consistent. It is essentially Christian, and is, on the whole, entirely harmonious with the known scientific facts and truths of this age."

At this point, Sadler's audience derailed the Sunday lecture and demanded to know more about this unsolved case, and its attendant philosophy.

That's when William Sadler invited his assembled colleagues and friends to submit their questions about the universe in written form to the "mysterious sleeper," now called the "contact personality." In this way they would be able to judge for themselves just how accurate the stories could be. Many of those assembled no doubt thought the whole thing was ridiculous, but some, apparently, did not. The group who returned the following Sunday had 4,000 questions among them. The Sadlers gathered these up, passed them on to the "contact," and revealed the answers the following Sunday.

This went on for some weeks. Guests would place their questions on slips of paper in a basket or fishbowl that rested on a chest of drawers in the middle of the sitting room. How the questions got from the dresser in the sitting room to the bedroom of the sleeper was a question much discussed by the Sadlers. The process had to be secret, to protect the sleeper's identity, but it also had to be somewhat transparent, to assure the group that the answers to the questions were actually coming from the lips of an anonymous man in a trance. A solution was proposed. Sadler; his wife; their son, William, Jr.; and their adopted daughter, Christy, would become the "contact commission"—the only ones allowed to transmit the questions, and to be present when the answers were first revealed. The people in the Sunday group trusted the Sadlers implicitly, or they wouldn't have been present at all. And it was thought that committee members could keep each other honest, should a dispute about the nighttime revelations arise.

So the four gathered dutifully by the sleeper's bedside, and asked the questions. He/it/they provided answers, Christy typed them up on yellow legal paper, and Dr. William Sadler read them back to the Sunday focus group. This reading provoked more questions and revision. And that's how the writing of *The Urantia Book* began, by committee. It took the group ten years of questions and answers before the celestial beings declared the first three sections of *The Urantia Book* to be complete, in 1934. In 1935, a fourth section, retelling the life of Jesus, was finished.

As it turned out, the Sadlers, rationalists though they were, had no trouble reconciling their belief in the scientific method with their belief in a higher, spiritual power that could communicate directly to humans. Or rather, they *did* have trouble, but they were determined, like Tse Tsan Tai, not to give up either reason or religion for the sake of the other.

William and Lena Sadler had both grown up in the Seventh-day Adventist Church, an American evangelical denomination founded in 1863. William had actually been an ordained minister before he went into medicine. The church's beliefs were about as far away from those expressed in *The Urantia Book* as possible. Adventists believed in the literal truth of scripture, in Christ's atonement, in salvation by faith alone, and in the creation of the world in six literal, twenty-four-hour days. Like Landon West's German Baptists, they practiced strict dress codes and dietary habits, and adamantly opposed the new invention of birth control. The church's founder, Ellen White, experienced mysterious trance states in which she claimed to receive prophetic visions from God, which in turn inspired numerous volumes of religious doctrine. But by the 1860s, people had started to see similarities between her works and other religious and philosophical tracts of the day. William Sadler, along with his mentor, Dr. John Harvey Kellogg, began to lose faith in White's integrity. Kellogg was officially excommunicated in 1907, and both Sadlers joined with a group of other disaffected Adventists to publicly accuse their former leader of fraud.

The fall of a beloved religious leader to science would seem to be exactly what was called for in the new "century of progress." Old idols fall; new truth emerges. And the Sadlers were all for moving onward and upward. But the quick demise of lifelong beliefs also leaves a hole in the believer. For the Sadlers, the fact that Ellen White, who claimed to communicate directly with higher powers via trance states, had turned out to be less than reliable, did *not* mean that such communication was impossible. Their disillusionment, paradoxically, gave the Sadlers the freedom to reexamine and rebuild their religious beliefs from the ground up. The original material for *The Urantia Book* came from the sleeper. Whether or not *he* got it from a group of alien spiritual beings is a moot point. In either case, the book is a collective creation that reflects the beliefs of those who participated in its writing. That's what made it interesting.

The Urantia Book is in constant dialogue with the Bible, re-imagining and reforming it in step with the accelerating pace of twentieth-century change. There were lots of Biblical ideas that *The Urantia Book* dispensed with completely—the virgin birth, the Trinity, and the atonement were all left out—but the Garden of Eden was still a necessity. The Sadlers and their guests wanted a chance to build Eden themselves, to start religion over in a world where, it seemed, everything else was brand new. That way, they could control what was in it.

In the book, Adam and Eve needed to establish a new head-quarters for their worldwide moral rehabilitation mission—somewhere *on* Urantia, but not *of* the corrupted planet, a place where they could incubate new life safe from evil Caligastia's reach. The Garden did not yet exist on Urantia; it would have to be built. How would they find a suitable location? The higher powers convened a location committee, and they sallied forth in search of the perfect spot.

It took three years, but then the location committee returned with a proposal. They had scoped out three deserving sites. The first was an island in the Persian Gulf. That was immediately ruled out for its insufficient size. The second was the flat land just upstream of the meeting of the Tigris and Euphrates, in Mesopotamia. That region, however, had too many floods. True enough. The third option—a long narrow peninsula projecting westward from the eastern shores of the Mediterranean Sea, near Crete—was just right: not too warm, not too cold, with plenty of space. The vote was almost unanimous, and by majority rule the Mediterranean peninsula was declared to be Eden.

Sometimes *The Urantia Book* offered dazzling riffs on religion; sometimes it just made everything seem unnecessarily complicated, Byzantine even. Eden, for example, was to be created in the center of the peninsula, surrounded by a ring of mountains, which were in turn surrounded by a moatlike circular sea; this sea fed into a large river flowing eastward along the twenty-seven-mile-wide neck of land connecting Eden to the mainland and preventing it from being completely isolated.

Once this river of Eden hit the mainland, it did indeed split into four tributaries, as in Genesis, but *The Urantia Book* doesn't bother to name them. There were indeed precious stones in the mountains surrounding Eden, but Eden's residents didn't pay them very much attention. Such petty details were unimportant. The Tree of Life, however, was real. It was a magical shrub that absorbed antiaging space energy and then mysteriously released this life-extension force of the universe when eaten—sort of like an intergalactic battery.

The Tree wasn't the only element in the Biblical Eden story that the Urantians plucked from oblivion and nursed back to health. The name Melchizedek, though it sounds rather futuristic, is actually a minor Biblical character who appears twice in the Old Testament: once in Genesis, as a king who brings bread and wine to a victorious patriarch; and once in the Book of Psalms, where someone is referred to as "a priest on the order of Melchizedek." On such scant material vast libraries are built. Various thinkers have claimed, variously, that Melchizedek represents either an incarnation of Jesus, or an incarnation of the Holy Ghost, or possibly the Jewish messiah yet to come. Or maybe just a priest. In any case, *The Urantia Book* embraced this walk-on priest-king, and invited him and his order to play a much larger role in their new sacred universe. Likewise, they invited the Bible's angel Michael to have his name above the title: He was actually the Son of God, known on this planet as Jesus Christ.

Everything about *The Urantia Book* was much larger than the Bible. Over many Sundays, the group that gathered at the Sadlers' house, which came to be called "the Forum," developed a vast cosmology with millions of inhabited planets, all symmetrically organized and classed in neat hierarchies: mansion worlds, material worlds, architectural worlds. *The Urantia Book* has a fondness for numbers—the bigger and more specific, the better. Its cast of thousands easily rivals those of its cousins the Old and New Testaments. Whereas the Bible moves in a cozy little circle dotted with Canaanites, Elamites, Egyptians, and Hebrews, *The Urantia Book* boasts heavenly hosts of angels, material sons, and "midwayers," all materializing and dematerializing across unfathomably large swaths of space. All this had been revealed to the Forum in what it called the Fifth Epochal Revelation of the Universal Father—that is, God.

But for a group with such grand ambitions, the Forum was surprisingly modest. There was no proselytizing. People could come and go freely as they saw fit. On joining the group, they did have to sign a pledge of secrecy—they were not to reveal anything about the Urantia revelations until these were complete and ready for publication, to which end members contributed a small amount of money every week. But even the secrecy came with a humble explanation: it wasn't fair to let someone experience the Urantia revelations secondhand. If friends of a friend happened to hear through word of mouth about the Sunday activities, they were welcome to come and experience the revelation for themselves. Humility was also the expressed reason for the secrecy surrounding the identity of the "contact personality." The members of the contact commission did not want this person to become a de facto saint. They'd seen what happened to Ellen White. No, their mysterious sleeper was just a vehicle for the divine message, and should not be idolized. The term "Forum" itself was borrowed from the nonreligious Chautauqua movement, and the Forum's members were called "readers," not "believers" or "the faithful." The whole enterprise had the feel of corn-fed self-improvement. Urantians were simply engaged in the rational activity of reading and studying a book, together.

After all, *The Urantia Book* did encourage belief in some very reasonable things. One was the difference between science and religion: "Science deals with facts; religion is concerned only with values." Contrary to the teachings of the Seventh-day Adventists, Jesus was not so concerned with whether or not you ate meat, or drank alcohol. "It is not that which enters into the mouth that spiritually defiles the man, but rather that which proceeds out of the mouth and from the heart." In this *The Urantia Book* agreed with the New Testament, Matthew 15:11. Jesus *did* care about pride, cruelty, oppression, and hypocrisy.

The mood on Sunday afternoons was confident and content. Faraway worlds seemed to blend quite comfortably with the real one. From 1924 all the way through 1942, families dressed in their Sunday best brought their children, and everybody listened diligently to the Fifth Epochal Revelation. During their breaks, the readers would step out onto bustling Diversey Parkway, where they could purchase a soda or a snack, then go back to revelation. Every year, they celebrated Jesus's birthday with a picnic.

Study groups formed, study guides were written, and scholars emerged. One bespectacled young woman, Marian Rowley, who was not a member of the contact commission, attained such mastery of the cosmology and theology of *The Urantia Book* that William Sadler himself would refer the earnest questions of other readers to her. As the story goes, a fellow reader telephoned Rowley at ten-thirty one night struggling to remember the location of the midsonite world because she couldn't find it mentioned in any lists of the headquarters clusters. Rowley answered immediately and matter-of-factly: the midsonite world wasn't an architectural world but an evolutionary world, located in the local universe. Her friends liked to joke that Marian probably had lunch with celestial beings every day. Marian and the others seemed to leap eagerly at the chance to master an arcane body of knowledge; they saw it as their chance to help build a brave new world.

As *The Urantia Book* told it, eighty-three years before Adam and Eve's scheduled arrival, a dedicated corps of 3,000 volunteer workers began to prepare the land of Eden for settlement, while Adam and Eve received supplemental training in intellectual advancement. After peaceably evacuating the peninsula's previous residents, they built a brick wall across the neck of land to separate it from inferior civilizations. In the center they built an exquisite temple to the Universal Father; to the north they established Eden's administrative headquarters; to the south were homes for the workers and their families. To the west, they broke ground for Eden's educational system. And in the east of Eden? Adam and Eve's personal dwelling, of course. There was never a more carefully designed Garden.

Adam and Eve's arrival in Eden was cause for much joyous celebration by the residents of Eden—workers, teachers, gardeners, families—who had been preparing for this day for so many years. Adam and Eve themselves caused wonderment as they processed down the main avenues of Eden. Members of the new, superior "violet" race, they were more than eight feet tall with pale skin that glimmered with holy purple light. Most of the time the holy light was covered up with clothing—as opposed to fig leaves—but the violet auras emerging from the tops of their heads were the source of our idea of saints with halos. Adam and Eve were happy with the general plan of Eden—although privately, they did make many changes to their own house. They held conferences, built schools, and ate vegetables, and Eve gave birth to 1,647 children, who were pure violet, with superior spiritual ability, imagination, musical ability, a sense of humor, and a love of adventure. The idea was, eventually, to interbreed the violet race with humans so we could have the benefit of their talents.

Adam and Eve's achievements in Eden went far beyond the imagination of the Forum's meager earthlings, far beyond anything that has been accomplished on Urantia ever since. Like William Warren and Landon West, *The Urantia Book* had much invested in humanity's more perfect prehistory. If our ancestors were ten-foot-tall divine creatures living at the North Pole, we had a lot to live up to. If even a primitive race of Mound Builders had enough religious sophistication to build a giant reminder of man's sin, who were we poor fools to ignore it?

But there was one major difference between these more conservative visions of the descent of man and the forward-thinking Urantians. Warren and West thought we didn't have a prayer of reaching the enlightened state of our ancestors in this lifetime, and all we could do was not slide backward. The members of the Forum saw things differently. In the late nineteenth century and the early twentieth century, they believed, man *was* again ascending up toward the heights of Eden. And they could get there soon, given the extraordinary scientific progress the world seemed to be making every day.

It's easy to see why they felt so upbeat. The 1920s saw the invention of the first television, the first talking motion picture, the first solo transatlantic flight, and the first liquid-fueled rocket. That's not to mention antibiotics, vaccination, frozen food, hearing aids, automatic soda-dispensing machines, and the vast proliferation of the automobile, thanks to Henry Ford and the Model T. Clearly we were heading into a mechanized universe, one in which human ingenuity could save us from virtually any enemy, including ourselves. Likewise, the Urantian Eden was a vast improvement over the previous models.

William Willcocks would have been proud to know that Eden on Urantia contained thousands of miles of advanced irrigation ditches. The residents of Qurna, who lacked sufficient sanitation, would have been better served in the Urantian Eden. In *The Urantia Book,* there were dedicated sewage inspectors to make sure Edenites scrupulously buried or composted all their waste, dramatically lowering their rates of disease. Eventually they figured out how to construct covered brick conduits that ran beneath Eden's walls and emptied waste into the one river of Eden almost a mile beyond the outer walls of the Garden. Somehow, Urantians even managed to keep the drinking water of Eden wholesome with strict sanitary regulations.

Technical advances like these, the Sadlers and the Forum believed, would provoke social advances. On Urantia, slavery had been abolished 100 years before Adam and Eve's arrival, and women were given equal status in all areas of life. Or rather, Adam *tried* to teach the Edenites sex equality, but they were a tough crowd. Before Adam and Eve's arrival, they had looked at women only as vehicles for producing and nourishing babies. But Eve was a role model: the way she worked side by side with her husband made a profound impression on all the Garden's dwellers.

In 1920, the Nineteenth Amendment, allowing women the right to vote, was finally ratified after decades of struggle. (The Equal Rights Amendment, proposed in 1923 to end discrimination on the basis of gender, still hasn't passed muster.) When Dr. Lena Sadler found out that the Medical Women's Club was not to be included in the "Century of Progress" exhibit at the great 1933 Chicago World's Fair, she was outraged. Without women, what kind of progress could there possibly be? She immediately and astutely raised the funds for an exhibit by soliciting sponsorship from various manufacturers of maternity clothing.

Despite civilization's advances, it was important that human beings not be left completely to their own devices. That was how evil lord Caligastia had been able to take over the planet Urantia to begin with. Freedoms had to be reasonably curtailed. According to *The Urantia Book,* the perfect democracy must strike a balance between liberty and control. A chief executive should be elected by universal suffrage, with no third term allowed. Both voting and military service should be compulsory for all adults over the age of twenty. Charity destroyed self-respect; it should be replaced by government entitlement programs. Some ideas in the book anticipated Roosevelt's New Deal; this wouldn't have surprised the Urantians—a celestial being, especially the one called the Seraphim of Progress, could be expected to stay somewhat ahead of the curve.

Indeed, not much took the Urantians by surprise. Later studies of *The Urantia Book* uncovered liberal borrowing from many other, earlier, texts. Unlike Ellen White, however, the higher beings made no secret of their plagiarism: they proudly claimed to have gathered the most forward-thinking human knowledge—including the work of the Sadlers themselves—to present to humanity. Some of the studies that might appear to debunk the divine truth of Urantia were actually written by believers themselves, in order to reinforce this idea.

But not everything in the book was so worldly and enlightened. In a 1932 lecture, Lena Sadler recommended severe eugenic measures to stem the tide of human degeneration. She was in favor of federally enforced sterilization of the "feebleminded," and believed free medical help for welfare mothers should be withheld, because we don't need to save every weak child in the world. Doctrines like these also made it into the pages of *The Urantia Book*. One higher intelligent being chides the earthly readers: "It is the false sentiment of your partially perfected civilizations that fosters, protects, and perpetuates the hopelessly defective strains of evolutionary human stocks." In Urantia, the government should segregate persons of "subnormal intelligence" in colonies where sex for procreation is forbidden.

The Sadlers weren't the only progressives who saw no conflict between their new era of enlightenment and the advocacy of eugenics. Margaret Sanger, the birth control pioneer, whose clinic's motto was "No Gods, No Masters," also became involved in promoting eugenics later in her life. Likewise, William Sadler's medical mentor, Dr. Kellogg, became a eugenics proponent, founding, among his many other enterprises, the Race Betterment Foundation. Controlling the population seemed to some like a natural extension of their other efforts for social progress. If humans had to take the world into their own hands, they had to go all the way.

Likewise, then, it followed that people of extraordinary intelligence were to be encouraged to breed abundantly. Back in Eden, Adam and Eve worked to carry out the divine plan of the Universal Father, which was simple, if time-consuming. They were to have as many children as possible, so that vast new generations of their superior race could take over the corrupt world outside the Garden and move it into a higher stage of planetary development. But outside the secluded mountain walls of Eden, the rest of planet Urantia had a long way to go. Too much evil had been bred into the population.

This was also true in the world immediately outside the safe confines of 533 Diversey Parkway. Chicago seemed a case study in personal freedom gone horribly awry. The city was embroiled in mob violence and serial killing. The new prevalence of automobiles and alcohol led to an epidemic of drunk-driving accidents. Even the freedom of the press had a dark side: in the "circulation wars" of the 1920s, reporters and deliverymen battled to the death for their rival newspapers' circulation numbers.

In *The Urantia Book*, the evil outside world concocted a plot to disturb Eden's blissful perfection. First Serpatatia, leader of a particularly advanced tribe outside Eden, contacted Eve—still considered the more suggestible of the two reformers—and inquired as to whether any collaboration was possible. Discouraged by the slow pace of progress, Eve began to attend breakout sessions with Serpatatia.

The meetings were unauthorized, but Eve's quest for progress was in earnest, and for the ends of the Universal Father all means were justified. The sneaky Serpatatia offered impatient Eve a shortcut for creating utopia. The plan was simple. At Serpatatia's suggestion, Eve cheated on Adam with a man named Cano—the father of Cain—in hopes of spreading the good genes of the violet race faster that way. Then, distressed at what she'd done, she told Adam. Adam's reaction? He disappeared for thirty days, during which he picked out a particularly brilliant non-violet (and presumably nonviolent) partner to have sex with, so that he could share Eve's fate, even though he didn't yet know what that fate was.

On Earth, bigger trouble was brewing beyond Chicago, and there, "racial development" was part of the problem, not the solution. In Germany, the theoretical anti-Semitism that Delitzsch had pioneered in service of the kaiser in 1903 had taken on a life of its own. Delitzsch had died in 1922 and the kaiser was now in shameful exile in Norway after his many wartime misdeeds, but a new generation of Germans was still trying to make world history into Aryan history, and world geography into Aryan geography. In 1924, in *Discovery of Paradise,* Franz von Wendrin had argued that the Garden of Eden had been in Germany, but that the Jews had falsely claimed it for Asia. Along with maps, his book included exhortations to his countrymen to liberate their homeland from the "inferior races." Soon, it became clear that this was not just rhetoric for Germany. Everyone feared the worst; war was coming.

On Urantia, Adam and Eve waited, crestfallen, for their dalliances to be discovered by the Universal Father. They knew they would be punished, but they didn't realize that the suffering wouldn't stop with them. Adam and Eve's loyal followers blamed the evil Serpatatia for tempting Eve. They massed together and turned in a rage against Serpatatia's settlement outside the Garden, destroying it completely. Adam and Eve did not know what to do; this misapplied vengeance just made them feel guiltier. Then their heavenly chaperones, the Melchizedek receivers, who had zoomed off to outer worlds once they had safely entrusted the Tree of Life to Adam and Eve's care, suddenly returned to Eden. This was a bad sign. Clearly the higher authorities were prepared for an epic battle between good and evil. But Adam and Eve were nonviolent. So they decided the best course of action was to pile everyone into a caravan and hightail it out of Eden before Serpatatia's allies took revenge.

On May 31, 1942, while the Germans were advancing on Stalingrad, and the Jews of France were being forced to wear the yellow Star of David, the official organization of the Forum ended. The manuscript of *The Urantia Book* had been typed up, although, for obvious reasons, no authors were listed on the title page. The group had even contracted with the printing company R. R. Donnelley to create printing plates. But the book wasn't actually set into type until 1949. Why the delay? It could have been because of paper rationing; everybody had to sacrifice for the war effort. Or maybe, owing to the momentous events that had happened in the meantime—Hiroshima, Nagasaki, Auschwitz—last-minute revisions were necessary. The world now knew it had the capacity to destroy itself, and many people of all faiths were reevaluating their relationship to God.

The Urantia Book was finally published in 1955, during another forward-looking era, though this period was somewhat less innocent than the 1920s. The book retained the characteristic optimism of its creators. The crew at 533 Diversey Parkway had simply picked themselves up, dusted themselves off, and begun anew. Likewise with their Adam and Eve. After their exile from Eden, the couple had naturally consulted the location committee's original advice, and found their way to Paradise, Plan B: the Euphrates valley in Mesopotamia. There, they got to work tilling the land with the sweat of their own brows. It was quite a pathetic sight to witness angelic Adam and Eve and their ever-increasing troop of children growing their own produce and building towers out of mud brick, but Adam and Eve were determined to make a contribution to civilization.

Upon publication of their magnum opus, the earnest ranks of Urantians allowed themselves a moment to dream. After thirty years of work, during which more than 400 people had passed through the doors of 533 Diversey Parkway, finally, finally, the words of the Fifth Epochal Revelation could reach outside those steel-girded walls. They trusted that the strength of the wisdom contained in the 2,000-page tome would soon spread to the rest of the world. Promotional ideas were discussed. Someone suggested offering *The Urantia Book* for serialization in *Life* magazine, but this was considered too evangelical. So instead they just sent copies of the freshly printed volume to major figures whom they respected, including Aldous Huxley, Edward R. Murrow, and Eleanor Roosevelt, hoping that these wise leaders would see the light and help spread the word. Sadly, as reported in the next month's newsletter, nobody responded.

It was true that the once glorious Adam and Eve and their children looked out of place in muddy Mesopotamia. But don't be fooled: man did not "fall." Man cannot "fall." Man can only progress. The fruit of knowledge is here, right in front of us; what's to fear? Like William Willcocks, the Urantians minimized the role of sin in Eden. Adam and Eve did not sin, because sin requires evil intent. Adam and Eve "defaulted." They had only the best of intentions. True, they went against the divine plan for peace and harmony, thereby bringing chaos upon themselves and their families and followers. But to err is human, so no atonement or blood sacrifice is necessary. Eventually Adam and Eve received official pardons. And despite their setbacks, they still contributed vast amounts of learning to human society. Their eviction from the idyllic first Garden taught them many valuable lessons. First among these lessons: it's not civilization that makes people; it's people who make their own civilization. Unlike Willcocks, the Urantians had learned that you could not force civilization on anybody. People had to come to it for themselves.

The first Urantian Garden of Eden, out in the middle of the Mediterranean, eventually disappeared. The volcanic mountains surrounding the Garden suddenly became active, turning the floor of the Mediterranean into a giant seesaw, gradually raising up the western side, which became today's coastline, and sinking the eastern side, and with it, the entire Edenic peninsula. And thus, the most beautiful natural creation Urantia will ever see was lost. But still, there was no reason to despair. The loss of Eden wasn't Adam and Eve's fault. It wasn't even a bad thing. In fact, the celestial beings noted, it hardly seemed to them a coincidence that Eden's disappearance "was timed to occur at just about the date of the accumulation of the reserves of the violet race for undertaking the work of rehabilitating the world peoples." The old world had to die for the new one to be born. Adam and Eve's race had finally reached a critical mass, thanks to the widespread interbreeding of those 1,647 children.

They had been patient, and they had been rewarded. Patience wasn't just *a* virtue for the Urantians; it was *the* virtue. Rehabilitating the world would take some time, but it was possible. Eden had been taken from us not because we had sinned and were no longer worthy, but because we were *so* worthy that we had no need for it anymore.

9

Mother Eve's Great Decision

IN THE BEGINNING, Adam didn't know what to do with himself in Eden. He just sat there all day—idle, naked, unemployed—under a Florida grapefruit tree. God had given him immortality, so what was the rush? One day, though, he realized he needed more from life. And that's when Eve showed up.

On Elvy Edison Callaway's hand-drawn map of northwest Florida, the Jim Woodruff Dam over the Apalachicola River looks like the narrow wrist of a giant hand. Just north of the dam, near the Florida-Georgia border, the Apalachicola splits into four fingers. Callaway has neatly labeled each river with its Florida name and its Biblical name: The Chattahoochee would be the Tigris, Fish Pond Creek the Pishon, Flint River the Gihon, and Spring Creek the Euphrates. In 1956, Callaway, a bespectacled lawyer who had been born in Alabama, announced that this four-river system "proves beyond all doubt that the Bible account is true, and that the Garden was in the Apalachicola Valley of West Florida." Callaway spent the next thirty years trying to convince the world that he'd found paradise in the flat piney swamps of the Florida panhandle. He knew this was a hard sell. But he figured he could convince the skeptics—after all, he'd been one himself most of his life.

Biblical truth was not the message one would expect to hear from a man who was named after the father of American invention, Thomas Alva Edison, and who, as a lawyer, had taken Clarence Darrow's side in the legendary Scopes trial. Callaway's skepticism about religion extended all the way back to his youth. It began with a girl.

Back home on the farm in tiny Weogufka, Alabama, young Callaway had wanted little to do with his father's hard-line Baptist
church, and he wasn't afraid to make his feelings known. Just
before Christmas 1908, when Elvy was eighteen, a young female
schoolteacher arrived in town. She was boarded in a respectable
Weogufka household, but was not yet a member of Elvy's church.
Still, he saw no harm in befriending her and transporting her in
his horse-drawn buggy to local (non-Baptist) square dances.

Since Baptists were forbidden by their church to actually dance,
Callaway would simply "take a seat in the corner and look on."
But after several nights as a spectator, speculating all the while on
the relative morality of dancing, he "finally reached the conclusion that any God who would condemn a young man to eternal
damnation for what appeared to me an innocent amusement was
a monster instead of a loving father."

Callaway did not pretend this was an entirely theological point.
"My interest in the young lady helped me to reach this decision."
And he "entered whole-heartedly" into the dance for the next three
weeks, throughout the Christmas holidays, until the fourth Saturday
of January, when, his father insisted, he had to go to church. After
a ninety-minute sermon on "the pearly gates and golden streets,"
the preacher opened the floor to the congregation, and somebody
said what everybody was thinking.

"I hear that young Brother Callaway has been dancing during the
holidays, and I think he should make an apology to the church."

Callaway stood his ground. "I danced with a young woman who
is good enough to teach your children and boards in one of the
best homes of the community. I have not committed any wrong
and I do not intend to apologize." The congregation remained
unpersuaded. A motion was made, and seconded, to charge Callaway with "revelry" and start proceedings against him. Callaway
responded with the declaration: "I have no desire to associate with
a bunch of ignorant bigots." He then picked up his hat and walked
out, to the heartbreak of his parents, who felt he had "joined the
ranks of the Devil."

As Callaway told it in his 1934 book *The Other Side of the South,* this was the moment when he converted to secularism, the moment when he turned directly from ignorance to knowledge. Without the pressure of the church, he studied and read whatever he could get his hands on, being careful to hide his books in the woods and barns to keep his parents from destroying them. It was only a short step from book-reading to Jacksonville State University in Jacksonville, Alabama. And he had women to thank. He left for school that very year, 1908, and by 1911 he had married Annie Levie—who may or may not be the good woman from the square dances. He had Annie to thank for keeping him out of World War I. Though he registered for the draft, he claimed exemption on the grounds that with his burgeoning law practice in Lowndes, Mississippi, he was the sole provider for his wife and their young son, William.

Soon they moved south to Lakeland, a good-size town in central Florida, about halfway down the peninsula. There, in the 1920s and 1930s, he argued cases for the newly formed NAACP. Callaway claimed a long lineage of forward thinkers. He wrote that his great-grandfather—who had built the church from which he made such a dramatic exit—had freed his 103 slaves in 1856. Callaway's views on "the situation of the Negro" were progressive for his time and place, as were his views on the separation of church and state. He claimed friendship with Clarence Darrow—though Darrow, thirty-two years older, most likely considered the lanky Alabaman more of a disciple. Callaway supported Darrow's pro-evolution position in that defining trial. Both these positions—pro–civil rights and antireligion—would have been minority views in central Florida.

To Callaway, evolution was an appealing idea. Like others of the time, Callaway took the scientific term in a social sense. Evolution meant social progress, and clearly in the impoverished, racially divided South, progress was needed. Callaway was optimistic: "The strongest evidence of the evolution of man is that throughout every age there appears in some mysterious way men and women of deep emotions and peculiar visions to lead us away from the false and cruel customs of the past." He considered himself one of those peculiar visionaries.

In his opinion, two forces were needed to save the bereft and broken South, America, and the world: religion and reason. Ever the lawyer, he reserved the right to define these timeworn terms. "What I mean by religion is love, patience, toleration, sympathy, kindness, vicarious service, honesty, truth, a love of and for the beautiful, a hunger for knowledge and wisdom, a belief that right thought, right conduct, right example is a magnet sufficient within itself to attract men and women away from excesses and evils." Who could argue with that? He did not stop to define "reason," perhaps because he hadn't spent so much time battling against it. Reason needed no definition.

"If we can ever have both religion and reason," he continued, "the South will be the 'Garden of Eden' of this earth." Callaway was speaking figuratively here. He meant that the South had potential for perfection, though it was hard to see at the time. How Callaway got from a figurative Garden of Eden to a literal one is a story that begins in politics.

Ever since his teenage rebellion over the square dance, Callaway had had a strong contrarian streak. He wasn't comfortable unless he was swimming against the current of popular opinion. By 1929 he was chairman of the Florida Republican Party, in a state so Democratic that Callaway wrote: "It is known to every informed Southerner that one who opposes, questions or criticizes any President branded, like a cow in the woods, with the designation 'Democrat,' commits an unpardonable sin and is looked upon as a traitor to all that is sacred and holy." Callaway chafed at anybody's telling him what was or was not a sacred cow.

The Depression was an awkward time to be a free-market libertarian Republican, to say the least. Unemployment had gone from 4 percent to 25 percent, and in 1932 the Democrat Franklin Delano Roosevelt was overwhelmingly elected for the first of four terms. He spent his first 100 days in office meeting with Congress daily in a marathon lawmaking session, during which it granted every one of his requests for aid and regulation.

Callaway was suspicious of exactly this kind of Democratic party-machine unanimity; it offended his pride as an individualist and an entrepreneur. He opposed everything that Congress and Roosevelt favored—except the repeal of Prohibition, which he was all for. In 1936 Callaway ran for governor of Florida on an anti-welfare platform. He was proud to viciously denounce Roosevelt's wildly popular New Deal. He wanted the return of the gold standard. He wanted the new banking regulation reversed. He lost, dramatically, and never quite got over it.

Two years later, in a letter published in the *Washington Post,* Callaway accused the New Deal Democratic Party—"economic royalists" all—of buying a Florida Senate election by insinuating that Roosevelt would deprive Florida of the millions of dollars in graft that the party had plundered from the government. He even claimed that the party machine told the Florida citrus growers that President Roosevelt had promised to pay for that year's damage done by the Mediterranean fruit fly, but only if the party's candidate won. This, wrote Callaway, was not progress, but ignorance. But nobody seemed to pay attention.

He returned to his law practice in Lakeland. Life went on. America got into another war—yet another mistake by Roosevelt, as far as Callaway was concerned. In 1942, his son William, age thirty, was drafted into the National Guard. Before he could be called to serve abroad, William followed his father's example and got married. Ten months later William's first child was born and named Cal Elvy Callaway. A year and a half later, William's second child was born. Six months later, in August 1945, the war ended.

That October, Elvy Callaway paid a visit to one Dr. Brown Landone in Winter Park, a central Florida town not far from Lakeland. The ninety-eight-year-old Landone had once been a medical doctor in New York City. Now, in his Florida retirement, he had taken up metaphysics. With the help of a large secretarial staff, he produced prodigious quantities of inspirational literature. Among the titles: *The Methods of Truth Which I Use, Transforming Your Life in 24 Hours, Spiritual Revelations of the Bible,* and, in 1940, *Prophecies of Melchizedek in the Great Pyramid and the Seven Temples.* Landone's followers felt that he had a special talent for bringing scientific rigor to mystical problems. Callaway describes his meeting with Landone as a "calling."

It is unclear whether Callaway's calling happened before or after he got a divorce. But also in October 1945—after more than thirty years of marriage—Elvy and Annie Levie split up. At such a delicate point in his life, Landone's call to Callaway to "close his law offices and his home in Lakeland," must have seemed particularly expedient.

Landone ordered him to move to a different part of Florida, somewhere farther north, where he would receive the mystical knowledge necessary to perform an unspecified sacred mission, sponsored by the Order of the Melchizedek.

According to Landone, Melchizedek, whoever he was, gave his name to a mysterious order of priests that might or might not exist, and might or might not operate by means of the "Teleois Key," a numerological system relying on the numbers 1, 4, and 7 to transmit wisdom throughout the ages. Callaway claimed to have no idea what Landone was talking about, but he was willing to make the leap. "It appeared that there was nothing for me to do but to give [the wisdom of Melchizedek] to humanity."

So that's what he did, leaving Annie in Lakeland along with their son William, back from the army; William's wife, Betty; and two young grandsons, Lance Arthur and Cal Elvy. Perhaps Landone's neat formulations of life and truth appealed to Callaway's developing sense of reason and his idiosyncratic sense of religion. Perhaps his wife, Annie, had been the "reason" to his "religion," and without her he came unmoored. In any case, for the first time in almost forty years he was without the influence of women in his life, and for the first time in almost forty years he began to lean again toward religion—albeit a faith of his own making.

By 1946 Callaway had purchased a patch of farmland in the township of Bristol, 300 miles north of Lakeland along the Apalachicola River. At first, the time did not seem ripe for the wisdom of Melchizedek. Bristol was both the county seat of Liberty County, and the county's only town. Two-thirds of Liberty County was considered wilderness, habitable only by gators, wild turkeys, and the occasional rattlesnake. In the other third, there were only 3,000 people—about four per square mile. Florida's swamp dwellers were just as isolated from the predominant American culture as Iraq's Marsh Arabs were from, say, the residents of Baghdad. And much to the chagrin of anti-prohibition Callaway, Liberty County, despite its name, was a "dry county," where no alcohol was sold. Callaway's theoretical Eden of progress seemed just as far away as Warren's Eden at the North Pole. But that was exactly the kind of challenge Elvy Edison Callaway was prepared for.

And, sure enough, in 1952, surveying his Panhandle land with a tax assessor, Callaway found the inspiration for his mission for Melchizedek: the Torreya yew tree. *Torreya taxifolia* goes by many names—including Florida yew, "stinking yew," and "stinking cedar"—although it's not at all a cedar. Yew trees in general can be found all over the world, and many pre-Christian cultures ascribed mystical powers to the evergreen, which could live as long as 2,000 years. But Callaway was probably the first to equate the yew with "gopher wood," which is, according to the Bible, the species of tree that Noah used to build his Ark.

The King James Bible leaves the Hebrew word "gofer" untranslated. (Though it's often spelled with a "ph," it's safe to say that "gophers" have nothing to do with Noah's Ark, except, of course, as passengers.) Since it appears only once in the Bible, and nowhere else in Hebrew literature, the word "gofer," like "Melchizedek,"— or "Eden," for that matter—has been an object of an enormous range of speculation. Some say it's based on the Babylonian word for cedar beams, or on the Assyrian word "gapiru," which means "reed." The previous generation of European Orientalists including Delitzsch, Sayce, and Willcocks, would have assumed that their

Mesopotamian Noah's boat was made out of Mesopotamian materials that were still prevalent: tightly woven bundles of marsh
reeds covered with that recurring magical substance, bitumen. But
there's also a Methodist theologian who insists the word "gofer"
is related to the Greek word for "cypress," and Callaway's theory,
though undeniably idiosyncratic, had perhaps as much to recom-
mend it as any in the tail-chasing confusion of Biblical translation.

Torreya taxifolia is an authentically primeval tree, an evergreen that
survived the previous ice age in what's called a "pocket reserve"
along the Apalachicola River. That is to say: just as a survivor of
Noah's Flood should be, Torreya is a holdover from a now vanished world that existed before a huge geologic event. Its needled
branches look like truncated palm leaves, and its tiny dark-purple
fruit is reminiscent of its Middle Eastern cousin, the date, except
that when you crush this fruit it emits an unpleasantly pungent
odor, which gave the tree its "stinking" nickname.

If Callaway had wanted, he could have nominated Torreya for the
Tree of the Knowledge of Good and Evil—its leaves are tempting,
but its fruit is poisonous—or even for the Tree of Life: it's recently
been discovered that the Torreya contains the cancer-fighting
compound taxol, which helps prolong the life of chemotherapy
patients. And, like anything valuable, *Torreya taxifolia* is also rare.
Once, Torreyas as tall as sixty feet could be found all over south
Georgia and north Florida. But their wood was especially dense
and good for shingling, furniture, and fuel, and by the nineteenth
century the tree was already so endangered that a famous naturalist called his visit to its habitat a "pious pilgrimage." By the
1950s, after a mysterious outbreak of fungus, there were only a
few hundred individual trees left, on the banks and bluffs of Torreya State Park, and most of these were in immature stands only
about two feet tall.

Callaway saw that there was something special about this tree,
and he looked to both religion and science to figure out what it
was. He asked a biologist with the state forestry service, one Dr.
Nieland, to affirm in print the Torreya yew's biological uniqueness.

This was done. Then he consulted a local geologist who told him that the Appalachian mountain region—of which the Apalachicola is the southernmost remnant—was one of the oldest landmasses in the world.

And then Callaway set about feeding all the information he had about the Torreya yew into Dr. Landone's mysterious "Teleois Key." And it was the Teleois Key, wrote Callaway, which allowed him to "conclusively prove" one of the "definite facts" of the Bible: that the Torreya yew was the gopher tree mentioned there. How did he know? "From the Teleois Propertionals of the design of its leaves, the grain of its wood, its strength and weight." That's when Callaway, like the Reverend Landon West before him, concluded that the Ark must have been built in America and floated by Noah down the Mississippi and across the Atlantic to Mount Ararat in Armenia during the Flood. (Callaway calculated a different rate of speed and a different arrival date than did Reverend Landon West, but he still had no doubt that Mount Ararat was the destination, not the starting point, of Noah's journey.) Callaway would have protested against accusations of hocus-pocus. He was *not* a mystic but a practitioner of "teleology," which he defined as "the science of arriving at the truth of any one thing by its complete harmonious relation of other things." Teleology was his most reliable source.

Landone's dubious mystical philosophies had given Callaway the "out" he needed from traditional Southern Christianity. They let him believe he was practicing reason and that he was therefore a force for progress, not ignorance. But teleology also freed his religious imagination, shaking up a deep-seated need that had gone unmet since he'd left the Baptist church half a century before. As with William Sadler, his early religious disillusionment had led to new, unique religious seeking. Teleology, whatever it was, was *not* the hard-line dogmas of his childhood. With the zeal of a convert, Callaway began applying his mystical methods to religious concepts that he felt were stale and outmoded. God Himself—like American economics, politics, and race relations—needed serious revision in order to keep up with the future.

Many people, Callaway realized, had an idea of God that resembled a child's idea of Santa Claus, "a white-haired, long-whiskered old gentleman coming around at Christmas time distributing presents." (As Callaway himself had aged, his vision of God had too: from "father" at the square dance to well-meaning grandpa.) It was no wonder there were so many atheists and communists in the world, if Christianity relied on such a ridiculous idea. Callaway thought about an alternative. If, as he believed, "God is Spirit and Spirit is Law," then God is Law. Or actually, God is four laws: the law of energy, law of life, law of intelligence, and law of love. Who could object to these four qualities? Callaway's vaguely inclusive theology could bring all those intelligent atheists into the Christian camp—and maybe even some of those mysterious Russian communists.

Encouraged, Callaway applied his four disembodied laws to the question that preoccupied him: human origins. He acknowledged that in the 1925 Scopes trial, "evolution won the battle," and he accepted the idea of evolution as progress. But still, like so many others, Callaway felt a need to assimilate the Book of Genesis into his "scientific" thinking. Traditional Biblical literalism of the kind that William Jennings Bryan tried to defend could not stand up against the new truths of science. But maybe Callaway's new mystical-logical teleology could bring the two closer together. He began to revisit the Biblical details that had helped bring down Bryan. How long were those six days of creation? Bryan had admitted that they might not be regular twenty-four-hour days, and on this matter, Callaway agreed with Bryan. The Bible doesn't specify twenty-four hours. A Biblical day was, according to Callaway, much more likely to have lasted "thousands of years."

Callaway read the newspapers. He knew that humanlike fossils were being discovered by evolutionists the world over. How to account for them? God created man twice. The first creation took place, according to Callaway, late on the sixth "day," long before the Garden of Eden existed. God created early man in the Appalachian area of the United States "because all informed geologists admit that

it is the oldest land mass on earth." He created these early people
without souls. A "soul," by the way, as Callaway defined it, meant
the power of choice. These first, soulless people also provided Callaway with an answer to another of Darrow's trick questions from
the Scopes trial: where did Cain, Adam and Eve's evil son, find a
wife—as the Bible says he did—if there were no other humans
yet? Well, that's simple: after the family left Eden, Cain migrated
north from Florida to the Atlantic Appalachians, otherwise known
as the land of Nod, and married a woman who didn't have the
power to say no. (Conveniently Cain, his unfortunate wife, and all
of this first robotic creation would be destroyed in Noah's flood.)

Also on the sixth day of creation, the new Appalachians were
covered with fruit trees—of which Callaway was particularly fond.
In 1934 he had advocated the Florida grapefruit as "the best tonic
I know," and in 1938 he'd defended those poor citrus-tree growers
against libel by the Democratic machine.

And on the seventh day, or "long period of time," God rested.
But "rested," notes Callaway, does not mean, "stopped." No, during that time, "the Appalachian Mountains eroded down and the
plains and the valleys were formed." Once rested, God began his
second round of creation.

This time, God made only three things. First, he created Adam,
a much-improved human with a soul. Adam was created about
a mile outside Bristol, Florida. Then God created the Garden of
Eden, along the Apalachicola River, near Bristol. This time, along
with the fruit trees, God created other tree species "pleasant to the
sight," like the majestic gopher wood, with its dark green needles
and bright red berries, and also magnolias, anise, mountain laurel,
and hydrangea.

And all was good, except that Adam was lonely among the magnolia trees. Callaway sympathized: "The Lord God said, 'It is not
good that the man should be alone. (Every bachelor I have known
was lonely) I will make him a help mate.'" The final element of
the second creation was, of course, Eve—or, as Callaway calls her,
Mother Eve. A lonely bachelor himself at the time, Callaway was

particularly focused on this vision of feminine hope and promise: "She was the last and best thing He created." Eve was created from Adam's rib—not because she was inferior to him, but so that "she might be his exact equal in the right of liberty."

Callaway was against a lot of things: Prohibition, welfare, labor and farm regulation, Roosevelt, the abandonment of the gold standard, World War I, World War II, and communism. But if there was one thing he had always advocated, ever since his square-dancing days, it was women's liberation. He was pro–women's suffrage, pro–women's education, pro–birth control, and against women being pressured into shotgun weddings by an ignorant church. So now, here in Liberty County, Florida, he could hardly stand by the traditional scapegoating of Eve as the original sinner, tempter of men, and bringer of curses.

Still, Callaway found the elements of temptation and the snake too essential not to include in the story. Like the idea of God, and the soul, "original sin" needed a radical revision. As Callaway saw it, God gave Eve two options, and the power to choose between them. She could continue as an immortal, but she would be living "as a beast or a totally insane person," that is, without the ability to progress. Or she could eat the fruit of the Tree of the Knowledge of Good and Evil, which allowed her the possibility of improving human life through knowledge and progress—in return for giving up immortality. God, says Callaway, *wanted* Eve to eat from the Tree of Knowledge. The serpent, which was most certainly "not a serpent, but a Communist or a welfare-statist," wanted to keep Eve, as it were, barefoot and pregnant, forever. Instead, Eve ate the fruit of empowerment, and Callaway for one "blesses her forever for her great decision." Callaway's women's liberation was really women's libertarianism: women had every right to help themselves, but God forbid they be "tempted" by social welfare programs.

Callaway's Eden, like the Urantian Eden, had no original sin. "I have often heard it preached that we are all born in sin—natural crooks. It is a slander of God to teach any such doctrine." Had Elvy

Callaway sat down with Reverend Landon West, chaos no doubt would have ensued. They both belonged to the Baptist church in some form, and they both located the Garden of Eden in their respective American backyards. But to West, an Eden without sin simply didn't make sense. West did his preaching at the turn of the century, in a hardscrabble, ascetic environment of poverty and struggle on the edge of the jagged, ancient Appalachian mountains. Progress was coming, but it was a frightening prospect, rather than a promise to be embraced. West did eventually relinquish his youthful zealous view that everybody who so much as touched a modern convenience was going to hell. But sin hadn't gone away. There was still time for it all to fall apart. There was still need to repent.

Fifty years later and 800 miles to the south, Elvy Callaway didn't see all that much to atone for. His new home, the Apalachicola region, was appropriately named: it marked the intersection of two natural regions: Appalachia and Pensacola. Here, the northern pines gave way to southern palms, and West's northern Puritan streak gave way to a more easygoing southern disposition. Callaway had of course lived through two world wars and the Depression, and he saw the cold war on the horizon. But he'd lived through all of it on his terms, in Florida, and for him progress and industry were still the only answer. Drunkenness, adultery, speaking the Lord's name in vain—all these offenses were forgivable, as far as Callaway was concerned. That was small stuff. There was only one unpardonable sin: not to avail oneself of the opportunities provided by Mother Eve's great decision. Mother Eve would be very disappointed in you. "If you think you can fritter away your time and talents, whatever they are in this life, and then be right with God in the afterlife, you will be woefully disappointed." To summarize: Mother Eve, Adam's equal in the power of choice, was tempted by the demon of communism, but chose instead the American way of progress.

Since there was no sin, there was no exile. In his first act of decision making, Adam simply chose to leave Eden one day, and

Eve decided to follow him. ("She has been following him ever since.") And what about the angels with the flaming swords? If the Tree of Knowledge of Good and Evil represented progress, the Tree of Life represented the other necessary pillar of Callaway's civilization: liberty, which had to be protected at all costs. So Eden's guardians were there not to keep people out of Eden, but simply to protect the Tree of Life, Liberty, and the Pursuit of Happiness from any who would harm or misuse it. Callaway's angels, then, look more like the founding fathers—maybe Paul Revere on a rearing horse, or Patrick Henry with his fighting words. Thus the fearsome cherubim received their most bizarre makeover since William Willcocks declared them to be puffs of bituminous smoke. Such patriotic protectors would, presumably, keep only communists, welfare-statists, or Democrats out of Eden. Everyone else was welcome to come visit.

Callaway opened Garden of Eden Park in 1956, on his land along a bend in the Apalachicola, within the very small geographical range of the endangered *Torreya taxifolia*. He set up a ticket kiosk along Highway 12, a two-lane road running east-west across the Panhandle. There, visitors could pay the $1.10 admission fee and head down a 3.75-mile hiking trail called Garden of Eden Road. The dirt road snaked through flat plains covered by wire grass and longleaf pine, and populated by deer, rabbits, and gopher tortoises. Down at the banks of the spring-fed Kelly Creek, you might find salamanders and crayfish. Past the sand hills and on toward a cliff 135 feet above the Apalachicola, plant and animal species unchanged since before the last ice age still grew undisturbed. A vast population of migrating birds—including that guardian of Liberty, the bald eagle—called the Apalachicola home. To supplement these natural wonders, Callaway had gone into the woods and dug up three petrified logs of gopher wood, which he claimed were cast-offs from the building of the Ark. He had taken three friends with him to the woods to confirm his discovery. These logs were on display in the kiosk on Highway 12. Other exhibits related to the

Torreya yew were in the works: a believer all the way from Illinois was apparently engaged in building a gopher-wood replica of the Ark nearby.

But despite all these attractions, Callaway's Garden of Eden took a while to catch on. It was harder to lure visitors to a patch of flat swampland than it had been for E. O. Randall to rustle up attention for Serpent Mound. In February 1956, a visiting columnist for the *Chicago Daily Tribune* found only one pair of customers—a Mr. and Mrs. F. R. Wentworth of Valdosta, Georgia, a two-hour drive away. These intrepid tourists were thwarted by a recent rainstorm, which had washed out the sandy parts of the Garden of Eden Road and made it difficult to progress toward the scenic view. Wentworth received a refund, and claimed he would return in better weather. (Callaway went out of his way to point out that he had "no financial or material interest at all" in the land of Eden. Admission fees would be used only for explicitly religious and educational purposes, and the park would remain a "non-profit shrine" in perpetuity.) The *Tribune's* columnist reported, generously, that the Garden of Eden would have been "an excellent place for an aging serpent to raise a family."

Still determined, Callaway came up with a brilliant publicity stunt. In 1964, after Lyndon Johnson overwhelmingly won the presidential election, and passed a mandate to revive the New Deal Callaway so despised, Callaway publicly offered the defeated Republican Barry Goldwater a retirement home in the Garden of Eden. This was not because he wanted Goldwater to retire—quite the contrary—but because Callaway wanted to give a consolation prize, in memory of his own defeat at the hands of the "welfare-statists" in 1936. Retirement homes were all the rage in Florida, and having a celebrity like Goldwater around Apalachicola would also, of course, be good for business, profitable or otherwise. Goldwater did not take Callaway up on his offer. Nonetheless, the Garden of Eden Park seemed to be making some headway. In her 1967 book about the Panhandle, *The Other Florida,* Gloria Jahoda noted that

Callaway's claim had taken hold among "a surprising number of north Floridians."

In 1971, Callaway founded a nonprofit organization, In the Beginning (ITB) Associates, to publish his book also titled *In the Beginning.* Following in the long tradition of Eden seekers beginning with William Warren, Callaway gathered testimonials from anyone he could find, including a couple of scientists, though their endorsements, like that of Sayce for Warren, were highly provisional. Several local ministers wrote that they hoped having the Garden so close by would provide a relief from the "spiritual confusion" afflicting the world around them. The nearest major Florida paper, the *Tallahassee Democrat,* saw things more practically. It diplomatically refused to weigh in on the Biblical legitimacy of Callaway's claim, but a 1972 editorial allowed that Callaway's park would be "a tourist boon to the state's least populous county." Salvation was already at hand. Come to Florida, where it's warm all the time! See the U. S. A. in your Chevrolet, no penance to be paid!

The county certainly needed a boon from something. In the early 1970s, Liberty County did not have much stake in the bustling Florida tourist industry, or in any other industry, for that matter. So when government-allied businessmen came up with a proposal to dredge parts of the Apalachicola River to make it passable by larger ships and, therefore, open to commercial transportation, people were listening. Ecologists however, who were just beginning to have a public voice, argued that dredging the river would not be progress, but a step backward. Without taking a public stand on the issue, Elvy Callaway could use even this as an opportunity for publicity.

When the *New York Times* came down South to cover the dredging controversy, it used Callaway's proclaimed Eden as an engaging lead: *Here's this local character who thinks North Florida is the Garden of Eden, and maybe he's right, because the place is that beautiful.*

For Callaway, though, anything that brought people to his corner of paradise was all to the good. Couples from Georgia, shrimp boaters from the Midwest, even reporters from New York—all were welcome in the Garden of Eden. Callaway was especially proud of the funds donated to ITB Associates by the "famous inventor and philanthropist" Everett P. Larsh. The book contained a public service announcement from one of Larsh's other investments, the East Ridge Lutheran Retirement Center, which still exists in Miami.

Though Callaway praised Mother Eve's great decision to forfeit her God-given immortality in favor of progress, one of the most visible fruits of that progress was the ever-longer human life span, and the growing Florida retirement industry fit right in with Callaway's hopes for Eden. Eat of the Tree of Life—that is to say, American libertarianism—and if we can't exactly guarantee you eternal life, at least your last days will be filled with fresh fruit and sunshine. Come to Eden, and with the help of good old-fashioned ingenuity, you can put off death. You may not be "like God," yet, but it's progress.

10

Back to the Land

IN THE BEGINNING, God created both man and nature, and He thought they would stay together forever. But man grew dissatisfied in Paradise. Man wanted progress, and on the seventh day, while God rested, man took over. Man banished himself from the Garden, and has been trying to get farther away ever since. Or *most* men have, but not Thor Heyerdahl.

In 1936, at age twenty-two, the Norwegian explorer, with his new wife, Liv, decided to go back to Eden. As legend had it, when Thor first met Liv, he announced his intention to go "back to the land" and asked her what she thought—as a pick-up line, and as a test. Said Liv, "Well, it would have to be *all the way* back." Thor married Liv right away, and they immediately began scouting around for the most perfect, the most unspoiled, the most abundant natural landscape they could find, so they could reverse the footsteps of Adam and Eve. They sailed out of Larvik, Norway, clothed in evening wear. Two months later they dropped their luggage on the beach of Fatu Hiva—a tiny island three weeks from Tahiti by ship, in the Marquesas thousands of miles west of South America—wearing not a stitch.

They had reversed the Fall of Man; they had risen from the depths of corrupted, materialistic civilization to the spare spiritual heights of what they unabashedly referred to as "primitive" life. And for a while, it worked. Island natives helped them build a hut out of bamboo and banana leaves. They ate red bananas and fresh fish. Thor stopped shaving. Every day, they swam naked in streams overhung with hibiscus. They wanted for nothing—except modern medicine. Soon, both Thor and Liv contracted serious cases of elephantiasis, their legs swelling enormously. They had to brave fifteen-foot waves in a canoe to seek treatment on Tahiti. That was the end of the new beginning. Said Thor to Liv, disappointed: "There is nothing for modern man to return to. . . . Paradise has no geographical location."

The Garden of Eden is, again, part paradise, but only part. Eden also has to be the place of origins, the starting point, the zero hour, home. And in that sense Heyerdahl never gave up his search for a geographical Eden. He turned all the idealism and energy he'd invested in the search for the perfect place toward the search for the first place. In fact, paradise and home were intertwined. Back on Fatu Hiva, an elderly South Pacific islander had told them how his people came to be: a god named Tiki had sailed to the island from the east, on a raft made of balsa wood. This origin story seemed to satisfy the older man, but for Heyerdahl it provoked a question: the island people had come from Tiki, but where had Tiki come from? Heyerdahl instantly connected this tale with a piece of Peruvian folklore about a king, called Kon-Tiki, who had left Peru on a raft for parts unknown. Could it be that the Peruvian story of exile and the Polynesian story of origins were the same story? Did the king Kon-Tiki leave Peru as a refugee and arrive in Polynesia as a god? Could it be that South Americans had populated Polynesia?

No one else thought so—those cultures had had no contact with each other; they were too far apart, and the balsa rafts were not strong enough for the rough Pacific seas. But Heyerdahl was not deterred by scholarly opinion. He and Liv, now pregnant, settled into a small cabin in rural Norway, not unlike the one where he had grown up, the only child of a Christian father and an atheist mother who ran the local natural history museum. Heyerdahl spent every waking moment working on his theory. He was convinced that ancient South Americans could have populated Polynesia, but since he had no scientific degree—only a few years of zoology at the University of Oslo—nobody was listening. Heyerdahl was determined: if he couldn't convince the establishment, he would simply appeal directly to the public.

In 1947, Heyerdahl recruited five fellow Scandinavians, several of whom he had met during his short tour of duty in World War II. He did consider bringing Liv aboard—how, after all, could South Americans have populated Polynesia without women? But he decided that the spectacle of one woman on a raft with five men might attract unwanted publicity. So he took his all-male crew to South America, where they built a raft under the tutelage of the Aymara Indians: they lashed together nine forty-five-foot-long balsa tree trunks with hemp rope, and fortified them with bamboo and pine, using only what would have been available locally in prehistoric times. The only metal onboard was survival gear donated by the U.S. Army. Heyerdahl reasoned that this army gear would not affect whether or not the raft could survive the experiment; it would affect only the survival of the raft's occupants.

They didn't need the gear. One hundred and one days and 4,300 miles later, Heyerdahl and his crew gently ran aground on a tiny Polynesian island. Word reached the world by radio, and immediately this tall Norwegian with ragged blond curls and a long, regal-looking nose became a folk hero, a pioneer, an example of postwar pluck, a harbinger of the antiestablishment movements of the 1960s and 1970s. His book about the journey, *Kon-Tiki,* was translated into sixty-seven languages and eventually sold 20 million copies. The documentary film he made from footage shot on the voyage won an Academy Award in 1951. Heyerdahl has even been given the dubious honor of starting the 1950s craze for all things Polynesian, including tiki torches, Hawaiian vacations, and surfing.

Meanwhile he and Liv—Eve to his Adam—had essentially lived separate lives since he had set out for military training in Canada in 1939. (They were together long enough to conceive a second son, born in 1940.) Liv and the two boys had lived out the war years in the home of a friend in New York. From Liv's perspective: she got sick of Thor's absentee fatherhood, and the fact that he seemed more concerned with gigantic publicity stunts like the *Kon-Tiki* than with their family. From Thor's perspective: Liv's time in America had insulated her against the wartime horrors; she was growing more conservative, and had become a devout atheist, something Thor the seeker could not abide. Life after Eden had changed both of them, and Adam and Eve divorced calmly. Liv even wanted to be introduced to any girl Thor was likely to marry, so that she who knew him so well could judge the girl's appropriateness for him. Liv got this chance not long afterward; she approved of young Yvonne, who became the second Eve.

Over the next thirty years, Heyerdahl made several more voyages on primitive watercraft, always looking backward for the first of everything: the first settlers on the Polynesian islands, the first South Americans to make it west across the Pacific, the first settlers on Easter Island, the first Africans to cross the Atlantic, the first Egyptians to sail toward Asia. So it was only natural that eventually Heyerdahl's quest would take him to Mesopotamia. This was his chance to finally go "all the way back" to man's original home.

Iraq had been through a lot since the tenuous peace under King Faisal and the League of Nations had collapsed in 1941. In 1946, despite World War II, the second British occupation, and the second breaking of Qurna's Tree of Knowledge, cautious optimism prevailed in the home of civilization. This time, the West was determined, the repair of Iraq would be permanent. On New Year's Eve, 1946, exactly twenty-six years after the Inland Water Transport sappers first broke Qurna's Tree of Knowledge, the *London Times* published its final letter on the subject, from Norman C. Wright.

Wright, who would go on to become a knight, and the first deputy director general of the Food and Agriculture Office (FAO) of the new United Nations, had at the time of his letter just returned from Iraq. He had been there on special assignment with the Scientific Advisory Mission to the Middle East, had seen the

Tree in Qurna for himself, and he was above all petty speculation about its age, state of health, and Biblical provenance.

"The antiquity of the tree itself has been clearly disproved, and the authenticity of the site as the original Garden of Eden is (to err on the side of understatement) open to serious question." Wright knew the Tree was "not real." But he didn't care. He *did* care that the Tree was ugly and abandoned, its appearance "far from romantic . . . reminiscent of a series of ill-kept cabbage patches."

Wright had sent a photograph, which the *Times* reprinted on page 6. There was the same dead tree trunk, now fallen out of its pedestal, whose concrete reinforcement had long since crumbled. On top of the pedestal, someone had placed a hand-painted sign that read "The Original Garden of Eden," and in Arabic, *Janat 'Adan.* "It would be unfortunate," wrote Wright, if "some attempt were not made to preserve for posterity this traditional abode of our earliest ancestors."

Wright had a plan. "To replace a single tree (reported by your correspondent to be the intention of the local administration) hardly appears consistent with the lavish resources of our modern civilization." No indeed. Wright felt it was in man's power to "re-establish" the complete garden—a veritable Garden of Eden—with multiple trees, flowers, and fruit. Surely this ambition "would be more in keeping with the times . . . a visible sign that we had truly used the fruits of the Tree of Knowledge to improve and increase the fruits of the earth."

Ten years after Wright's letter to the *London Times,* it looked as though his dream of a peaceful, abundant Iraq had been achieved, thanks once again to Britain, chaperoning its fledgling government into a western-style industrial future. On the occasion of a state visit by King Faisal II to Spain in 1956, Iraq's directorate of propaganda had a limited-edition glossy pamphlet, *The Land of Two Rivers,* printed (in England). Among the other tokens of progress depicted—tweed-clad Iraqi scientists looking through tiny binoculars, giant concrete irrigation works, women in white cotton uniforms working at sewing machines—is a photograph of the

Tree of Knowledge. No longer a dismissed shrine on the outskirts of town, this Tree—very likely the same one the "local authorities" planted in the 1940s—is flourishing, a bouquet of tiny green leaves overgrowing the space allotted to it, and butting up against a mud-brick building next door. The new tree and the old mud pedestal, and various other local plants, are enclosed within a fence made of painstakingly woven bundles of reeds, which extends all the way around the trees, except for a small arched doorway just tall enough for a person to walk through and pray at the Tree. Outside the fence, a tall man in a polo shirt and gray slacks and a woman with a neatly cut hairdo, in a sleeveless sundress and sandals—tourists—stand looking in at the Tree from a safe and respectful distance.

But two years later, Faisal's government collapsed in the bloody revolution of 1958. After three more violent transfers of power, the government of Iraq finally landed in the hands of the Ba'ath Party, officially the Arab Socialist Ba'ath Party. This party was originally founded in Syria in the 1940s to encourage Arab nations to stick together in the face of increasing American and European encroachment. Its secularism gave it flexibility in the religiously diverse population of Iraq; its nominal socialism allowed Iraq to seek alliance with the Soviet Union. The young Ba'ath Party set about refurbishing, publicizing, and profitizing anything that could bring Iraq revenue—including the Tree of Knowledge.

Norman Wright's delicate reed park seemed too old-fashioned for a new era of national renewal. So, instead, officials built a ninety-by-thirty-foot concrete plaza the size of a basketball court around the Tree. A branch from the venerated 1920 Tree was rumored to be on display in the National Museum in Baghdad, still going strong fifty years after Gertrude Bell's death. The new Tree, planted in 1946, had gone the way of its predecessor; it was dead but still standing. People tended to call it Adam's Tree.

The park, despite its unfortunate concrete aesthetic, was a peaceful place. There was a fountain with a wishing well. Someone erected a bilingual sign, which helpfully if elliptically explained the site's religious context: *On this holy spot where Tigris meet Euphrates this holy tree of our father Adam grew symbolizing the Garden of Eden on earth. Abraham prayed here two thousand years B.C.* Iraqis still visited the Tree to meditate, tie green fabric around the branches, and light candles. And just a few hundred feet away from Adam's Tree and the surrounding park, on that little spit of land between the two great rivers, someone saw fit to bulldoze the old mud-brick customhouse to the ground and build a hotel: the Garden of Eden Rest House.

Qurna's ambitions for tourism were small: the Garden of Eden Rest House had only three guest rooms. Still, its giant dining room and terrace attracted locals—the mayor of Qurna, schoolteachers, elderly men—who spent weekends and holidays relaxing there, drinking an Iraqi beer or a cup of tea while looking out at the view. But even these modest aspirations collapsed sometime in the mid-1970s, as infighting in the Ba'ath Party grew deadly. What had begun as an intellectual movement had become highly militarized. "Arab unity" became a euphemism for oppressing non-Arab minorities, and "secular socialism" began to acquire the destructive dogma of dictatorial religion. The new Iraqi regime closed the country to tourists. But it left the door open a crack for science and industry, and that's how Thor Heyerdahl got into Iraq in 1977. Truth be told, Heyerdahl's Iraqi experiment, like his earlier voyages, lay somewhere between tourism and science. He planned to build a ship exactly like what the ancient Sumerians would have built, and use it to find out where human civilization really began.

Like his English predecessor Sir William Willcocks, Heyerdahl bypassed scholarship when it didn't suit his purposes. Willcocks had scoffed at anyone who did not study a subject "on the spot." Heyerdahl liked to use the word "armchair" before a scholar's academic title, as if to emphasize their inevitable narrow-mindedness: armchair biologist, armchair archaeologist, armchair anthropologist. He even saw "a touch of religious fanaticism" in these scholars' insistence on their positions. The two boatmen also shared personality traits: Willcocks's blunt practicality would have matched Heyerdahl's stubbornness. But their politics could not have been further apart. Whereas Willcocks earnestly believed in the civilizing power of European colonialism, engineering, and development, Heyerdahl virtually renounced his citizenship in modern Europe, believing that the profit motive and the greed of empire had sent humanity down a dangerous path. If paradise consisted of complete harmony between man and nature, then building dams along the Tigris would take us *farther* from Eden, not closer to it. Eden lay not in the future, but in the past. After World War II, Heyerdahl had seen what happened when man tried to surge forward, betting on ever newer and ever more powerful technology. That line of thinking would lead straight to nuclear war. Instead, Heyerdahl and others wished they could turn back the clock to a time before man had eaten from the Tree of Knowledge.

In order to reach Eden, Heyerdahl believed, you had to travel backward, back through the testimony of primitive cultures—which were not really primitive at all. Like William F. Warren, Heyerdahl subscribed to the old religious idea that we humans have fallen from a great height, and have lost—rather than gained—knowledge from our past. So he began to investigate the Sumerians, who gave Mesopotamia its reputation as the "cradle of civilization." But he soon realized that in the Sumerians' own origin myths, Mesopotamia was not the first stop on the journey. Their ancestors had arrived by sea, from a land they called Dilmun. This surprised Heyerdahl. Of course, people couldn't come from nowhere. But he had been holding out hope for an actual beginning of everything, and Sumerian sailors arriving by sea in Mesopotamia just didn't fit the bill. As Heyerdahl wrote, "This is no real beginning. This is the continuation of something lost somewhere in the mist." The location of Dilmun—indeed, whether or not it was a real location—had long mystified Assyriologists and archaeologists. Some scholars equated Dilmun with the Garden of Eden, and placed it on an island in the Persian Gulf, or in Saudi Arabia, or somewhere near Pakistan.

In 1974, while Heyerdahl was in the midst of planning his Sumerian voyage, a large cloud surrounding human beginnings was swept away all at once. Paleontologists digging in Ethiopia's Awash valley uncovered the small female *Australopithecus* skeleton they called "Lucy," then the oldest hominid primate known to have walked upright—3.2 million years ago. Her brain was much smaller than that of her descendants *Homo sapiens,* but she represented a major step in the evolution of humanity. Lucy opened the gap between the origin of hominids with some human characteristics, millions of years ago, and the beginning of western material culture generally credited to the Sumerians, thousands of years ago. This was exactly the gap between "origin of man" and "origin of civilization" that William Warren refused to believe in. Lucy became the original first woman, a newly minted ancient celebrity, and she had every right to steal some of Eve's thunder.

Remarkably, this huge advance in the science of human origins made only a small splash in the search for the Garden of Eden. Africa had long been known to contain some of the oldest human settlements. And yet—aside from the tentative advances of the anthropologist Henry Seton-Karr in 1897, advances that were publicly ridiculed by Harvard professors—almost everyone seeking Eden had left Africa alone. Why this disconnect? If hominids were the first men—or rather, people—and they appeared in Africa before they appeared in Europe, then wasn't Africa the first place? But the vast Judeo-Christian mythology of Eden just couldn't change that fast. Lucy was too new. Unlike Eve, this first woman came with no baggage, no sin. Culturally speaking, Lucy was created ex nihilo, with no myths of origin except one: she was named after the Beatles' song "Lucy in the Sky with Diamonds," which was—so the story goes—played at an impromptu celebration under the stars in the Ethiopian desert on the night of her discovery.

There's no denying the impact of racism here. Before Darwin, "Adam" and "Eve" were still stand-ins for the first people on Earth, and Adam and Eve simply had to be white. Well into the twentieth century, after Darwinian evolution became commonly accepted scientific knowledge, there were plenty of educated thinkers who had trouble separating the science of evolution from the theology of Genesis. Adam and Eve were so strongly identified with American and European culture that Delitzsch couldn't even let them be Babylonians—a dark-haired, more Semitic-looking tribe. Landon West had to invent an entire fictional Native American population so that his Edenites would not be "red."

Even Heyerdahl, an enlightened advocate of developing countries, did not immediately switch his itinerary to Ethiopia upon the discovery of Lucy—he too was more interested in the myth of origins than the fact of origins. He knew he couldn't fill in 2 million years of history, to find the "real beginning," so he would try—as he had tried with the Tiki legends—to connect the mythology and history of various ancient cultures to one another.

Beginning at Qurna, he would follow the travels of the Sumerians backward as far as he could, using the scant archaeological record. He'd sail south through the Persian Gulf, around the axe-head-shaped Arabian Peninsula and across the Arabian Sea to Pakistan, where a little-known ancient culture called only the "Indus Valley Civilization" had sprung up around the same time as the Sumerians had, in 3,000 B.C. Then he'd sail west, across the Indian Ocean, past the Horn of Africa and up the Gulf of Aden between Ethiopia and Yemen, to the Red Sea, which would take him all the way to Egypt, the third of the three major ancient civilizations. He would see whether the footsteps of Adam led back to the pharaohs, if not to Lucy. There were all kinds of obstacles to this plan, both scholarly and logistical.

Scholars who considered the question at all assumed that Sumerian ships, built out of reeds, would not have been able to survive such a treacherous journey. Navigating the narrow passage out of Basra and down the hazardous Persian Gulf to the open ocean took great skill. But there was an even simpler objection: reeds absorb water. What was to stop the ship from sinking, gradually, across a long ocean stretch with no shore in sight? True, the *berdi* reeds of the Mesopotamian marshes made a convenient building material for many things—fences, mats, houses—but the dense pulp inside the tall grasses acted like a sponge. The ancient canoe-like reed boats of the Marsh Arabs had always been covered with a liberal layer of—what else?—bitumen.

Heyerdahl was as skeptical about bitumen as he was about its distant modern cousins petroleum and asphalt. He'd seen images of Sumerian ships etched into clay tablets, and these ships showed reed ribs, not the smooth silhouette of the bitumen-covered *mashhufs*. The Sumerian carvings showed ships shaped like a crescent moon, with symmetrically upturned bow and stern, big enough to seat at least six men with oars. In Baghdad, he consulted the scientists at the National Museum, who were supportive. And he checked in with the Ba'ath Party's ministry of information, because he had to. Such a bizarre project must have seemed harmless enough to the Party officials. But they did send a "minder" back to the marshes with Heyerdahl just in case. And with tie-clad bureaucrat in tow, the long-haired experimental anthropologist headed south to Qurna, determined to find someone who could help him design a Sumerian ship.

He'd made a couple of earlier scouting missions to the Mesopotamian marshes, where life bore a striking resemblance to the ancient descriptions left by the Sumerians on their baked-clay tablets. Back then, though, the Baghdad officials had been "a bit reluctant" to let him into the marshland, home territory of the marsh Arabs, called Madan. It wasn't because the Ba'ath thought the Madan were dangerous, Heyerdahl reported; it was just that they were "not in step" with the modern Iraq the government wanted to portray to outsiders. But it was exactly the premodern Iraq that Heyerdahl longed to explore. He persuaded the officials to let him in, and he was rewarded for his efforts. On that trip, Heyerdahl had found an elderly Madan with crucial information about boatbuilding: harvest your *berdi* reeds in August. That's when they're pliable enough to build with, but not old enough to develop the sponginess that could sink a ship. Use August *berdi,* and you don't need bitumen. This was possibly apocryphal knowledge, but Heyerdahl had made a career out of taking oral history and folklore seriously, and he wasn't about to stop now. So he came back to the marshes in 1977, in August.

This time, Baghdad's attitude toward the Madan seemed to be improving. Heyerdahl attributed the Ba'ath Party's new open-mindedness to western explorers like himself, who had emerged from their marsh journeys "full of admiration" for the natives there. This time, the party practically pushed him to enter this once iso-lated territory. Heyerdahl wrote: "I was even encouraged to use a film camera and to bring as many Madans as I needed out of the marshes to my shipbuilding site near the rest house."

Heyerdahl floated around this silent alternative universe built on reeds, entranced. Finally, it seemed, he was headed back to the land, all the way back. "With each calm punt stroke by the two silent marshmen I sensed that I was traveling back through time, not into savagery and insecurity, but into a culture as remote from barbarism as ours and yet incredibly simple and uncomplicated." And his minder from the ministry of information? According to Heyerdahl, he was "as fascinated as I was."

Heyerdahl got to work: arranging for the harvest, drying, and delivery of enough August *berdi* to build the giant, sixty-foot-long bundles that would be the raw material of the reed ship, the *Tigris*. Just south of the marshes in Qurna, the Garden of Eden Rest House, long boarded up, was reopened for Heyerdahl and anyone involved with his project. Besides his minder and a translator from Baghdad, Heyerdahl had also hired Aymara Indians from Peru to plan the boat's construction, Madan to do the construction, and a couple of dhow sailors from India to do the navigation. That's not to mention his German sail designer, American cameraman, and Russian and Norwegian crew members. The *Tigris* party more than filled the three guest bedrooms in the Garden of Eden Rest House, so they set up camp beds and mattresses in the vast din-ing hall, and began the actual boatbuilding in the space between the Rest House and Adam's Tree. Somewhere in the chaotic early construction, when the empty lot next to the Rest House over-flowed with truckloads of reeds and supplies, two of the fence posts surrounding the enclosed Trees were knocked over.

While the *Tigris* party labored, the infamous annual rains began, raising the level of the river so much that Heyerdahl was afraid the reed boat might get flooded before it was even launched. Along with the rain came stories of a cholera epidemic, and a mysterious fever sent the entire team to their beds, to rest and shake off whatever infernal bug had bred in that sea of mud. Having stayed in Qurna long enough, even the pacifist Heyerdahl got fed up and started to sound like the British military men of World War I. "If this was the Garden of Eden," he wrote later, "someone had some explaining to do."

The *Tigris* was to be launched on November 11, 1977. Word got out to all the foreign journalists in Iraq, who seemed to flood the Rest House all over again. The *Tigris* was up on blocks, ready to be pushed out into its namesake river—after the Madan anointed the ship with the blood of a goat sacrificed for the occasion. Heyerdahl tried to talk them out of it, but to no avail. This was done, and the big moment arrived. But no sooner had the moon-shaped ship left the riverbank than its back end started to drag far below the appropriate waterline. It looked as though it might sink before it ever reached the ocean. How had it become so unbalanced? Heyerdahl sent his Japanese scuba diver into the water to find out. It turns out that some of the wooden boards used to hold the ship off the ground before the launch had come unnailed from their pile and had attached themselves to the stern. So Heyerdahl had to un-launch the ship and spend two weeks repairing the stern with more reeds before the *Tigris* could be, anticlimactically, launched again.

Finally out of the Garden of Eden, the crew of what Heyerdahl affectionately referred to as "the haystack" immediately encountered other obstacles, but none that the ancient Sumerians would have had to endure. These were twentieth-century hazards: errant fishnets, unmanned freight barges, mysterious clots of orange-red fuel oil that seemed to come from nowhere. They even had to sail through the foamy discharge of a paper factory near

Basra—chemicals designed exactly to dissolve reeds into pulp, Kryptonite to the *Tigris*. The buoyant ship survived. But Heyerdahl, who had been sounding the early warning about ocean pollution ever since his *Kon-Tiki* days, was aghast at the extent of the industrial waste in the Gulf waterways. "From a paradise of a kind our golden ship had suddenly found herself in an inferno.... Sumerians would have been horrified to see the environment modern man prefers."

Along with industrial waste, the *Tigris* ran up against another by-product of twentieth-century civilization: cold war politics. For this, too, Heyerdahl was ill-equipped, but he managed to slide through. As one story goes, before World War II, when he was in the wilds of British Columbia studying Native American canoe building and someone told him that Norway had been invaded, he asked, "By whom?" Heyerdahl didn't pay much attention to national borders himself. He had spent his lifetime on the ocean: an interdependent ecosystem operating on its own laws of tides, currents, and trade winds. And he thought that land should work this way, too. He sincerely believed that nationalism and its attendant "bloc politics" were part of civilization's problem. In 1966, Heyerdahl became vice president of the Association of World Federalists, an organization founded after World War II to prevent future international warfare through world unification. But Heyerdahl's ideals sometimes blinded him to reality. As the haystack made its way south out of the port of Basra, its crew made a political gaffe. On the HAM radio they used to communicate their whereabouts, they referred to the "Persian Gulf."

This angered their Iraqi sponsors, who were not Persian, and preferred the term "Arabian Gulf." But to use the term "Arabian Gulf" would be an act of aggression toward the Persian government of Iran, whose shoreline the crew could see from the *Tigris*'s deck. Diplomats and funders had no good answers for Heyerdahl, so he insisted on calling it the "Sumerian Gulf" from then on, harking back to what he considered a more authentic history—ancient, peaceful, unified.

World unity has always been a common theme among Eden seekers. What good is a myth of origin that doesn't explain everybody? It may take elaborate family trees to prove such a myth— Warren made a hierarchy of civilizations; Tse Tsan Tai drew tables of the generations of Noah; *The Urantia Book* divided the world into color-coded factions—but eventually, somehow, Eden has to be the source of all of us.

All Heyerdahl's voyages, from the *Kon-Tiki* to the *Tigris,* sailed under the blue-and-white United Nations flag, which happens to use the same North Pole–centric projection of the world map that William Warren did in *Paradise Found*. Heyerdahl also flew a flag with the famous photograph of the Earth from space, looking like a blue-green-and-white marble against an ocean-blue background. He wanted the *Tigris* crew itself to be sort of a mini-United Nations. His eleven men, he proudly reported, spoke nine languages and had a broad range of national origins—Russian, American, British, Mexican, Italian, Japanese, Norwegian, Danish, German, and Iraqi. A few weeks into the voyage, however, they had all spent so long on the bamboo deck of their tiny reed ship in the sun-baked Middle Eastern seas that their skin was bronzed, and hair bleached, to almost identical shades of tan and blond, respectively. Decisions still had to be made by multinational consensus, but this could be done over dinner, in their swimming shorts.

Sometimes, Heyerdahl's belief in world unity was so strong that he would not let facts—or a lack thereof—stand in his way. The first major stop on the *Tigris*'s route was Bahrain, an island kingdom off the coast of the Arabian Peninsula that had long been considered for the role of "Dilmun." The Sumerian texts describe Dilmun both mythically and literally—it's the place where Ziusudra, the "Noah" of Mesopotamia, was granted eternal life by the gods after he saved humanity. It's lauded as "holy and clean" in an epic poem. But Dilmun figures also in the Sumerians' less literary documents. Here, it's a fondly remembered hometown, a good trading spot with abundant freshwater and massive stone quarries. Heyerdahl confused the literal and the figurative. Visiting an archaeologist uncovering a desert burial ground, he became reverent about the possibility of visiting Noah's grave. Delitzsch, who insisted that the Sumerians kept their literature and their science separate, would have been appalled.

A tiny island off the shores of Bahrain was supposed to have even older archaeological sites, but it was inconveniently owned by the son of the emir—and operated as a prison for government dissidents. Heyerdahl lobbied the ruling royal family for weeks for permission to visit. And here again modern politics came into play: though the crew of the *Tigris* had bonded into a renegade multinational cohort, the men's individual national origins still seemed to be important to other people.

The members of the royal family of the emirate were not on speaking terms with the Ba'ath government of Iraq, which they felt was too closely aligned with the Soviet Union. They did finally grant permission for Heyerdahl's party to visit the outer island, but only if the one Russian member of the crew would stay behind.

After exploring the island briefly, Heyerdahl was satisfied that he'd found Dilmun. And if he could make it here with his reed ship still intact, maybe the Sumerians could have come from even farther away. He was ready to move on, into the treacherous narrows of the southern Gulf.

There, the *Tigris*'s lack of modern nautical technology started to seem less appealing and more just plain silly. In order not to drift aimlessly toward dangerous shores, the *Tigris* had to procure a tow from a giant Russian freighter. (In this case, the crew members were glad they had a Russian-speaker on board.) In order to get through the Strait of Hormuz, one of the busiest and narrowest shipping channels in the world, the *Tigris*'s cameraman had to shinny up the mast and attach strips of tinfoil to the rigging of the all-natural ship in hopes that larger ships would then be able to pick up the *Tigris* on their radar. Archibald Henry Sayce, who'd given up his wooden Nile houseboat rather than share space with steamships, would have sympathized. Meanwhile, the *Tigris* looked so non-threatening that crabs and tiny fish attached themselves to its reedy bottom, and it traveled so slowly that even the drowsiest of sea crea-tures—and one mystified Iraqi mouse below decks—could keep up.

Finally the *Tigris* made it to the sultanate of Oman, on the south end of the Arabian Peninsula. Here Heyerdahl wanted to locate Makan, an important Sumerian copper-trading post even farther afield from Mesopotamia. Not surprisingly, he succeeded. A friendly scientist cautioned him that Oman might very well be Makan, but that he himself hadn't found any definitive evidence of Sumerian contact. Heyerdahl was not disturbed. "Even if no Sumerian vase is ever found in the barren landscape of the *wadi* and the surrounding mines, geography and geology combine to argue with rather conclusive strength that northern Oman was the copper country of Makan to the old Sumerians."

After some zigzagging back and forth across the Arabian Sea to deal with broken cameras and lost crew members, Heyerdahl finally decided to steer his haystack toward Pakistan, to visit the recent excavations of an ancient inland city, Mohenjo-daro. The city had been laid out in a perfect grid sometime around 3000 B.C., and at its height housed about 35,000 people. Heyerdahl found it to be "a monument of the age-old unity of mankind, a lesson not to underestimate the intellect and capacity of other people in places or in epochs remote from our own." It validated his long-held view that humanity had not progressed in any essential way from those ancient days. "The citizens of Mohenjo-daro and their uncivilized contemporaries would have learned to drive a car, turn on a tele-vision set and knot a necktie as easily as any African or European today." Having spent more time than he'd planned scoping out archaeological sites, Heyerdahl found his funds running low. So he decided to head straight west across the Indian Ocean toward Africa without many more stops. For weeks, Heyerdahl and his crew relished being out in the open sea, far away from dangerous shorelines and narrow channels.

But then the internationalist haystack bumped blindly into an obscure corner of the cold war. Clustered around the narrow en-trance to the Red Sea from the Gulf of Aden, five small Arab and

African nations were playing out the large-scale conflict between the communist Soviet Union and capitalist United States. To the east of the *Tigris,* the Arabian side, capitalist North Yemen and communist South Yemen conducted armed border conflicts with each other. To the west, the African side, Soviet-aided Somalia was at war with American-backed Ethiopia, home of Lucy and possibly the entire human race. All of the European governments in the area warned the flimsy reed ship to stay away, for security reasons. (Heyerdahl at first found it laughable that the major military-industrial powers would be afraid of the bedraggled *Tigris,* until he realized that everyone was actually afraid *for* him and his hapless haystack.)

Unable to complete his journey by sailing up the Red Sea and entering Egypt, thus tying all three of his major ancient civilizations together, Heyerdahl was frustrated. He knew he could go no farther. He couldn't even take his ship back out the way it had come; nor could he transport it to the Kon-Tiki Museum in Oslo to join his other surviving reed boats. Only the new and still neutral African republic of Djibouti, a former French colony carved out between Somalia and Ethiopia, would let him and his crew land. It was symbolically perfect: like the *Tigris,* Djibouti was an underdog surrounded by hostile parties, either very brave or very naive. Because he wanted to make a dramatic ending—and because he couldn't bear to let the *Tigris* sit and rot in Djibouti—Heyerdahl decided to torch the ship.

Heyerdahl felt he had proved that the Sumerians came from the sea. He had tried to chart a reverse course from Adam and Eve and Noah, in Mesopotamia, back to the Indus Valley, and Egypt, but he hadn't quite made it. Heyerdahl was dwarfed by the wide scope of the task he had set himself. Even if he had made it to Egypt, where did the Egyptians come from? There were still millions of years to cover between Lucy and Cleopatra. Paleolithic primates like Lucy had had millions of years to evolve into Sumerians, and this vast transition was only beginning to be understood. "With the total collapse of accepted dogmas concerning man's antiquity as a species, we have to move on tiptoe and not be blindly wedded to existing assumptions on the age and spread of civilization. We know too little."

Heyerdahl, like Sayce, wanted to hold open the possibility that new relics would be found—possibly buried under old coastlines, deserts, or volcanoes—to answer the question of origins once and for all. Sayce believed Christianity would be proved true and correct by future archaeological finds; Heyerdahl wanted the new science to endorse his philosophy of international cooperation. As more ancient trade routes, cosmopolitan cities, and complicated watercraft were discovered, a more cooperative, civilized ancient world would emerge, a world that could serve as a model for the present one. This idea, Heyerdahl insisted, was borne out not only by his eleven-man international crew, but by the ancient history they'd explored. Before he set the *Tigris* on fire, he wrote a statement to the secretary-general of the United Nations: "We have shown that the ancient people in Mesopotamia, the Indus Valley, and Egypt could have built man's earliest civilizations through the benefit of mutual contact with the primitive vessels at their disposal 5,000 years ago. Culture arose through intelligent and profitable exchange of thoughts and products. Today we burn our proud ship . . . to protest against the inhuman elements in the world of 1978 to which we have come back as we reach land from the open sea." Explaining the circumstances of their abortive landing in Djibouti, Heyerdahl concluded: "We are all irresponsible unless we demand from the responsible decision makers that modern armaments must no longer be made available to the people whose former battle axes and swords our ancestors condemned." And then he set the *Tigris* ablaze.

It's always smart to be modest about answering questions of ancient history. Sayce and Heyerdahl knew enough to realize how much more there was to learn. But hoping that future science will bear out one ideology or another is just wishful thinking—a matter of faith more than reason. A new cuneiform tablet, a new ancient city, or a new hominid skeleton is likely to raise many more questions than it answers. And the link between ancient history and modern politics is always going to be subject to interpretation.

Heyerdahl's anthropological assumptions about the interrelatedness of Sumer, Egypt, and the Indus Valley are no longer considered radical. In fact, they are practically commonplace. In 1982 a shipwreck was discovered off the Turkish coast dating back to 1400 B.C., a free-floating example of Heyerdahl's "intelligent and profitable exchange of thoughts and products." The wreck, known as the *Uluburun,* carried twenty tons of trading cargo from at least eleven different nationalities: Cypriot, Egyptian, Canaanite, Assyrian, Mycenaean, Romanian, Kassite, Italian, Bulgarian, Hittite, and Afghan. In fact, relics from so many different places were found that no one has yet determined for sure where the ship itself originated. The ship dates from well after the beginnings of the Sumerians, but it reveals such an elaborate and well-developed culture of exchange that the discovery does seem to leave open the possibility of a long-standing relationship between these ancient cultures.

Evidence of trade in the ancient world does not necessarily mean evidence of peaceful cooperation. Spearheads and swords were found in the *Uluburun* along with the incense, jewels, and ceramics.

And even if *Uluburun* had been a relic of an entirely peaceful ancient world, the historical facts would not come with the ramifications Heyerdahl hoped for. Knowledge of a cooperative past does not necessarily bring improved cooperation in the present. Heyerdahl's wholehearted prayer for peace—even his burning of his own ship—went unnoticed by the world. Within a year of the *Tigris's* proud end, the leaders of both North and South Yemen were assassinated, and the cold war between the United States and the Soviet Union intensified. In July 1979, Saddam Hussein acceded to the presidency and control of the Revolutionary Command Council (RCC), Iraq's supreme executive body—by killing many of his opponents.

By 1980 Iraq was entrenched in what would be an eight-year war with Iran. No more tourists came to Qurna, which is situated just west of the Iran–Iraq border. Numerous lives were lost, and hundreds of Qurna's precious date palms remain scarred by gunfire. The Iranians sealed off the Shatt al Arab, the waterway that flows past Qurna and forms the southern border between the two countries; this closure effectively paralyzed the whole region of southern Iraq, which depended on the Shatt for transport. Anyone who wanted to escape the front lines—Marsh Arabs, Shia villagers, Iranian infiltrators, dissidents against the Ba'ath Party—took refuge in the marshes. This development gave Saddam Hussein an excuse to do what there's reason to believe he'd been planning for some years, even while Heyerdahl was lobbying the ministry of information for permission to visit the primitive Madan: he drained the marshes.

Hussein took a page directly out of William Willcocks's old playbook. The reclamation, he told the public, was strictly a civil engineering maneuver, meant to reclaim hundreds of acres of valuable farmland. Bit by bit, Hussein had dozens of dams built across the Tigris to the north of the marshes, depriving them, slowly, of the floodwaters that had enabled the Madan for centuries to grow rice, raise buffalo, and build houses, ships, and whole islands from *berdi* reeds. By the early 1990s, he had taken apart the Garden of Eden completely—destruction by means of construction, destruction in the name of progress.

Heyerdahl, who lived long enough to regret his innocent wooing of Ba'ath Party officials, felt personally betrayed by Saddam Hussein. He had truly believed Hussein wanted what was best for the Marsh Arabs. Progress, Heyerdahl knew, was not always progressive. There was a huge difference between "progress" and "civilization." Progress just meant moving forward; civilization meant moving forward wisely, with the fruits of progress being used for good.

Industry, which Willcocks believed had magical healing powers, could also destroy the planet it depended on. Liberty, the sacred Tree of Life of Elvy E. Callaway, had not been sufficiently protected by its guardian angels; it morphed too easily into Tse Tsan Tai's old enemy, militarism. The world in 1980 was no closer to being "fit to be federated," as Tse had put it in 1914. The Garden of Eden was not abundance, sunshine, and plantations of fruit trees. It was parched, abandoned, and torn apart by war. And original sin, the essential curse that had been edited out of Eden by William Willcocks, the Urantians, and Callaway, began to creep back into the picture. Only now, it wasn't our invisible ancient ancestors who had sinned beyond repair—it was us.

PART IV

Exile

II

An Evolving Creation

I N THE BEGINNING, everything was just where the world had left
it after the Scopes "monkey trial" in 1925. Science was leading
America into the certain perfection of the future. Old-time religion had been sent back to the woods of the Deep South with
its tail between its legs, never to be heard from again.

Or so it seemed for a while. Throughout the 1930s, 1940s, and
1950s, Christian fundamentalists disappeared from the public sphere.
There were few protests about the unflattering portrayal of their
side of the Scopes trial after the movie version, *Inherit the Wind,*
came out in 1960. American popular culture was a Babylon they
wanted nothing to do with. Historians now look at this period as
a kind of political and cultural exile.

As anyone who's watched an epic film knows, an exile so complete will set the scene for a sequel in which the excluded party
returns, even bigger and stronger. That's certainly what happened
to Christian fundamentalism in America in the second half of the
twentieth century.

When I first heard the rumor that my great-uncle—WASP, professor, New York City allergist—had been searching for the literal
Garden of Eden in the 1950s, the cognitive dissonance was immediate. That's because I had grown up in the 1980s and 1990s during *Scopes II: The Culture Wars.* I associated people who thought
the Book of Genesis was a map to the real world with minimal
education and ultraconservative politics. I thought those people,
the Christian conservatives, *they* must believe the Garden of Eden

is a real place. *They* think they know where it is. Not my family. I didn't realize then that religious life in America hadn't always been so polarized. My uncle could see both sides. In his offices at Columbia University, he dreamed of Eden; in the pews of his Presbyterian church, he dreamed of science. But that kind of peaceful middle ground didn't seem to be possible anymore. The two origin stories that had clashed so dramatically in 1925—creation and evolution—were returning for rematch after rematch.

In May 2007, an organization called Answers in Genesis—slogan: "Genesis: Believing it. Defending it. Proclaiming it"—opened the Creation Museum, a $27 million center in rural Kentucky designed to show that God created man in six literal days, 6,000 years ago, and that everything afterward happened just as the Bible said. This museum was hardly the first outpost of strict Biblical literalism in American history. But it was the grandest, the most expensive, and the loudest—designed, apparently, not to hide in the hills but to get the most attention possible.

It had my attention. By 2008, I had spent four years following Eden seekers to Gardens far and wide. Biblical literalism no longer seemed monolithic to me. In fact, one thing I knew for sure after reading dozens and dozens of interpretations of those four verses of Genesis—was that there was no one "literal" way to read the Bible. To me, however, this made the various readings more interesting, not less. If visions of Genesis didn't have to be "all true" or "all false," there was room for individual personalities to come through. I wanted to test my newfound equanimity on the first and most powerful brand of literalism I'd encountered in my life: late twentieth-century Christian fundamentalism. The Creation Museum seemed a perfect opportunity. I felt sure that if I immersed myself in this particular map of Genesis, if I could find out where on Earth this Eden was, the "other side" of this polarized world would no longer be mysterious to me.

As I drove past the Cincinnati airport into the mountains of northern Kentucky in the fall of 2008, there wasn't much to break the rural scenery, only a few abandoned factory smokestacks and blown-out ghost towns. The museum itself was completely hidden behind a jagged mountain peak, but along the highway, its colorful roadside signage—"Prepare to Believe!"—stood out.

At the entrance desk, I was the only single-ticket customer behind throngs of families and tour groups bused in from nearby churches and schools. They were all there to see the museum's permanent exhibition, the "Walking Tour of Biblical History," which re-created the Book of Genesis, according to what the museum called the "Seven C's of History": Creation, Corruption, Catastrophe, Confusion, Christ and The Cross, and Consummation. Somewhere in these stations of the creation, I figured, I was bound to find out where the Garden of Eden was.

Before I could enter the exhibit hall, an enthusiastic white-haired man wearing a safari vest and a museum ID around his neck urged me to stand on a particular spot on the floor, in front of a green video-projection screen, so he could take my picture.

I must have appeared mystified— how was I supposed to pose? —because my guide pointed up above my head a few feet away. "Look up there!" he suggested, grinning. A small crew of fierce-looking dinosaurs stared down at me from behind a Plexiglas wall; I was supposed to cower in fear, but I was confused. What were sixty-million-year-old creatures doing in a young-earth creationist museum? They slowly opened and shut their animatronic jaws, continually letting out elephant-like roars.

Dinosaurs, unlike other discoveries of modern science, such as human genetics or microbiology, were too well known and too beloved by children for creation science to erase them completely. But the Creation Museum did more than acknowledge the existence of dinosaurs: it embraced these wonders of paleontology as a challenge.

Dinosaurs, the museum stated, had existed, and had died out only a few thousand years ago. Therefore, if the Earth was 6,000 years old, humans and dinosaurs must have coexisted. Every exhibit in the Creation Museum set out to reinforce this idea: in the lobby, a tiny model caveman child stood giggling next to a tiny velociraptor, a benevolent prehistoric pet.

Dinosaur and human coexistence was such a new idea that not even all of the creation-science theme parks—and there are several—agreed on the details. Dinosaur Adventure Land, a park whose owner, Kent Hovind, was imprisoned in 2009 for tax fraud, contended that the dinosaurs were all killed by Noah's Flood, neatly explaining their extinction. The Creation Museum posited that dinosaurs *did* make it onto Noah's Ark, and were saved. Later, they turned against each other and most were killed, except a few surviving stragglers, which we know as dragons. (Yes, dragons are real. How else could Saint George slay them?)

The Creation Museum didn't really try to prove scientifically that dinosaurs went extinct thousands—rather than millions—of years ago. Instead, it did an end-run around science itself. A side-by-side interactive exhibit showed how "mainstream" scientists look at dinosaurs versus how scientists working "from a Biblical perspective" might approach the same fossils. "Mainstream" scientists read the data and determined that dinosaur remains may be up to 60 million years old. Creation scientists, instead of looking to the fossils themselves to ascertain their age, simply started from a prior assumption: the Earth was created 6,000 years ago. So that was how old the dinosaur bones must be.

I found all this profoundly discouraging. Before I'd even arrived at "In the beginning," the brazenness of the Creation Museum had stymied my attempts to reduce it to a manageable size. How could responsible parents tell their children that dinosaurs and humans coexisted? It was unimaginable. I plodded on into the "Walking Tour of Biblical History," where I sat alone on a low, carpeted bench in the Six Days of Creation Panoramic Theater and watched a six-minute video re-creation of the Earth's beginnings, complete with thunderous background music. This was the version of our origins that, according to a 1991 Gallup poll, 47 percent of Americans believe: Earth—and human beings—were created specially by God, recently; a "young Earth" creation. That 47 percent became the basis of the voting bloc known as the "religious right," who were widely credited for the contentious election of George W. Bush in 2000. By mobilizing this last untapped group of potential Republicans, Karl Rove had completed the process of returning religious fundamentalists from their post-Scopes exile. And this time, believers in the latter scenario could not entirely be dismissed as "yokels." They held positions of power.

In the Bush era and afterward, America had officially reached a point in the culture wars that any earlier Eden seeker could have predicted would be untenable: we had two competing origin stories, and the gap between them seemed unbridgeable. Either we're descended from apes, or we're a picture-perfect creation of God dropped from heaven. Either the brain secretes thoughts like bile, or God washes your mouth out with holy soap. I was definitely not equipped to bridge this gap. There had to be people who had really believed both stories, and I needed to talk to them. It took me a while, long after I left the Creation Museum, but I finally found someone who could help.

Lee Meadows teaches science education at the University of Alabama in Birmingham, and he grew up in Oxford, Mississippi in the 1960s, in a fundamentalist world. At public school, his favorite classes were those in science. But in his home, a literalist interpretation of Genesis was taken completely for granted. He shied away from biology in order to avoid the inevitable cognitive dissonance between science and his religion. As a kid, Dr. Meadows said, he was "a six-day creationist to the core."

He was in junior high school in the 1970s, when the antievolution movement in America was gathering steam. While belief in a God-created universe had, of course, been around since the beginning, "creationism" as an organized, conservative Christian belief system was a more recent creature, which had evolved in a complicated two-step with modern science.

In the 1950s, shaken by *Sputnik,* the American government began extensive new initiatives to improve science education, especially in biology; these included $100 million in new funding from the National Science Foundation, some of which went toward strengthening the teaching of evolution. Partially in response to government-sponsored science education efforts in the 1960s, Christian fundamentalism got organized. We think of the 1960s as a freewheeling, socially liberal era, and they were. That ethos was one of the many factors driving these Christians back from their cultural exile. Fundamentalist leaders saw the cultural chaos of the 1960s—the shifting roles of women, the availability of birth control and abortion, and the ever-present threat of nuclear war—as obvious evidence that the world as they knew it was in grave danger. And so they emerged, like Rip Van Winkle, into a world of carbon dating, genome mapping, and social change.

Gradually, fundamentalists began to develop their own alternative explanations of human origins, borrowing the language—if not the methodology—of science. In 1961, John C. Whitcomb and Henry M. Morris published a hugely influential book, *The Genesis Flood,* in which they asserted that the fossil record had not been deposited over millions of years, one layer of sediment at a time, as geologists had repeatedly proved. No, it had been created all at once by a catastrophic worldwide event—a Flood of enormous proportions. And the Flood became a crucial part of creation science. Like William Warren, the creationists envisioned a flood that resembled an earthquake or a spasm, sputtering everything into the shape we now find it. "I think they're having to invoke the flood as the way to explain science," said Meadows. The Flood was a vessel for everything creationists couldn't quite deny: extinctions, plate tectonics, climate change. Between 1961 and 1987, *The Genesis Flood* would go through twenty-nine printings and sell 200,000 copies.

By 1971, the televangelist Jerry Falwell's *Old-Time Gospel Hour* was having a $1 million year. Morris had left his day job teaching at the Virginia Polytechnic Institute to start the Institute for Creation Research (ICR) in San Diego, with his colleague Tim LaHaye—later to become famous as coauthor of the wildly popular *Left Behind* novels. The ICR churned out creationist books and pamphlets as if there were no tomorrow, which, for believers in the apocalypse and the rapture, made sense. One of the ICR leaders, Ken Ham, started his own spin-off organization, Answers in Genesis (AiG), which would eventually build the Creation Museum.

It was the Answers in Genesis books that Lee Meadows read as a kid. "I was on the ICR and the AiG mailing list, and this was before the Internet, so I was probably writing off to get [this material]." And for a kid who loved science classes, did the creation science literature make an impact? "Oh, yes. I remember thinking, 'Why doesn't my teacher talk about this?' I wanted the science." Meadows remembers asking science questions at church, and being shut down. Then he asked church questions at school, and was shut down again.

Meanwhile evangelical Christians were beginning to make their presence known, and creationism was coming out of the closet. In 1977, ICR opened America's first "creation museum" in San Diego. In 1981, bills were introduced in twenty states to require that public schools give "equal time" to teaching creationism in science classes, reminiscent of the flurry of antievolution legislation in statehouses in the 1920s. In 1925, after Scopes, only two states—Arkansas and Mississippi—still managed to pass antievolution laws. In 1981, only two states passed "creation science" laws: Arkansas and Louisiana. In a trial known as "Scopes II," the Arkansas law was overturned, thanks to the testimony of clergymen, who believed in the separation of church and state, and to philosophers of science, who succeeded in separating science from non-science. The Louisiana law was also overturned.

But the continuing string of legal failures did not dissuade creationists. When the ACLU sued the publicly accredited Liberty Baptist College for teaching creation, Falwell agreed, after a lengthy battle, to teach evolution instead. Liberty's professors did teach evolution—as an unproved theory—in their biology classes. But

Falwell simultaneously made it a requirement that all students at Liberty also take a course in Creation Studies—taught as fact. This rhetorical coup allowed Liberty's graduates to be qualified to teach high-school biology wherever they wanted to, and it got the ACLU off Falwell's back.

As a teenager, a college student, and later, Lee Meadows lived a double life. Though he walked around in the world of science, he still felt himself, as a Christian, to be an outsider. He had to protect himself from the non-Christian world, which, he had been taught, was a threat to his beliefs and way of life. It wasn't until Meadows was in his late twenties that this anxiety began to break down. He was at the University of Georgia, studying for his doctorate in science education, and there, he was required to take a course in the history of science. "That's when I started to realize—why would I *expect* science and religion to agree? They have such different historical reasons for what they come up with . . . so why would I expect them to line up? This was very freeing for me, opening up, not to have to make the two meet in a nice neat little box."

Meadows planned to return to teaching science himself, but he got caught up in another conversation about the nature of scientific inquiry, with his colleague David Jackson, a "Yankee, liberal, agnostic, Democrat." Eventually they cowrote an article that investigated the troubled relationship between science and religion in classrooms across the American South.

Jerry Falwell hadn't been the only one to avoid teaching evolution. Lee Meadows found that this was commonplace in public schools where there were large populations of kids whose religious beliefs make them resistant to the idea. Teachers in public schools simply ignored the topic, or made a series of compromises. "They might teach natural selection, but leave out evolution of species. . . . Some textbooks don't have the topic at all. Some won't use 'the e word' and instead say 'change over time.'" Evolution was an intimidating subject for even the most scientifically-minded teachers. "They know that if evolution is not presented well, [the parents of their religious students] will step up and say, 'That's not right, they're teaching against the Bible, they're telling lies!'" And it's not just the parents. Meadows told me that there were children who show up in their public-school biology classes with tracts in their hands: "Things like '10 Questions to Ask Your Teacher' or '7 Problems with Evolution Your Teacher Doesn't Want You to Know.' They have been prepared. They have been coached. They will name a church. And they want to defend the other children, those who may have been misled, from this teacher who's going against the Bible."

This was one of the points in my conversations with Meadows where I had to stop and remind myself that, for those who object to evolution, this is not a casual fight. It's essential to understand this. It may be easy for a secular person who's always been taught evolution to visit the Creation Museum and treat it like a campy joke. But for believers like those kids and their parents, in order for the one essential piece of Biblical information—the New Testament's promise of Christ's crucifixion, atonement, and everlasting life—to be true, every single word of Biblical text, all the way back to "In the beginning," also has to be inerrant. For such believers, as Meadows put it, "everything hangs together." The virgin birth, the resurrection, eternal life—if one falls, they all do.

"If you don't take Genesis 1, 2, and 3 at their word, that tears down the whole thing; because it's not just about Genesis, it's about everything in their worldview." That's why creationism has become such a huge marker of evangelicals; it's a litmus test. If you believe in creation, you are a Christian; if not, you're not. Children take this ultimatum extremely seriously. For them, the debate over creation and evolution is a life-or-death issue. If a science teacher dismisses those kids' concerns about evolution, he or she may lose their respect on more than just this one issue. On the other hand, a teacher who acknowledged creationism or intelligent design in a science classroom was also doing more harm than good. If you cared about your students, you had to respect them and respect science, and this was a difficult balancing act to pull off. Meadows's and Jackson's article won the "Article of the Year" award from the National Association for Research in Science Teaching. This warm reception of his work helped convince Meadows that his religious background gave him a valuable perspective on his chosen field of science education.

Throughout the late 1990s and early 2000s, Meadows was busy earning tenure, learning new techniques, building a consultancy, doing the work of establishing an academic career. But all along, the teaching of evolution—or the lack thereof—was nagging at him. The results of this neglect were beginning to show elsewhere in the public sphere. In 2005, a new mutation of creation science called "intelligent design" nearly worked its way into the official science curriculum of the public schools in Dover, Pennsylvania, bringing to the state courts yet another Scopes-like trial, *Kitzmiller v. Dover*. Intelligent design did not rely on the Bible directly, but rather on a tenuous redefinition of science to include the possbility of super-natural interference. The ACLU's attorneys commissioned an all-star cadre of scientists, and the courtroom turned into a classroom. The federal judge, John E. Jones III, who had been appointed by Bush, got an education in evolutionary biology that he may never have received in school.

He learned, for instance, that calling evolution "just a theory, not a fact," as creationists often do, makes no sense in the scientific world, where a theory is more important than the facts it's com-posed of. Gravity and electricity are also theories, but no one is trying to overturn them. He heard that Darwin's theory of natural selection was borne out a century later by the new science of genetics. He was shown slides of Tiktaalik, the newly discovered "fishapod," a 375-million-year-old transitional fossil that showed characteristics of both fish and amphibians. Kevin Padian, one of Tiktaalik's discoverers, said later, "The reporters were just amazed: 'how come we've never learned this?' And the reason is: it's not in the textbooks because creationists have fought so hard to keep it out, and that's been a big influence." The journalists had learned, and so had the judge. Jones wrote a spirited decision of more than 100 pages, finding that "intelligent design," like "creationism," was certainly not science, and did not belong in the classroom.

Various forms of creationism had failed in court many times in the past, ever since the Supreme Court overturned Louisiana's "equal time" law in 1987. But if there was one thing all the players on both sides of *Kitzmiller v. Dover* could agree on, it was that this would not be the last battle.

It was around this time, in 2006, that Lee Meadows began to get back to evolution. It wasn't because of current events; he just knew he was uniquely qualified to address the situation, and he had waited long enough. "It was an integrity issue for me, a moral imperative." He set himself the task of mediating between the two worlds. He began showing teachers ways to engage students who resisted learning about evolution. He spoke at conferences and spent time in middle school and high school classrooms. I asked him where on earth he began. Were there particular sticking points for these resistant kids, points that teachers would have to learn to address?

"Oh sure," he said. "'I didn't come from a monkey.' You hear that one a lot. And in fact it reveals a basic misunderstanding of the process of evolution, because we didn't descend directly from monkeys."

How could teachers counteract misunderstandings such as this one? A simple reliance on dogma—"that's just how it is"—would antagonize those students who had already been told that the Bible was the only explanation they needed. Instead, Meadows's mission was nothing less than to reintroduce the concept of science.

"You have to make [evolution] inquiry-based, so that it's about collecting data and drawing conclusions. Midway through the unit on evolution, I ask teachers to step back and have kids take a look at how science is limited to natural explanations. Now, that doesn't mean that science says there is *no such thing* as a supernatural explanation. But science can never make a supernatural argument. And science is an amazing thing . . . but there are other ways to know the world." After his talks, Meadows told me, "teachers always come up and thank me; they say, I've never thought about that before."

Meadows wanted kids to have the same liberating moment that he had had in college: the freedom to look at science and religion next to each other and not necessarily have to make them match. This was tricky. Kids inevitably saw conflict between what their church told them and what they learned in school. It was hard enough for adults to learn to live in "a two-idea world," but for kids it was nearly impossible. Meadows believed that if teachers could get them to understand the evidence for, and the process of, evolution—well, that was a start.

"There are kids—and I know because I was one—who struggled just to understand the evidence." Meadows clearly relished the challenge of overcoming that struggle. "If you can get a kid to see that there's this amazing blue whale that came from a creature in the marshes of the Middle East, if they can get that, that's good stuff."

For a student to say, of the blue whale, "I don't buy that," Meadows could live with. It was imperative to start somewhere. He contends that everyone needs a basic understanding of evolutionary processes just in order to get along in today's world—to understand, for example, why you need a new flu shot every year, or how DNA information gets passed down. The rest of the work of integrating scientific knowledge with religious belief could happen slowly over a lifetime, as it did for Meadows. But for kids never to be exposed to evolution at all? "That bothers me. That bothers me a lot."

Opened two years after the latest legal defeat for creationism at Dover, the Creation Museum seemed designed to show that the idea had not gone away. In a 2007 follow-up to their earlier polls, Gallup found that 66 percent of surveyed Americans believed that young-earth creationism was "definitely or probably" true. Just a few weeks before the Creation Museum's grand opening in May 2007, three Republican candidates for the presidential nomination publicly agreed that they did not believe in evolution. A spokesman for Answers in Genesis, Mark Looy, told the *Washington Post* that, with the exception of three $1 million donations, the $27 million raised to build the Creation Museum had come mostly from contributions of $100 or less. So creationism was hanging on tenaciously. But what did it have to say? When I finally arrived at the museum's Garden of Eden, I thought I'd figure that out.

Pushing through thick plastic curtains, I left the main exhibit hall and went into a steamy, climate-controlled garden. It was easy to think I had actually been transported to a tropical paradise. The teeming plant and animal life seemed to come right up against the guardrails and overwhelm the walking path. The museum brags about the professional quality of its exhibits, designed by Patrick Marsh, who created two attractions—"Jaws" and "King Kong"—at Universal Studios in Florida. And while the grandeur of the place isn't quite on that level, the Garden of Eden did feel enormous and strangely realistic. The dim light and piped-in birdsong evoked a greenhouse or botanical garden—in which every plant was carefully modeled plastic.

The story of Eden unfolded in chronological order in separate life-size dioramas starring lifelike models of Adam and Eve. In the first scene, a dark-haired Caucasian Adam named the animals. He reached one hand forward toward a deer and an elk. In the crook of one arm he held a tiny lamb, both symbolizing Christ and conveniently covering his private parts. At this point of course Adam was still naked and unashamed, but the viewers were not. A penguin stood in the foreground amid a bed of country wildflowers; possibly it was waiting in line to be named. It would have to wait behind the ape—whose presence was meant to show that, from the beginning, humans and apes, like humans and dinosaurs, existed simultaneously, not sequentially. There was also a dinosaur here, bending his great reptilian head down to the ground to eat a pineapple. All the beasts of the field in the Garden of Eden were happy, healthy, and vegetarian.

Each new scene came with a placard matter-of-factly stating Biblical interpretation as if it were an explanatory caption. The next time I saw Adam, Eve had showed up—with black hair long enough to cover her breasts. Adam and Eve submerged up to their abdomens in a peaceful-looking pool of water: "Eve was made from the side of Adam. God created men and women fit for different roles from the beginning." Adam and Eve in a birch forest, sheltered by modesty-protecting ferns: "The special creation of Adam and Eve is the foundation for marriage: one man and one woman."

Nowhere did any of the plaques or posters mention *where,* geographically, Adam and Eve were supposed to be. This surprised me, since everything else was so specifically laid out—well, specifically and vaguely at once. It was as if in the quest to make this origin story "universal" and therefore true, Answers in Genesis had cut out pieces of familiar objects and pasted them together in an awkward collage. The Tree of Life, for example, had the elaborate trunk of a mangrove, the heart-shaped leaves of a beech, and luminous orange fruit that resembled mangoes. The museum's designers wanted the exhibits to look realistic, but not quite "down to Earth." If they were to offer a location for Eden, I imagined that it, too, would be an odd composite: a desert oasis in northern Europe, glaciers at the equator, the Californian Alps.

The Tree of the Knowledge of Good and Evil—narrow willow leaves, dark purple bunches of currant-like fruit—appeared near the end of the path, in front of a disturbingly bright orange backdrop. Wound around one of the tree's upper branches was a venomous-looking red serpent with a white underbelly and bright green eyes. Its scales were like those of a desert snake; its face looked more like that of a sea snake.

Suddenly, all went dark. The path narrowed. I had been able to stroll through the pastoral scenes of Eden at my own pace, but after the entrance of the snake of sin the story sharpened dramatically. I filed past smaller, framed exhibits, which broke down the Fall of Man in the way a parent trying to make sure a child understands crucial information emphasizes *one word at a time.* Frame one: a dimly lit diorama of the snake alone, its jaws open, pulsating red, inset into the black-painted walls like a picture in a gruesome gallery. Frame two: Adam and Eve in a darkened box, Eve with fruit in her open hand—the next "C," *corruption.* Frame three: a truly terrifying spectacle—Adam and Eve, hair disheveled, faces ashen, stand before an altar piled with incredibly bloody, skinless lambs, their glassy eyes rolling upward. Adam and Eve are draped in the bloody skins of the creatures they have sacrificed. "The entrance of sin into the world brought about sickness and death in our once perfect world." These were the wages of sin, and it was enough to make anyone long for the herbivorous days of Eden.

Then I was out into the light again, the fluorescent faux sunshine of Noah's boatyard. It was full of elaborate, animated-model people—climbing up on the Ark's framework, hammering boards, carrying water, and weaving baskets. Everyone was cheery, with the exception of one old man, the designated skeptic, who repeatedly shook his head and muttered, "I don't know about that Noah!" I crossed footbridges to inspect the construction and viewed a model of the Ark—to scale, not one of those cute "bathtub-size" re-creations. The Museum's founder, Ken Ham, believed that toy-like Arks encourage people not to take Biblical literalism seriously.

And it should be taken seriously: despite the bright, industrious atmosphere, Noah's Ark was actually the centerpiece of one of the most important C's of history: *catastrophe*. The flood was of course catastrophic for all those summarily drowned by God for their sins. But the Ark was much more than that; it was a foreshadowing of apocalyptic events to come. According to Ken Ham, "The Flood is a reminder that one day there will be another global judgment, but next time by fire. All who have ever lived will stand before a Holy God." Again, the Creation Museum may look to me like a theme park, but its purpose could not be more serious: to keep evangelical Christians who live in the modern, scientific world within the fold. And in at least one case, Lee Meadows told me, it's succeeding.

Meadows hasn't been to the Creation Museum himself, but he understands how effective its arguments can be. An acquaintance of his, a PhD in health sciences, traveled to the museum and reported, "It changed my life. It was amazing." The lack of scientific method didn't seem to bother her. The museum is presented as legitimate, as an "alternative" viewpoint. As Meadows put it: "They can say, 'You can go to the American Museum of Natural History and see *their* science, then you can come here and see *our* science. Or more likely they say 'the REAL science.'" Because of the lack of understanding of the scientific method, their theology can pass as science. Discouraging, yes, but all the more reason for Meadows to help teachers get back to science.

In 2007, after Meadows gave a presentation of his work at a science teachers' conference, an editor from the esteemed educational publisher Heinemann approached him about writing a guide for teachers teaching evolution. Meadows's moment had come, and he wasn't shy about accepting—"I'm a Presbyterian," he said, "I believe in providence!"

In the fall of 2009, Heinemann published his book: *The Missing Link: An Inquiry Approach for Teaching All Students about Evolution.* Meadows believes that the "inquiry-based" educational techniques— which focus more on evidence and experimentation than on rote memorization and dogmatic presentation—can help unravel the tortured politics of teaching evolution, and he's eager to get his ideas into the hands of teachers.

Meadows is now an associate professor in the University of Alabama's school of education, where he works constantly to interpret the two worlds to each other. If he ever got an opportunity to speak in front of a conservative Christian group, he said to me, he'd tell them: "When you say 'I don't believe in evolution,' [a non-Christian] just heard you say 'The earth is flat.' You just told them, 'I'm stupid.'" On the other hand, he wanted secular public-school science teachers to realize that their religious students "are not stupid. And their faith is not crippling. It's actually something that adds a great deal of beauty to their lives."

How to connect that kind of personal faith with the big, shiny theme-park aura of the Creation Museum? Did one really represent the other? The final attraction of the "Walking Tour of Biblical History" was the Last Adam Theater, where visitors who had not already done so were encouraged to accept Christ as their personal savior. Sin had followed us from the Garden, to the Ark, and on to the Tower of Babel; that's why everyone dies, because everyone is a sinner. But according to the Creation Museum, humanity had one more opportunity to redeem itself: *Christ and the cross.* "Because sin brings about death, God sent His Son Jesus to die in our place and rise again to defeat death. Jesus' crucifixion was His act of paying the sin debt for all." I happened to walk by while a show was in progress and the theater doors were closed, so I tiptoed on to the food court, ignoring the giant red LED clock counting down the minutes to the next presentation.

But I thought about it: Christ as the "last Adam." This idea connected Eden seekers all the way back to Augustine. If Christ was the antidote for Adam's sin, then the redemption of Christ should cancel out the destruction of Eden. Once all of us were free of the debt of sin, we could live forever in the Garden of Eden, naturally. That is, we could if we knew where to find it.

I was not the only visitor to the Creation Museum to wonder about the location of the Garden of Eden. Answers in Genesis had considered the question. It had an official answer: the Garden of Eden "was destroyed in Noah's global cataclysm and we do not know where it was."

I found myself wishing that in this one instance the literalists would be more literal. What about the Pishon and the Gihon rivers? What about the lands of Havilah and Cush? Those were real words, used in the Bible. Didn't the things they signified have to be *somewhere*? Abstraction seemed uncharacteristic of a belief system so confident conclusions that it could put dinosaurs on the Ark. The Creation Museum's Garden of Eden was not totally opaque: it had penguins; the snake climbed trees; Adam and Eve were white with dark hair. But in this one crucial detail, Eden, the centerpiece of the story of sin, remained unclear. Why? There was theology here. The Garden of Eden had to support Noah's Flood, or rather, Noah's global cataclysm. If Eden *could* still be found on Earth, even deep underwater or high on a mountain, this would mean that Noah's Flood wasn't Earth-shattering. And *that* would mean God's punishment wasn't really very severe, hardly a reminder of the brutal trials and tribulations to come.

And that's what the museum was all about: a heavenly afterlife. It's the seventh and final C in history: *consummation.* "God promises in Scripture to do away with the corruption of man by creating a new heaven and a new Earth where death and suffering no longer exist for those who have followed Jesus Christ." This was more than your average redemption—a new heaven *and* a new Earth. Earth was not to be venerated; Earth was just a temporary home. Evangelical Christianity had excised even the possibility of Eden on Earth in order to re-create a more perfect Garden in heaven, after the apocalypse and the rapture.

As ideas about the Garden of Eden go, I found this empty, invisible Eden disappointing. Mongolia, Ohio, the North Pole—these locations, however far-fetched, were human. They represented possibility, even in the face of disaster. Tse Tsan Tai's country was on the chopping block in the midst of World War I, but he still held out the Garden of Eden as a dream of world peace. Thor Heyerdahl was convinced that man had ruined Eden, yet he still worked for world cooperation and environmental stewardship. William Warren believed in original sin, but he loved the northern lights of his abandoned Polar Eden; at the very least it could be a good source of electricity. The Creation Museum's empty Eden brought to my mind another "C," coldness.

What was at the heart of the Creation Museum's religion? Its prescriptions all involved things Christians should fight against: sex outside marriage, the theory of evolution, the reality of climate change. But what did Christians fight for? William Jennings Bryan, venerable hero of the old-time fundamentalism, was a devotee of the "social gospel," whose faith drove him to lobby for the poor, for laborers, and for women's suffrage. The only activity the Creation Museum actually endorsed was evangelism: spreading the Word endlessly, so that more people could be spirited up to heaven for the rapture.

In the early twentieth century, if you wanted to protect the religious status quo from Darwin's advances, you planted a flag on a spot on the globe, declared it to be the Garden of Eden, and held your ground. Locating Eden on Earth—anywhere on Earth—was basically a conservative position, even if it took some highly creative leaps of logic to get there. But after the culture wars, it seemed, the tide had turned. In the late twentieth century, drawing a map of Eden was a way of saying that there was hope for us in the here and now, down on Earth, not just the afterlife.

Lee Meadows hasn't drawn a map of the Garden of Eden. But in a way, that's exactly what he's trying to do. For him, it's not about the wages of sin, the global cataclysm, or eternal life; it's just about being fair to kids. "My passion is the public school. And for the religious kids whose parents put them in public school: that says something." Meadows wanted to reach these kids where they're at—even those kids with tracts in their hands. With a shift in perspective, even the stubborn misperception "I didn't come from a monkey" could be instructive.

"I would say [the monkey misconception] is a smoke screen, but it's actually not. It's actually a very deep idea in Christianity that we are created in the image of God....There's a really fundamental resistance to the idea that humans could be 'random products.' And there's a real passion [in that resistance] that I want to honor."

As I read the plaques at the Creation Museum, which casually explained why fundamental tenets of science were not only incorrect but immoral, it was very easy for me, a believer in science and also in morality, to become indignant and defensive. But did I really believe that every third-grade kid in the group-ticket line was out to destroy me personally, and my belief system? Did I really think that 47 percent of Americans deserved my disdain? What good could more polarization and more court trials do? The two sides, says Meadows, "have been in entrenched warfare all the way back to the Scopes trial. And I'm trying to find a third alternative." Perhaps the way out of the war over origins was to try to reach the individuals beyond the rhetoric, to place humanity over ideology.

Meadows is reaching out; his goal is to be invited to give keynote addresses at science-teaching conferences in the Deep South, where he can really work with teachers who are in a position to put his ideas into practice. It's an intimidating prospect; he stands in the middle of some highly contested territory. Teachers might be relieved to have his tools at hand, but lots of other people resent what he's trying to do. "I've been called a creationist [by science teachers]; I've been called an evolutionist [by creationists].

"Just recently I was even called an atheist, and that was from the Christian side, so it really hurt." For the record, Meadows is a Sunday school teacher and an elder in a Presbyterian church in Birmingham. The Presbyterians are what's called a "mainline" Protestant denomination, one which, unlike most "evangelical" denominations, encourages the kind of thinking Meadows wanted to do. It's the same denomination, incidentally, that my great-uncle the Eden seeker belonged to in the 1950s.

Meadows knew his dream of reconciliation would be a very long-term process. But he believed in getting started now. As he put it, laughing, "I'm a ready-fire-aim kind of guy." Yes, he lives in a no-man's-land between religious conservatives and secular liberals. But there's nowhere else he'd rather be. Actually, he wouldn't really see it as a no-man's-land. "I live in *both* worlds," Meadows said, "And I have to tell you, I kind of like it!"

12

The Once and Future Eden

IN THE BEGINNING, saith the Lord your God, this place called Independence was Eden, the Garden of the Lord. Behold! Go forth to the promised land of Missouri as speedily as can be, and purchase tracts of land!

The Mormons would seem to have the Garden of Eden figured out. Joseph Smith, who founded the Church of Jesus Christ of Latter-day Saints, as Mormonism is officially called, claimed to communicate directly with God. And God revealed to him exactly where Eden was: Independence, Missouri. That was all Mormons needed to know.

Between 1829, when he was first visited by the angel Moroni in Palmyra, New York, who told him of the existence of *The Book of Mormon,* and his death in 1844 at the hands of a violent mob in an Illinois jail, Smith delivered hundreds of revelations on theological and practical topics. His announcement of the location of Eden was both.

Eden in Missouri made sense in Mormon theology: according to the elaborate origin story in *The Book of Mormon,* Christ visited prehistoric America, and much of the Bible took place there. In the early 1830s, Smith's followers in New York and Ohio, who called themselves Saints, were in danger, and Smith needed to move them to a safer place. In retrospect, the Mormons' migration through the Midwest—from New York to Ohio to Missouri to Illinois—appears to be a sort of dress rehearsal, since we know they eventually found a permanent home in Utah. But during Joseph Smith's lifetime, Utah was outside the borders of the United States, and not on the itinerary.

Jackson County, Missouri, was thought to be safe, and Independence was the major town in Jackson County. This is not to say that practicality trumped God's word. For the young church, the two were inextricably tangled up. Its God—born of the revivalist "burned-over district" in northern New York state—was a living, speaking God who responded to events in real time.

So Mormons during Smith's lifetime had every reason to take Smith's word—God's word—that Eden was in Jackson County. Even after Smith's death, Brigham Young, the new leader who would eventually lead the Mormons to Utah, said that it was just as necessary for good Mormons to believe Adam and Eve lived in Missouri as to believe Joseph was a prophet of God—which is to say, absolutely necessary. And for generations after that, the Saints still venerated the Missouri chapters of their history.

So why was it that here in Independence, on the official tour of the Mormon visitors' center, there was no mention of Eden?

After the tour, I asked our guide, Hermana (Sister) Cameron, a young blonde Mormon from Newport Beach, California, serving a two-year mission in Independence, "Is it true that Independence is the Garden of Eden?"

"Yes!" she said. "Isn't that amazing?"

But she also said that she hadn't known Eden was in Missouri until she was assigned to her mission—and even here, Eden wasn't one of her talking points. She had picked it up from older visiting Mormons. Back in California, Hermana Cameron said, if she thought about Eden at all, "I thought it was in the Middle East somewhere!"

At first, I could see why she'd be confused. Today, Independence, Missouri, is clearly not a perfect paradise. In the late 1990s, the city became a hub for methamphetamine abuse. Missouri was second only to California in production of this drug, sometimes called "redneck cocaine." Meth production went on, undisturbed by the ghost of Independence's hometown hero, Harry Truman. Trumanalia is memorialized all over Main Street: there was the Truman Courthouse; the Truman Statue; and Clinton's Soda Fountain, where Truman had his first job. But otherwise, there's not much here. Behind the Truman Memorial Building, the Wild Bill Hickok Memorial Parking Lot is empty. The pizza place across the street does not sell slices on weekends; it's not worth their while. You have to buy the whole pie.

However, none of these facts are entirely inconsistent with a Mormon Eden. The Church of Jesus Christ of Latter-day Saints, is not simply another branch of Christianity with another reading of the same Bible. The works of Joseph Smith—*The Book of Mormon; The Pearl of Great Price;* and especially *Doctrine and Covenants,* an anthology of Smith's many revelations—are at least as influential for church members as the Old and New Testaments. And in these Mormon scriptures, Eden plays a different role. The Garden of Eden is not about abundance and perfection.

The Garden of Eden is also not about creation. Mormons believe that although God gave Adam and Eve physical form in the Garden of Eden, they had existed before Eden as purely spiritual beings. In fact the Earth could be much older than the Garden of Eden. Mainstream Mormonism, unlike evangelical Christianity, does not have a hostile relationship with the science of human origins. Duane Jeffery, who is a practicing Mormon and a former biology professor at Brigham Young University, told me that in his regular evolution classes, "only rarely did I have a student bring up the Missouri Eden story." In short, according to the church, "It is evident that the Lord did not intend the opening chapters of Genesis or other scriptures about the Creation to be textbook sections on geology, archaeology, or science."

The Garden of Eden isn't even about sin. In the Mormon church, humans are not born with original sin. Adam and Eve did eat the forbidden fruit, and God did kick them out of the Garden—but they didn't have to pay for their sin throughout eternity. God actually pardoned them. According to *The Book of Mormon,* you need the bitter to have the sweet. If Adam and Eve had stayed in the Garden, "they would have remained in a state of innocence, having no joy, for they knew no misery; doing no good, for they knew no sin."

For Mormons, the Garden of Eden *is* about exile. It's the place they were kicked out of. And, just as important, it's the place they will come back to—when Christ returns to Earth to usher all faithful Saints up to heaven, where they will live forever with their families in a state of perfection known as "Zion." As a Mormon hymn puts it, "Zion will be where Eden was."

Between the downfall of Eden and the rebirth of Zion, Independence itself didn't have to be anything special. Eden doesn't have to be perfect, beautiful, or lush. It just has to be waiting—with its meth labs and empty streets.

Mormonism is young. Most Jews and Christians are used to having their religion comfortably shrouded in a deep haze of time, which allows all kinds of reasonable people to be religious without necessarily having to come face-to-face with the "historical" events of their faith at all. For example, in order to believe in the commandment to honor thy father, it's *not* necessary to believe that the Ten Commandments were written on stone tablets and carried by Moses down from Mount Sinai.

But Joseph Smith founded his religion in 1830, and died in 1844. You can still find cast-iron frying pans that old. And having a frying pan from the same era as the founding prophet of your religion—not to mention endless letters, journals, newspapers, and public records—makes belief complicated. The church has a deserved reputation for secrecy about its temple rituals, but its history is mostly in the public domain—warts and all.

This lends Mormon faith a sort of defiance. Yes, the believer knows that Joseph Smith—the Prophet, Seer, and Revelator—was arrested for fraud not long before he received his visit from the angel Moroni revealing the gold plates. Yes, the believing Mormon knows that *The Book of Mormon* contains all sorts of language and plotlines lifted from nineteenth-century fiction. This doesn't necessarily bother Mormons, just as the plagiarism in *The Urantia Book* did not disqualify its wisdom in the minds of Urantians. Religion, after all, is not science. A leap of faith is just that—a leap.

At first, this stalwart quality of belief made the Mormon Eden seem to me irreconcilably different from all the other Edens proposed by other seekers. The others challenged themselves to prove their faith using the rules of reason. The charm of their stories was in the details, proofs, and interpretations. Mormon believers, who had already made the leap of faith, did not require elaborate maps and rationalizations. So, what fun were they?

But really, every Eden seeker, no matter how much of a scientist he considered himself to be, always had that little moment of faith on which their whole idea hinged. Some moments were not so little. Warren's article of faith: the North Pole was once land. Delitzsch's: rivers are really canals. Landon West was absolutely convinced that sin had taken over the world. Sayce believed a freshwater river was really salt. Willcocks: irrigation and civilization are the same thing. Heyerdahl hopped into a reed boat that could easily have turned into a sponge and sunk, only on the basis of an unproved belief: that reeds harvested in August wouldn't absorb water. *Believe this much, and I can lead you the rest of the way.* Joseph Smith's leap of faith may have been a mile wide, and Sayce's just an inch or two, but once faith is involved—as it must be when you are talking about the Bible—how different could two Eden seekers really be?

What made Smith's Eden unique was that unlike Sayce, Delitzsch, or Tse, Joseph Smith had hundreds of followers who believed that he was in direct communication with God, and his words were enough to move them to action. So this Eden story was writ especially large, and its repercussions were long lasting. It began in the 1830s, when Smith's followers picked up and moved from New York to Ohio to Missouri.

This was a big deal. Missouri's proximity to Indian country made it both dangerous and enticing—one of the main goals of Mormonism was to convert the Indians, whom they called Lamanites, and whom they believed to be descendants of a wayward ancient prophet. Smith declared Missouri "the promised land" before he'd actually been there. When he did make a scouting trip, with a small band of trusted leaders, he could see that the place had problems.

"Although [Missouri], according to the prophets, is to become like Eden or the garden of the Lord, yet, at present it is as it were but a wilderness and desert." The Indians weren't interested; the country was unfriendly. Nevertheless, he maintained his position that Missouri was the "center place" where Christ would return to Earth, and the city of Zion would be built in the last days. And to mark the territory, he planned to build a temple. The land purchased for the temple lay on a small hill half a mile out of town and just south of the existing road.

With much pomp and circumstance, Smith and his small advance team assembled to lay the cornerstones. The best shrub-oak tree that could be found nearby—about ten inches in diameter at the stump end—was chopped, trimmed, and cut off at a suitable length. After numerous speeches, twelve men, representing the twelve apostles, carried the tree to the temple lot.

One of Smith's companions selected the best small rough stone he could find, carried it in one hand to the spot, prepared a place in the dirt for it, and then—after one last speech—placed it in the ground. The twelve men then rested the shrub oak on the stone and raised it up. Ezra Booth, one of Smith's companions, described the ceremony for a local paper. "And there was laid down the first stone and stick, which are to form an essential part of the splendid city of Zion." From objects as lowly as stones and sticks would come great kingdoms of God.

Passersby would be able to identify the splendid city by two carvings Smith made into the ground on either side of the shrub oak: T for "Temple," and on the east side the word "ZOM —for "Zomas," which, according to Smith, was the original word for "Zion." Whatever their etymology, these inscriptions stood for potential. Smith and his leaders returned to Ohio, bringing word of the new paradise ready to be found in Independence. Even then, it seemed a little hard to believe.

But streams of Mormons kept moving to Jackson County anyway, much to the anger of Missouri's "old settlers." Mormons kept to themselves, seemed to answer only to one man—Smith—and insisted on preaching to the Indians. Missouri was a border state, and the Mormons were antislavery, so their increasing numbers jeopardized any fragile balance the state had been able to maintain.

Tension rose, accusations flew, and on October 31, 1833, fifty citizens of Jackson County assembled in a mob ten miles west of Independence, and demolished the houses of twelve Mormon families. The mob sent the women and children screaming off into the woods, where they scattered in every direction. Two Mormon men caught unawares were beaten within an inch of their lives with stones and clubs. The mob dispersed at three o'clock in the morning, but struck again a few days later. This time, 150 women and children fled to the prairie, where they wandered for several days.

According to Joseph Smith's official history of his church, as the Saints fled Jackson County, the sky was full of light: "All heaven seemed enwrapped in splendid fireworks." It's not clear whether he was referring to shooting stars or to gunfire. But he is certainly describing the Garden of Eden. Streaks of light "cut and twist up like serpents writhing." The scenery "might be compared to the falling figs or fruit when the tree is shaken by a mighty wind." It's as if all the archetypal elements of the story of Eden—heaven, the fruit, the snake, the tree—had been whirled together in a tornado and released onto the Earth, where they seemed at once familiar and strange. The scene is one of terror, foreshadowing the devastation of the end-time, described in the Book of Revelation, "when the sun shall become black like sack cloth of hair, the moon like blood; and the stars fall to the earth." But there's also a certain beauty to the expulsion, and a sense of necessity.

Eden always had to be connected to the *next* destination. When Eden was ahead of the Saints, it was the perfect place, the land promised by their leader to his flock. When they arrived in Eden, it was an almost communist utopia: everyone's role was assigned, and people built houses together and went to church. When they were kicked out of Eden and moved on, it became their rallying cry. The exile from Jackson County seemed brutal and permanent, and the need for a new home close by was urgent.

But where to gather next? Having already declared Jackson County to be the former Eden and future Zion, Smith could not reuse the image for a new settlement. But there was another sacred place on Earth, waiting to be discovered. And this time the story came not from the Bible, but from the Mormons' own scriptures.

Before the place came the word: Adam-ondi-Ahman, which is supposed to mean something like "place of Adam" or "Adam-blessed-there." Smith claimed that this word, like other non-English words in *The Book of Mormon,* came to him directly from God. Some he translated. "Deseret" meant "honeybee," and it has come to be a symbol of Mormon industriousness. "Nauvoo," the name of an important Illinois settlement, meant "beautiful place" and was supposed to come from "old Hebrew."

In *Doctrine and Covenants,* the collection of Smith's revelations that is a crucial piece of Mormon scripture, God describes Himself as: "the holy One of Zion, who hath established the foundations of Adam-ondi-Ahman." But "Adam-ondi-Ahman" is more commonly heard among today's Mormons in a hymn of the same name, written in 1832. In it, Adam-ondi-Ahman has a magical, otherworldly quality. "This earth was once a garden place/With all her glories common/And men did live a holy race/And worship Jesus face to face/In Adam-ondi-Ahman." You don't get the sense that it's a real town on a map.

But, as tension between Mormons and Missouri's "old settlers" persisted, Adam-ondi-Ahman began, miraculously, to materialize. Danger seemed to heighten the nostalgia for a more perfect place and time. Smith knew his followers needed more than a hazy sense of theological security; they needed an actual home. Gradually but unmistakably, like the emergence of a color image on a blank sheet of photographic paper, that home appeared. In one of Smith's regular revelations from God—spoken and set into type in Ohio, then passed west by the Mormon press—the Lord, speaking through Smith in 1835, referred to Adam-ondi-Ahman as a "valley." It was the place where Adam called together his "righteous relations" and blessed them for the final time before he died, three years later.

But where was this valley? The following year, the Missouri state legislature agreed to set aside land "expressly for the Mormons," for their own safety. The legislature created two new counties, Caldwell and Daviess, about forty miles northwest of the Jackson County border, out of Eden. Mormons had settled rough land before, and they took up the challenge.

Two years later, in May 1838, Smith himself visited the home of one of these early pioneers, Lyman Wight. Smith approved of the spot, along a bend in the Grand River. He thought the tree-lined bluffs and rolling hills made the place suitable for settlement. And he revealed that this spot was hereby "named by the Lord Adam-ondi-Ahman, because, said he, it is the place where Adam shall come to visit his people." Once the place had been blessed by Smith, many settlers began to arrive, despite the pouring rain.

Only a month later, on June 28, a ceremony was held making Adam-ondi-Ahman an official church settlement. A president, bishop, and high council were appointed. Then everyone sang the well-known hymn "Adam-ondi-Ahman." The words, written six years before, must have seemed eerily right in their pristine, protected new home.

But no sooner could they get settled than trouble came again for the Saints. Despite the claims of the legislature, there were Missourians in the new counties who did not want the influx of Mormon settlers. Riots broke out in nearby Gallatin. In Adam-ondi-Ahman, Smith and hundreds of his Saints dug in their heels and prepared to defend themselves. Having given up on Eden, in Independence, Smith was not about to sit back and let Adam-ondi-Ahman be taken from him. The Saints formed militias, some still so controversial that the official church denies their existence, and pledged to drive all dissenters out of Daviess County—dead or alive.

In the midst of the military gathering, Smith paused to take a small group of church elders out for a walk just outside the main town plot. "Brethren, come go along with me, and I will show you something." They paused on a beautiful spot of land 300 feet above the Grand River. The perfect spring green spread out before them in all directions. Said an elder, "It was one of the most beautiful places I ever beheld." Smith asked them to follow him a little way off the path. He pointed out three outcroppings of stone, one above them, one ahead, and one slightly behind them.

"Here," said Smith, "is the place where Adam offered up sacrifice after he was cast out of the garden." Smith climbed up on one of the rocks and began to preach. In three tumultuous years, Adam-ondi-Ahman had gone from being a vaporous idea to being a specific rock. In Smith's conception, Adam's altar was a place of peace, an indication of gratitude to God for rescuing him from a tormented Eden—hardly the shameful bloodbath it was at the Creation Museum. Adam's altar was also the end of the road: he had stayed put and raised countless generations in this refuge, which now had his name. Not only had Adam sacrificed on this rock, so had the Nephites, a mythical ancient tribe from the Book of Mormon, when they passed through that exact spot in their exile. And now the Saints themselves had happened upon this stone in their time of trial.

But if Smith thought that tying the history of his Saints to the actual soil of upper Missouri would help keep them there, let them live out their generations in peace like Adam after he left the Garden, he was wrong. This time, the Mormons did put up a fight. But in the end, they were again run out of town. Once again, they had found perfection, and once again they were condemned to exile.

In 2007, Adam-ondi-Ahman was not on the regular Missouri highway map. But once I reached Gallatin on Highway 13, yellow-on-blue road signs started to appear, advertising the Historical Site of the Church of Latter-day Saints. The road continued through mostly flat farmland, where billboards address the road's customary travelers: "Want More Yield—Try

GenuTech!" "Winterize Your Lawn Sprinkler." The actual pre-serve, more than 600 acres of church-owned property, looked like a well-kept state park.

Turning off the two-lane highway onto winding, eggshell-colored gravel roads, cars are forced to slow way down. First I arrived at a small viewing point and picnic area called Valley Over-look. Behind whitewashed rail fences, groves of chestnut, oak, and beech trees had been planted at regular intervals, with uniform circles of mulch around each one. Four young missionaries lived in a tiny house on the grounds and took care of the place. Many signs discouraged "overnight parking or camping," and noted that the gates to the park area closed at dusk. And what about the altar? The rock where Joseph Smith stood to preach?

The official plaque for visitors did not have much to say. "The exact location of the structure is not known today and there is no visual evidence remaining." Since the overlook was still far from the part of Adam-ondi-Ahman thought to be the altar site, the sign seemed to discourage visitors from even looking for visual evidence of Adam's altar. Eden had vanished—though not as violently as it had in the Creation Museum. Instead of being washed away by a "global cataclysm," Mormon Eden was being taken apart quietly, piece by piece.

Joseph Smith had transformed Adam-ondi-Ahman from an idea to a thing when it suited his followers' needs. In 2007, the Church of Jesus Christ of Latter-day Saints was trying to reverse itself. The two Garden of Eden sites in Missouri—Independence (Eden) and Adam-ondi-Ahman (Zion)—both were being dematerialized. They had been places; now they were becoming ideas. That was what I had failed to understand at the visitors center in Independence.

Near the end of the tour, our guide, Hermana Cameron, asked the group, "What is Zion?" "What," not "Where."

Three somber-looking teenage girls, their parents, and I sat on rough-hewn but shellacked wooden benches in front of her. We faced an immaculate diorama of an early Missouri Mormon settler using a wood plane on a fence post. Hermana Cameron, in a navy blue dress that left only her head and hands visible, clutched her copy of *The Book of Mormon* and smiled encouragingly at the girls.

"It's a place where my family can be together," offered one girl in a black T-shirt, with a long, dark ponytail.

"It's where everyone is in the church so no one can hurt us anymore," said the oldest of the three. The third girl picked at her rolled-up jeans and mumbled something; the only word I heard was "spirit."

"Wow," said our guide, turning to the adults. "I don't mean to leave you folks out, but that pretty much covers it!"

Nobody mentioned anything about Zion's being a splendid city on a small hill just outside of town. At the final stop of the tour, I learned why. Hermana Cameron led us to a corner of the visitors' center where upholstered chairs sat facing a wall of flat-panel screens, watched over by a white plaster statue of Joseph Smith. "This is my favorite part of the tour," she said, and she started the video presentation, which was about the expansion of the church.

Church presidents gave speeches predicting that they would convert most of South America; then came footage of happy missionaries and natives, smiling, worldwide, after receiving the word of the Lord. The narrator intoned, "People around the world are learning to build Zion in their families and church communities, and to find Zion in their hearts."

In the twenty-first century, Smith's church is a vast institution with billions of dollars in assets and 13 million members worldwide. A religious institution like this doesn't want to be nailed down, so to speak. In the 1830s, Zion was not "in our hearts"; it was a city of "stone and stick" in Jackson County, Missouri. But if the church was going to make any headway in Montevideo, it was going to have to go easy on Missouri.

The Mormon Mitt Romney's 2007 campaign for the Republican presidential nomination put the Church of Jesus Christ of Latter-day Saints in an unfamiliar position: in the limelight. Reporters wanted to know just how crazy Mormons were, and they had several litmus-test questions for Romney: can you marry more than one wife? (No.) Do you have to wear sacred under-garments? (Yes, officially.) Is the Garden of Eden in Missouri? Romney hedged. Mormon experts disagreed. The church tried to focus instead on what Mormons had in common with evan-gelical Christianity, and therefore with a large chunk of the vot-ing public. They narrowed their promotional material down to only two talking points: "Jesus Christ and Strong Families." In the summer of 2007, an official statement simply declared the question of Eden's location unimportant.

"Some doctrines are more important than others and might be considered core doctrines. For example, the precise location of the Garden of Eden is far less important than doctrine about Jesus Christ and His atoning sacrifice." Historically, it's not surprising that the Church of Jesus Christ of Latter-day Saints would blur the edges of the map of Eden. The evangelical Christians had obliter-ated Eden in the Flood. Officially, Catholicism still endorses belief in the Garden of Eden as a literal place, but it does not specify a precise location. For Protestants, placing Eden somewhere in southern Iraq has become commonplace, but there are no church tours, no shrines, no mention of Qurna's Tree of Knowledge in any official church literature.

It's a good thing the Mormon elder Alvin R. Dyer wasn't alive to witness his beloved church's dismissal of Eden. In the 1960s, Dyer, a member of the Quorum of the Twelve Apostles, the highest level of church authority, convinced the church's president, David O. McKay, to purchase and preserve the land associated with Missouri's Mormon history. Dyer's book, *The Refiner's Fire: Historical High-lights of Missouri,* contains the fruits of a lifetime of research. Not only does he document "visual evidence" of Adam-ondi-Ahman; he maps, illustrates, catalogs, and cross-references mountains of it: Lyman Wight's original cabin, the temple lot, and the stone altars, both "Adamic" and "Nephite." During Dyer's lifetime, all these relics, except the altars themselves, still existed. But the disappear-ance of the three stones is the exception that proves the rule. By way of explanation, Dyer offers a bit of folklore that has nothing to do with worldwide expansion or political campaigns. It simply has to do with one old man named Clayt Barlow.

Barlow lived near Adam-ondi-Ahman and kept a small museum of objects he found there, including cast-iron pots, kitchen utensils, part of a rake, and shovels. Barlow claimed that in 1922, an itinerant farmer named Joe Miller passed through town—a good worker, but "kind of odd and strange," and given to rambling around the hills at night. Said Barlow, "I don't know what he was hunting for, but he found something and he shipped it away." Later, Barlow helped Miller unload some surprisingly heavy, mysterious packages from a wagon into a waiting boxcar. It took five men to lift them. Barlow didn't think anything of it at the time, and not until Miller was out of town did anyone notice that the sacred stones were gone.

The veneration of the altars, however, didn't disappear so easily. Like the older visitors who had told Hermana Cameron that Independence was the Garden of Eden, Mormon tourists at Adam-ondi-Ahman knew where to go to look for the altars, despite the discouraging blandness of the official sign. While the lore of the Missouri Eden is still around, this Mormon generation is suspended between the earthly history of Alvin Dyer and Clayt Barlow and the worldly rhetoric of church officials. A family from Independence—a father with three young sons and a bespectacled teenage daughter on crutches—told me that on a previous visit to Adam-ondi-Ahman, missionaries told them where to find the unmarked altar site. They offered to show me the way.

I followed them away from the gravel-lined viewing area, along a narrow footpath carved into the hillside, and down to the valley floor. We arrived at a small clearing that certainly looked less manicured than the designated parking areas. Whatever "visual evidence" there ever had been of an altar was now only rock, and rocks come and go. There's no one who can say whether the same rocks that Smith claimed for Adam are still there.

But there certainly were lots of rocks. Some of them were moss-covered and seemed to emerge from deep in the soil; others had been picked up and placed, not very carefully, on wet grass or in the middle of a path. Some people say that local farmers use the site as a way to get rid of troublesome rocks in their fields: just lug them over to this spot and they'll disappear into cars with Utah license plates. Other people deny that Mormon tourists would take holy relics as souvenirs.

The view from this rounded hill below the parking area was still perfect, completely green forests and fields unbroken by any human evidence, except the odd rumbling sound of farming equipment out of sight in the distance. After taking pictures of each other in the famous setting, father and daughter turned back up the path to return to their car.

"But Dad, I want to find the Nephite altar!" shouted the black-haired youngest boy over his shoulder as he ran farther down into the valley. His family paused and waited for him a moment longer.

The boy found a perfectly square rock that was inexplicably embedded in the ground, like a cornerstone. It was also a different color from its neighbors—yellower. He was convinced it must be part of the altar. Maybe because it was too big to unobtrusively remove, he wanted to take a picture of it. His father relented and brought him the camera.

The older sister hadn't said a word until that moment. "But, Dad," she whispered, peering down at the stone as her brother took its picture, "that might not even be *it*!"

"I know," said her father, and winked at her, "but it's good for him."

13

The Beginning or the End?

"IN THE BEGINNINGS" were going out of style. By the 1950s, everyone in the world of Biblical archaeology had finally agreed that the first eleven chapters of the Book of Genesis—including the creation, Eden, Cain and Abel, the Flood, Noah's Ark, and everything up to the Book of Job—were out of bounds for investigation. These stories came from Mesopotamian oral traditions. They had first been told before writing was invented, so trying to confirm or disprove them was like trying to retrace your steps in a game of "telephone." Genesis should be considered literature, not history.

Biblical archaeology had to draw such lines to separate itself from the bogus Biblical discoveries that continually showed up in the news, usually found by someone who resembled archaeology's fictional nemesis, Indiana Jones, a little too closely. It was an ongoing battle. In a September 2007 editorial in the *Boston Globe*—unfortunately headlined "Raiders of the Faux Ark"—Eric Cline, a distinguished professor and archaeologist, put it this way: "When most archaeologists and biblical scholars hear that someone has (yet again) discovered Noah's Ark, they roll their eyes and get on with their business." Real Biblical archaeologists, Cline wrote, have rules. They must present detailed research plans, submit proposals to peer review, and deal with the proper authorities. And you absolutely cannot get peer-review approval to find the Garden of Eden.

In contrast, Biblical archaeology *was* still trying to confirm the Book of Joshua, a section of the Old Testament that was compiled at a later date. Many serious studies have tackled the question whether Joshua did or did not fight the battle of Jericho, and whether the walls did or did not come tumbling down. But the Book of Genesis was out.

So I was surprised, to say the least, to find the name of a real live archaeologist in the pages of *Smithsonian* magazine in 1987 under the headline: "Has the Garden of Eden Been Located at Last?" Juris Zarins, a professor of archaeology at Southwest Missouri State University, contended that Eden had been located in southern Mesopotamia, under the waters of the Persian Gulf. Who *was* this guy, what was his game, and how had he gotten away with it?

In photographs, Zarins looked nothing like Indiana Jones. He was tall and skinny, with prematurely white hair falling into his eyes. By the time I started looking into his theory, he had retired from his university. But some of his classes there had been taped; clearly he was much more of a professor than Indy had been. In the classroom, he paced restlessly, cracking jokes, speaking in enthusiastic bursts, and constantly soliciting responses from his students. Friends and colleagues called him Juri. (The unusual name is one remnant of his Latvian heritage.)

Zarins would later become well known for his 1992 discovery of the Arabian city of Ubar, a center of the ancient "frankincense trail" long thought to be mythical; T. E. Lawrence had called the city "the Atlantis of the sands." Zarins's find made the front page of the *New York Times* and was named one of the top ten discoveries of the decade by *Discover, Time,* and *Newsweek.* But even then, Zarins demurred, always was careful to correct interviewers who called Ubar a "city." A lost city sounded glamorous, he said, but Ubar was in fact a whole region and a group of people: "People always overlook that." His wife may have thought he should take more credit. In an article in the *St. Louis Dispatch* from 1992, she was quoted as saying: "When we saw the first Indiana Jones movie, I said, 'Juri, they've made a movie about you.'"

This down-to-earth Midwestern professor's idea of Eden did not involve talking snakes or flaming swords. It had nothing to do with the biological origin of man. He left that to the paleontologists.

According to Zarins, the Eden story was "a highly condensed and evocative account of perhaps the greatest revolution that ever shook mankind: the shift from hunting-gathering to agriculture." How had he gotten here? Although Zarins's theory ended up at the Persian Gulf, it began in Saudi Arabia, in about 6,000 B.C.

Arabia would not usually spring to mind when you think of Eden. Much of the peninsula is now desert, the most forbidding part of which has been known for centuries as the Empty Quarter. It's also called the "anvil of the sun": this is the parched windswept expanse that nearly killed Lawrence in *Lawrence of Arabia*. Since 1932, when the Saud family took over a large chunk of the Arabian Peninsula, the new nation had been relatively closed to any exploration unrelated to oil. But by the late 1970s and early 1980s, huge oil wealth sparked an unprecedented construction boom, and archaeologists raced ahead of the bulldozers to survey the ancient desert before it was plowed under.

Zarins, like Heyerdahl, made a point of going where nobody else had gone. He had already been doing fieldwork in the Middle East, and one of his classmates from the University of Chicago, Dr. Abdullah H. Masry, had become Saudi Arabia's director of antiquities and museums. So off Zarins went to the Saudi desert. He spent ten years in the Empty Quarter, and found it not nearly as empty as everyone had thought. For one thing, it was full of dry riverbeds, called wadi in Arabic. Zarins also called them "fossil rivers," and indeed they turned out to be flowing with archaeological abundance. The wadis, Zarins learned, were integral to everything that had happened in early Arabian life. Along their banks, Zarins unearthed thousands of animal bones and stone tools, which dated from around 6,000 B.C.—clear indication of human occupation.

Human life was seasonal: when the rivers were high, food was plentiful; when there was less rain, fewer artifacts were created. For a time, along the riverbanks, these cycles continued. But then, sometime around 5,000 B.C., Zarins noticed, Arabia seemed to go through a more permanent drying up. Hunter-gatherers started to go farther and farther away from the rivers; fewer animal bones and stone tools were deposited. That's when the nomadic groups turned around and started to head east again, back to Mesopotamia, where, Zarins believed, they had come from originally. Zarins had worked in Iraq in the 1970s, and he was "fluent in cuneiform." So he, too, turned back to Mesopotamia and tried to figure out what happened next.

Migrating from Arabia to Mesopotamia would have been a good idea for the nomads. In 5,000 B.C., the rivers of lower Mesopotamia were flowing at their fullest; the Fertile Crescent was at its most fertile. That was Eden, the home of Neolithic Adams and Eves, who were heirs to its natural bounty. Southern Mesopotamia had everything they needed, "every beast of the field, every fowl of the air, every tree that is good for food."

Zarins knew from oceanographic studies that in 5,000 B.C., the region of southern Iraq had looked very different. The Persian Gulf—or the Arabian Gulf or the Sumerian Gulf, depending on your point of view—did not exist. There would have been small waterways, probably, rivers and streams, but the ocean came north only as far as the narrow Strait of Hormuz. That meant it had been possible for the hunter-gatherers to walk with their camels from Arabia, straight across to, say, Iraq, along the banks of those dry fossil rivers. All these lands were united; Thor Heyerdahl could have traveled to all of his ancient civilizations without a boat.

In the 1980s, Zarins used a new form of technology to show the route of this ancient exchange: aerial photographs from NASA's LANDSAT satellite-imaging program. Zarins's LANDSAT photographs zeroed in on the northern coast of the Persian Gulf, the place where Saudi Arabia, Iraq, and Iran meet. The Tigris and the Euphrates meet in the center of the image. To the right, the Karun River flows out of Iran to join them. To the left, Zarins and his crew had highlighted Wadi Batin, a fossil river stretching almost the entire width of the Arabian Peninsula, making an east-west beeline directly for southern Mesopotamia. Zarins named the Karun the Gihon and Wadi Batin the Pishon. Here were four rivers joining together into one river, which flowed together for a short distance until it emptied into the Gulf. If it weren't for the fact that it's covered by water, the land beneath the Gulf would indeed be in exactly the position of Eden in medieval maps, with the perfect four-armed river that so many early Eden seekers despaired of finding. How did it get underwater?

Eventually the hunter-gatherers from Arabia made it all the way along the Pishon back to Mesopotamia—only to discover that their old familiar haunts had changed forever. Agriculture had arrived. Somebody thought to plant a seed, instead of traveling in search of the plant. Though blessed with nature's bounty, Adam and Eve had chosen instead to experiment with creating it for themselves.

This was the moment where humans began to control their environment, instead of being controlled by it. What bigger transition could there be? All of human history depends on that first person who realized: *I can do this myself.* It's the source of all other major societal transitions: the end of nomadism, the iron age, the industrial revolution. But it's also one of the trickiest transitions to investigate, because it happened before the invention of writing. Archaeologists call it the "silent revolution." Scientists think agriculture began, roughly simultaneously, in perhaps half a dozen societies all over the world, including China and Mexico. And wherever there was a transition from one form of subsistence to another, said Zarins, there were signs of conflict. In the Middle East, he wrote, the gap between agriculture and writing was particularly wide. People "crossed over in a gradual way to agriculture" approximately 12,000 years ago. Writing from Egypt and Sumer appeared only 5,000 years ago, so "the events of the gradual agricultural evolution didn't enter the historical record." That was what made the Sumerian stories of their ancestors—as preserved in the Bible—so exciting. They were "likely residual stories" from this mysterious period.

Here's how Zarins's theory lines up with the Book of Genesis. To the Arabian hunter-gatherers, the Mesopotamian farmers must have looked like reckless heretics. They had eaten from the Tree of

Agricultural Knowledge. By harnessing the power of creation for themselves, they had "challenged God's very omnipotence." The sin: arrogance, putting their own knowledge above that of God. For this, they had to be punished.

In the Bible, the punishment comes from God: "Therefore the Lord God sent him forth from the garden of Eden, to till the ground from whence he was taken." To put it simply, God tells humanity: "If you think you can do better, go ahead and try; see how you like it." In Zarins's story, retribution came instead from other people: the nomadic hunter-gatherers. There must have been dramatic clashes—even battles—between the nomadic groups, defending their way of life, and the agriculturalists fighting to protect their lands. It must have been chaos, says Zarins: values and lifestyles were questioned, clans and tribes were dislocated. "Cursed is the ground for thy sake; in sorrow shalt thou eat of it all the days of thy life."

Then, to make matters worse, somewhere around 5,000 B.C., the seas beyond Mesopotamia began to rise, as they did around the world. Gradually, water covered that fertile flood bed of the four rivers with deep, salty gulf water. The Eden of the Neolithic farmers had been wiped out. Ahead of them were angry nomads; behind them were the rising tides geologists call the Flandrian Transgression.

Geologically speaking, a "transgression" is what happens when ocean levels rise past their accustomed shorelines, causing land to be flooded. This can happen if the land sinks, or if the level of water in the oceans rises greatly—say, as a result of melting glaciers. Scientists track transgressions by examining the different sediments present in the geologic record: some are associated with sea, some with land. The scientific word has entirely unintended Biblical associations: water "transgressed" its normal levels, just as man "transgressed" the boundaries God set in place.

This version of the Fall of Man was reminiscent of William Warren, whose Adam and Eve "coveted experimental knowledge," of Urantia's magical crops, and of Callaway's Eve, who bravely chose progress. But the pre-Sumerian legend is much sadder and more ambivalent. The agriculturalists—who, let's remember, are the survivors in this story—have still retained a legend in which they are the guilty party. They are both the hero and the villain.

As the displaced Neolithic farmers moved north, over centuries, the story of their lost natural paradise passed from the oral histories into the first written accounts of the Sumerians. "The Sumerians always claimed that their ancestors came out of the sea, and I believe they literally did," said Zarins. This was the prehistory of the Sumerians that Thor Heyerdahl had been looking for in his reed boat.

The Sumerians walked north ahead of the advancing seas, along the way telling stories of their vanished land. And eventually, about 3,000 years later, the stories were written down in the Bible. The writers of Genesis, whoever they were, spun the ancient stories into monotheistic terms, turning "Edin" into Eden, farmers into the sinning Adam and Eve, and fertile fields into forbidden fruit.

By then the physical Eden, the site of the agricultural revolution, was completely underwater. So, incidentally, were most of the other Edens of southern Iraq. Scientists believe that at its highest point, the Gulf would have completely covered the low-lying plain of Mesopotamia: past Sayce's salt river at Eridu, past Delitzsch's canals, past Heyerdahl's marshlands, past Qurna and the Tree of Knowledge, all the way up to the now landlocked town of Amara. (That's where William Willcocks was held captive on his river steamship.) This kind of theory has a strangely blanketing effect, making disputes over rivers, canals, and boundaries academic, water under the bridge.

Part of the reason I was fascinated with Zarins's idea is that I'd never seen it written about anywhere except in the *Smithsonian*. He'd never published his own version of the Garden of Eden theory—a theory that even the Biblical archaeology watchdog Eric Cline had called "reasonably plausible." (High praise, coming from him.) Instead, it seemed, Zarins had simply continued teaching classes, digging the Arabian peninsula, and writing scholarly reviews of early Mesopotamian archaeology. All this lent his idea a certain undogmatic appeal. The annals of Eden-seeking were full of Joseph Smiths and William Warrens, so modesty was a surprising quality, to say the least. Could this be true? To find out, I needed to find Dr. Zarins. In 2010, I finally reached him by phone in Dhofar, Oman, where he has continued to work as an archaeologist in his retirement from Southwest Missouri State.

I asked him why he'd never written up his theory of the Garden of Eden. "I never had time," he told me. "There was always something else to do." It is hard to get more modest than that. But his comment still didn't entirely explain why he wasn't out there trumpeting his theory to everyone who would listen. Zarins was content to let it lie there, under the Persian Gulf.

He'd never set out to find Eden in the first place. "I just sort of fell into it," he told me. "And then once you have one piece of the puzzle, it becomes like a detective thing," and you just get addicted to putting it all together. Plenty of other Eden seekers had tried this line: Callaway's remark, "It appeared there was nothing for me to do but give the wisdom of Melchizedek to humanity," springs to mind. But from Zarins, I bought it.

He certainly did not seem to have a religious stake in this fight. He wasn't out to prove that the Bible was the Word of God. "I think the Bible was written down during the Babylonian captivity, in about 550 B.C." And of course, Zarins told me with a chuckle, "The first eleven books of Genesis are all Mesopotamian. Plagiarized! Nobody gives them credit."

That was how he'd gotten away with investigating the books of Genesis that Biblical archaeology deemed untouchable: he wasn't a Biblical archaeologist. He wasn't trying to extrapolate all of human history from the pages of a religious text. He did feel that "archaeological evidence actually helps us understand aspects of Genesis 1–11." But since those books were essentially Mesopotamian, understanding them had "little to do with the Bible, but a lot to do with southern Iraq archaeology, history, and cuneiform studies." Fair enough. Symbolism and theology were far out of

Zarins's jurisdiction as a scientist. For him, Eden was a detective story, not a manifesto.

There was a moral to the story, however, one that even a pragmatist like Zarins could see. If the "sin" of Zarins's Garden was the control of nature, we were only now suffering the punishment. Several millennia later, human control of nature had become so pervasive that we were affecting the atmosphere, the oceans, and the glaciers. And it started, arguably, with agriculture. This Eden was not so much the beginning as the beginning of the end. As Heyerdahl learned on Fatu-Hiva, there was no going back to a life of preagricultural bliss, no more relying on bountiful nature, or God. So Zarins had every right to say, "I told you so."

"It's right there, in the text—agriculture is a curse! And it's caught up with us! Now, with the green revolution, we're coming around to realize this. . . . But the Sumerians knew for thousands of years that agriculture was no good for us."

And that was about as far as he would go.

Unfortunately, his entirely appropriate refusal to make ideology out of archaeology may have doomed Zarins to watch others do just that. In addition to its scientific credibility, it seemed to me that Zarins's Eden was theologically convenient—though he'd never think about it this way. It was underwater, as Eden should be after Noah's Flood. And it actually came with its own flood story, endorsed by science—the Flandrian Transgression. (The medieval idea that Eden survived the Flood because it was on top of a very tall mountain had long ago gone out of style.)

He had even used a new form of scientific technology—the satellite photograph—to answer the age-old question about Pishon and Gihon. This lent credence to the belief of Biblical literalists everywhere that Eden *would* be found, eventually, when people looked hard enough in the right place with the right tools. The Reverend Professor Sayce would have been proud. Thus it is perhaps not surprising to read Calvin R. Schlabach, writing in the conservative Christian magazine *Focus,* praising Zarins's discovery. It was specific enough to serve as "a confirmation of the accuracy, historicity, and literal veracity of the Bible," and yet still conveniently inaccessible, so that "whatever remained [of the Garden] in Noah's day was certainly erased by that catastrophic, worldwide Flood." Like the theologians who'd praised Delitzsch for work he thought they'd hate, Schlabach was using Zarins's science to confirm his own ideology.

I asked Zarins if he'd heard this line of religious argument; he had. Did it bother him? "Nope," he laughed. Of his idea, he said, "Once it's done, people are going do with it whatever they want." If he tried to argue with every possible perversion of his work, he'd never get anything else done. This struck me as a much healthier attitude than that of Delitzsch.

Zarins was even willing to entertain other seekers. I was just the latest in a long line of people who'd sought him out. "People have been calling me about the Garden of Eden for the past eighteen years," he told me cheerfully. All those journal articles he'd written, all those college classes he'd taught—thcy couldn't compare to that one *Smithsonian* story by Dora Jane Hamblin in 1987. Said Zarins, joking, "It's the biggest story I ever wrote!" Who called? "Oh, everybody—Bible thumpers, scientists, everyone wants to try out their ideas on me."

I knew about a couple of these people. In the late 1990s, David Rohl and Michael Sanders both claimed to have found the Garden of Eden—in two different places—using real archaeology. They both had much higher "Indiana Jones" quotients than Zarins, but that didn't keep journalists from lumping them in with him. After all, three of anything is a trend, which explained an article in the Israeli magazine *Jerusalem Report* in 1999, announcing a "new Edenist" movement.

Rohl, whom one reporter described as a "non-practicing Catholic," had no patience with Biblical archaeology's strict limitations on which Biblical stories were historical and which were not: "I consider the Bible a historical document just like the writings of Herodotus." In 1999, he promised to prove it, by searching for the Garden of Eden. As Rohl was well aware, all the previous scholars searching for Eden had been looking for a spot where the "one river" of Eden splits into four separate "heads." He'd seen Zarins's LANDSAT photographs, which, if one had been willing to accept the Persian Gulf as a river, showed just that.

But Rohl did not accept Zarins's evidence. He noted that in Hebrew, Genesis used the word "rosh" to refer to the four rivers branching off from one river. And "rosh," as he translated it, meant "beginning, source, head." Thus, he believed, we should be looking for Eden not where the four rivers end, but where they begin. And rivers begin in mountains. His Eden was *north* of Mesopotamia, in present-day Iran, where the Tigris and the Euphrates "emerge from the highlands" of the Zagros Mountains. His Gihon was the Araxes, and his Pishon the Uizhun, both of which also begin in the Zagros, and flow east into the Caspian Sea.

Oddly, Rohl began gathering evidence for this northern Eden where everyone else began: in the south, with the ancient Sumerians. At a lecture in 1997, he exhibited a slide of the same "Adam and Eve seal" that Delitzsch had relied on to prove his southern Eden almost a century before. Rohl told his audience, "This isn't a made-up image; it isn't somebody's fictional idea of Adam and Eve. This is a Sumerian cylinder-seal impression. It's a genuine artifact from the ancient Near East. It's extra-biblical."

There were two problems with using this artifact as evidence for Eden in Iran: (1) the artifact did not come from Iran, and (2) the cylinder seal actually had nothing to do with Adam and Eve. In the years since Delitzsch and Sayce had pored over the limestone cylinders in the British Museum, so many variations of the scene with the man, woman, tree, and snake had been found that the museum could definitely declare what it was: a 2,200-year-old image of a horned male god and his female worshipper, with the date palm and the snake between them possibly signifying fertility. The first eleven books of Genesis may be based on Mesopotamian mythology, but it was futile to try to trace a direct, specific connection between a horned god and Adam, or the snake of fertility and the snake of temptation. Besides, 2,200 years old was far too young for Eden. As the museum's materials put it: "There is no reason to connect the scene with the story in the Book of Genesis." Extra-biblical, indeed.

But Rohl proceeded doggedly, piecing together disparate ancient civilizations and borrowing Zarins's high-tech grand finale. In his documentary for the Discovery Channel, *In Search of Eden,* Rohl superimposed a four-square grid over a satellite map made by NASA, showing that his northern geography, too, conformed to the idealized four-quadrant geography of medieval Persian and European gardens.

His Eden began to appear in British, Canadian, Israeli, and American newspapers in 1999—along with his book, *Genesis: Legend of Civilization.* But even though Rohl called himself a Biblical scholar, other Biblical scholars gave him the cold shoulder. The journal *Biblical Archaeology Review,* which had published an article on Rohl's new theory of ancient Egyptian chronology in 1996, was having none of his Eden ideas. "The gist of our research back then was that he was wrong," the editor Stephen Feldman said, "so we have been reluctant to pay great attention to him now."

Rohl's only cheerleader in Biblical archaeology was David Ilan, a research archaeologist at Israel's Hebrew Union College. The same 1999 article in *Jerusalem Report* that had spotted the trend of "new Edenists" also reported that Ilan was organizing an "Eden in Jerusalem" conference to explore the trend, a conference at which Rohl would speak. Said Ilan: "In an era of so much uncertainty, of technology and confusion, people want to know where they come from. That's why this kind of science dazzles us." True enough. In September 1999, the *Montreal Gazette* reported that the "Eden in Jerusalem" conference had occurred. However, contacted in 2007, David Ilan admitted that it never had. "The idea was to get established archaeologists and Egyptologists to carry on a debate with David Rohl, but in the end, I couldn't convince them to play ball."

In 2007, Eric Cline wrote that Rohl's Eden argument was "not out of the question" but "seems no more probable than any other hypothesis," and less likely than that of Zarins. Zarins himself, asked to comment, felt he could afford to be gracious. "I don't discount what he is saying totally. There are interesting elements to his theory. But he's in the wrong place," he said at the time. "He's at the wrong end of the Euphrates." The Bible was a Sumerian story, and the Sumerians, it was universally agreed, lived in southern Iraq, not northern Iran. As Zarins told me, "[Rohl] has got the other end of it; he's confused." It was easy to get confused, Zarins allowed, because of the many disciplines you had to master to understand his theory.

"You have to be well-educated. If you don't understand the archaeology, if you don't understand the geology, if you don't understand the oceanography, the cuneiform, you are out of luck. All you can do is just put a statement out there and say, 'I believe it,' or 'I don't.' You have no way of checking." Zarins was after a logical explanation for events described in the Bible and elsewhere, an "independent" explanation that could be verified scientifically. Did the seas rise or didn't they? Did agriculture begin here? Were there clashes between agriculturalists and hunter-gatherers? These things can be investigated, with the Bible as a secondary source, without weighing in on whether or not God was involved.

Being at the "wrong end of the Euphrates" was about the best thing that could be said of the other "new Edenist" of 1999, Michael Sanders, the Yorkshire-born, California-based founder of the Mysteries of the Bible Research Foundation. Sanders was proud to be identified with Indiana Jones. Like Rohl, he was convinced the Garden of Eden lay at the northern end of the Tigris and Euphrates—in Turkey, though, not Iran. And he had the Indy-style overloaded résumé. Along with Eden, Sanders claimed to have found Noah's Ark, King Solomon's temple, the Tower of Babel, Sodom and Gomorrah, and the stone tablets of the Ten Commandments. There were, however, two essential differences between him and the mythical maverick who haunted the dreams of Eric Cline: "Indiana Jones has a stunt double. I do all my own exploration, and suffer all the injuries. Worst of all, Indiana Jones is better looking than me."

In March 2001, NBC broadcast two specials based on Sanders's expeditions: *Biblical Mysteries: Ark of the Covenant,* and *Biblical Mysteries: Sodom and Gomorrah.* Sanders explained that his expeditions were not religious endeavors. "I try to keep spirituality out of it. It's about scientific rational pursuit." Although he had no training in archaeology, and had been an early participant in Timothy Leary's LSD experimentation, Sanders, too, was frequently referred to as a "biblical scholar." He, too, had kept up with the work of other Edenists. He made extensive use of NASA's satellite photographs, like Zarins, and he shamelessly announced that because the technology is so advanced, there could be only one answer. "People have looked for 2,000 years to find [the rivers]. But new NASA satellite photographs show this exact configuration emerging from the desert in the north of the country."

Sanders, who placed a distant third in this three-way non-race for Eden, remained pugnacious toward Zarins, the front-runner. Sanders had not been to Turkey to check out his own Eden site, he wrote to me, because the Turkish government was "not pleased" with his desire to investigate something "pre-Islamic." Still, he was convinced that Zarins must be wrong. What about Zarins's perfect photograph of the four rivers? I asked him. Sanders was unimpressed. One river dividing into four, of which "even today two are named Tigris and Euphrates" would be "quite coincidental, to say the least." With that, Sanders put himself in league with William Warren, Landon West, and Tse Tsan Tai, seekers who dismissed present-day Iraq—and thereby most of modern science—out of hand.

"The problem with Zarins," Sanders wrote to me, "is the phrase, 'a river went out of/rose out of Eden.' Rivers originate in mountains, not in plains." Sanders was using another word from Genesis to back up Rohl's northern site. And yet, somehow, Rohl ended up to the east, in Iran, and Sanders to the west, in Turkey. Sanders claimed that his way was the only logical way to look at the words.

"The Biblical quote needs no 'interpretation' with this thesis, unlike every other one."

The Hebrew word "rosh" does indeed mean "head," or "beginning," (as in Rosh Hashanah, the beginning of the new year). But it certainly didn't follow that the Bible needs "no interpretation." Sanders's choice of "rose up" and Rohl's choice to focus on "rosh" instead of, say, the Sumerian word "Edin," which inarguably referred to lower Mesopotamia, struck me as just as much of an interpretation as anything else. By now, every word of the applicable verses had been subjected to this kind of scrutiny.

William Willcocks had "interpreted" that same phrase "a river rose out of Eden," to mean that water actually bubbled out of the ground, like a spring, in "Edin," Mesopotamia. And he would have bristled at anyone who accused him of not taking the Bible exactly at its word. There were plenty of one-word cautionary tales. Melchizedek could be the undercover emissary of Christ, or nobody at all. "Gofer" wood could be cypress, reeds, or yew. "Ararat" could be in Armenia or Iraq. "Mist" could be "free-flow irrigation." Just look how much trouble the various "literal" interpretations of the word "day" caused for William Jennings Bryan.

The trio of Zarins, Rohl, and Sanders illustrated something crucial about the search for Eden. Zarins had about the most legitimate evidence I'd ever seen, and that is saying quite a bit. But no matter how unassailable a theory of Eden seems, it will be assailed. The next Edenist will use your results as precedent, but violate all the assumptions that got you there. Gone are the days when Sayce and Delitzsch could carry on a subdued, scholarly disagreement about which of two similar canals in the same part of the same country might be the Biblical "Gihon." Now, if you're going to bother to put forward a theory about the Garden of Eden, it has to be big, and preferably on television.

Not just a revision is needed, but a total reversal of whatever came before: not the North Pole but Ohio; not Armenia but Florida; not Mesopotamia but Mongolia. Old knowledge must be flipped on its head. All of us are at "the wrong end of the Euphrates." That's because finding the Garden of Eden is, almost by definition, the creation of a new world.

Which may be why we keep doing it. I asked Juris Zarins one more time what was so fascinating about the story of the Garden of Eden. And he came right back at me: "You tell me, you're the one calling from halfway around the world!" He had a point.

14

Last Tree Standing

IN THE BEGINNING, long before the Sumerians arrived in their reed boats, Qurna was completely submerged. As time went on, the Gulf waters receded down to Basra, but Qurna didn't stay dry for long. Every few decades the Euphrates would explode beyond its banks, covering the Mesopotamian plains all the way to Amara again, leaving Qurna and its Tree of Knowledge entirely underwater.

When you read Qurna's history, a tidal feeling takes hold of the place: flood and retreat, flood and retreat. The much-beleaguered Iraqi marsh town always seemed to be a dividing line of sorts. It was the first place in Iraq captured by the British in 1916, and the place some wanted them to pull back to in 1921. Qurna got the best of whatever was coming and the worst of whatever was going. When Saddam Hussein briefly allowed foreign reporters into the country during the Iran-Iraq War, he brought them only as far as Qurna, close enough to Iran that he could blame its devastation on his longtime Persian enemies, but not close enough that they could see it was really Saddam himself who was wreaking havoc on his own country: eight years of war with Iran; the Kuwait debacle; the 1995 draining of the marshes; his attack on the Marsh Arabs, so vicious that the United Nations declared it genocide.

And then the Americans invaded. In the conflict that began in 2003 and surely will go on in some form for years to come, Qurna was once again an early entrance point for reporters, as if it were the center of a somewhat ill-advised publicity campaign. The stories that came out of Qurna after the invasion read eerily similar to those of generations of British and American travelers. Once again,

I went through the stark reports, looking for details that could tell me what had happened to this place, so central to the Eden story, a town where I still could not safely go and which, for all I knew about it, still felt as far away as the North Pole.

Older residents of Qurna still remembered their town's tourist past in the 1970s, when Thor Heyerdahl could attract an international crew and drink tea with the locals in the Garden of Eden Hotel. Even in the late 1990s, a few adventurous European travel companies were leading tours through southern Iraq. But in 2003, reporters seemed skeptical that such an hospitable atmosphere had ever existed. In a sure sign of disheartenment, the Garden of Eden Hotel was apparently renamed the Qurna Tourist Hotel in the late 1980s, then abandoned again. There were reports of an Adam's Ice Cream Stand, but nobody could find it.

Western journalists again professed surprise and disgust that nothing even remotely resembling a garden could be found in Qurna; there were only flat, trash-strewn lots. Once again, the town seemed like a sick joke perpetrated on the very idea of Eden—as one reporter put it, "about as far from idyllic as you can imagine." Dead fish floated on the river; human and animal feces littered the ground; even the sheep were dirty and mangy. The prevalence of disgusting details in the reports seemed to reflect a hope on the part of reporters that Qurna should have been somehow different or beautiful. Of course, Qurna looked like the contaminated battlefield it was.

But did Qurna's state of ruin make it less of an Eden? If the story of the Garden can be boiled down to origins, perfection, sin, and exile, then really the exile is the most important element, the one that makes all the other chapters fall into place. That's the essential paradox of the search. Eden has to be erased in order for it to be Eden. A paradise isn't paradise until it's lost. During the invasion, Qurna nearly had been lost.

By 2003, the town's population had swollen to about 250,000, with workers on the southern oil fields near Basra, making it really a small city. But the ratio of patients to doctors had actually gotten worse since 1920. According to the International Medical Corps Rapid Response Team, the eighteen doctors and sixty nurses at

Qurna's hospital served more than 500,000 people, from Qurna and the sprawling, makeshift villages nearby. In the immediate aftermath of the invasion, Qurna's hospital was thoroughly looted—electrical cables pulled out of the walls, doors torn off their hinges. Patients were afraid to enter the building, so the hospital shut down, leaving those 500,000 people to fend for themselves.

The bombings had killed hundreds, destroyed a bridge over the Euphrates, and left Qurna once again a city of crumbling mud huts along riverbanks, as it had been in Friedrich Delitzsch's time. So it was not a stretch to imagine, as I had, that the concrete park that had been built around the Tree of Knowledge would be wiped off the face of the Earth. After all, it was only made of wood and cement. True, the clearing on that spit of land between the Tigris and the Euphrates had been flooded several times since the 1940s, when Sir Norman Wright had designated the Tree an international symbol of peace. The park's tile and concrete floors, built in the 1970s, had cracked and warped; the stone walls were covered with graffiti—"Down with the U.S.A.! Down with Israel!"

The once famous wishing fountain contained neither water nor money. A set of stairs had been left, uselessly, in the middle of the plaza. Someone had built a raised prayer dais on one side of the park, but no one prayed there anymore. The sandbagged bomb shelter on the opposite side of the concrete expanse had clearly been of more use. The park hadn't escaped the desperate looting that was epidemic in the rest of the country after the invasion. Someone had removed the helpful sign explaining the site's convoluted history: apparently it was worth more as scrap metal.

Yet the park itself had survived. And so had the Tree of Knowledge—a bleached skeleton with yellowing branches that everyone called Adam's Tree. It seemed about to topple over, but it hadn't toppled yet. Qurna may have looked dismal, but every visitor to the place after 2003 seemed to find at least one Iraqi who still saw Qurna in a different light.

Kartan Adnan, a twenty-seven-year-old Qurna shopkeeper, insisted to a reporter that the Tree was "at least 2,000 years old and was here before the town was built." Reyahd al-Moussawi, who claimed lineage from the Prophet Muhammad, drew a neat synthesis between Eden in the Qur'an and Eden in Qurna: "The Garden of Eden is a paradise in heaven, but this is a part of paradise that came down to Earth." These people, survivors of at least two wars, a dictatorship, and genocide, called to mind the ghost of Sheikh Gubashi, who tugged on the British civil commissioner's sleeve in 1919 and expressed his earnest, urgent desire for something better.

An English teacher, Qassim Khalif, lamented the tragic state of the Garden: "Every generation was taught that this was the true Garden of Eden and this was Adam's Tree, the place where he first spoke to God. It is our truest hope that when peace comes to Iraq, the people of the world will come back here and pray again at Adam's Tree. They will be welcomed by us, as they always have."

When peace comes to Iraq, it could start in Qurna; everything started in Qurna. And Qurna starts with the Tree. It holds everything together, in its protected plaza in the center of the town, at the junction of the rivers, at the cradle of the world. Traditionally, it had been outsiders, like the soldiers of the Inland Water Transport, who didn't understand the Tree's unifying power. In 1919, they had looked on the Tree with amusement verging on derision. In April 2003, the soldiers of the First Battalion Royal Irish Regiment, who were the first to arrive and hold the town, seemed to have finally learned the lesson.

According to an embedded reporter, one of the regiment's early exploratory patrols took the soldiers up to the gates of the Tree of Knowledge Park. The kids who frequented the place invited them in, but they refused. Major Mike Murdoch, the officer in charge of the town, told his men of the humble concrete plaza, "It is no place for uniforms and weapons; it should never have been and it will not be now."

Could Murdoch be referring to the tree-breaking incident of 1920? Maybe that "storm in a teacup" had survived as a cautionary tale. The story had been buried in the archives of the *London Times*. No telegrams survived; no army reports mentioned it; nobody took pictures. Or maybe this was simply a gesture of piety: no guns in Eden, just in case. Either way, here was a small victory for Qurna and its Tree of Knowledge.

But another kind of invading party was coming to Qurna, one that the Royal Irish hadn't been expecting. In May 2003, some weeks after Major Murdoch made his announcement, officials of the Supreme Council for the Islamic Revolution in Iraq (SCIRI) took over the abandoned Garden of Eden Hotel. In the chaos immediately following the U.S. invasion, this Shia group, organized decades earlier in Iran, had moved smoothly to become the de facto government of all of southern Iraq. It did not, according to a reporter from the *London Times,* seem to appreciate the cultural significance of its Qurna headquarters. "Asked whether Ayatollah al-Hakim liked working in an office overlooking the Garden of Eden, one of his officials said disdainfully: 'It's not holy to Islam. It's only history you know.'"

Only history. In other words: *this nowhere town with its holy aspirations doesn't mean anything to me; I answer to Ayatollah Muhammad Baqr al-Hakim.* An offhand comment, to be sure, but one that put the official directly at odds with Qassim Khalif, Kartan Adnan, Reyahd al-Moussawi, and anyone else who'd professed a belief in Qurna's special status. The ayatollah's particular branch of Shia Islam would, in the coming months, crack down on things that Iraqis from Baghdad to Basra had regarded as completely normal—alcohol, music, unveiled women. Tree worship had always existed at the unofficial edges of organized religion. So if this ascetic, hard-line group considered the practice at all, it wasn't likely to be in a positive light.

For any ideologue, trees, stones, relics of any kind are suspicious, heretical. How can you control the meaning of a prayer to a tree? And yet, even in Qurna's darkest times, Iraqis still visited the Tree of Knowledge. A black-veiled woman named Zahra rode the local bus to Qurna with a friend; they took a few small pieces of the Tree's bark back with them, and left a prayer. A woman named Shalhub who came to pray at the Tree said, "My wish is that He will protect us from every disaster." Eleven-year-old Nasser Adnan knew the Tree's legend: "When I want to do well at school, I speak to it. It is specially put here by God."

"This is the tree of Adam. It is significant to all religions and to all people," said Hamida Mansour, age thirty. She lived in a small mud hut adjacent to the park, but she'd forbidden her five sons to play in it, for fear of causing damage. Her fears didn't come out of nowhere. In her lifetime, the park had been destroyed at least four times. And four times, at least, Qurna had rebuilt it, without fanfare.

Every time something happened that harmed the old Tree, a new Tree was planted, before the first one disappeared completely. By 2002, there were actually at least five sacred Trees growing in the park—a small grove of Trees of Knowledge.

This is an impossibility. There shouldn't be more than one Tree of Knowledge. Didn't it take only one sin to get us kicked out of the Garden? Yet here they are, together, pressed tight between the banks of the Tigris and the row of sagging mud huts, as if to support one another's weight.

One is just a decaying stump, possibly the last venerated remains of the 1920 tree. Adam's Tree, planted in 1946 under the benevolent sunshine of progress, had been dead for decades but still stood, its thick trunk twisted in the middle as if to avoid some invisible obstacle.

Two spindly Y-shaped olive saplings, with a few green sprigs each, were perhaps planted after Adam's Tree began to die. One young eucalyptus had taken on the name of Eve; it still had vibrant, real, green leaves.

Eden is like this, too. Before one dream of the Garden can die completely, a new one must be planted. It's unthinkable to be without Eden. We cultivate the dream almost automatically, even though it doesn't make sense. This Eden will thrive for a while, then eventually fade away, and another will appear.

It's not really the Tree, or its leaves or bark that are sacred; those are just tokens of something deeper. The Trees of Knowledge express the sacredness of the soil. God sentenced man to leave Eden and till the Earth. Thus the idea of Eden depends on our expulsion from it. If God removed us from perfection, He also gave us the gift of its memory. Those first steps *out* of the Garden, ahead of the avenging angels—that's where humanity truly began. And that's where Eden still exists, in the earth, the earth from which we all came, and to which we will all return.

Notes on Sources

Prologue

I have tried to rely on primary sources wherever available, but for this overview and throughout the book there were several general works on the Garden of Eden that proved invaluable. One was Jean Delumeau's *History of Paradise: The Garden of Eden in Myth and Tradition,* translated by Matthew O'Connell (Continuum, 1995). Delumeau covers everything from Augustine to Darwin with an open mind and ready wit. Alessandro Scafi's gorgeous coffee-table book *Mapping Paradise: A History of Heaven on Earth* (University of Chicago Press, 2006) was an inspiring resource. William Warren's *Paradise Found* (1885), for all its questionable logic, includes an admirably thorough history of searches for Eden, particularly that of Columbus. Quotations from the Bible are from the New Revised Standard Version, unless otherwise specified. Citations for other direct quotations and specific facts are given below. If there were additional sources that I mined for background information, these will be listed alphabetically by author below the quotations.

xiv   Augustine laid out the options . . . : Jean Delumeau, *History of Paradise: The Garden of Eden in Myth and Tradition,* trans. Matthew O'Connell (New York: Continuum, 1995).

xiv   probably in "the East" . . . : Ibid.

xv   "If the water does *not* proceed" . . . : Columbus, quoted in William Fairfield Warren, *Paradise Found: The Cradle of the Human Race at the North Pole—A Study of the Prehistoric World* (Boston, MA: Houghton Mifflin, 1885).

xvi   he called them "God's great plough" . . . : Louis Menand, *The Metaphysical Club* (New York: Farrar, Straus and Giroux, 2001).

xvii "Any school boy of twelve" . . . : Victoria Woodhull, "The Garden of Eden," in *Lady Eugenist: Feminist Eugenics in the Speeches and Writings of Victoria Woodhull* (Seattle, WA: Inkling Books, 2005).

xvii Livingstone from declaring . . . : David Livingstone, *The Last Journals of David Livingstone, in Central Africa, from 1865 to His Death, Volume II,* ed. Horace Waller (2 vols., New York: Harper & Brothers, 1875).

Carroll, Sean B. *Remarkable Creatures: Epic Adventures in the Search for the Origins of Species* (New York: Houghton Mifflin Harcourt, 2009).

Hecht, Jennifer Michael. *Doubt: A History—The Great Doubters and Their Legacy of Innovation, from Socrates and Jesus to Thomas Jefferson and Emily Dickinson* (New York: HarperOne, 2004).

Manseau, Peter. *Rag and Bone: A Journey among the World's Holy Dead.* (New York: Henry Holt, 2009).

Morris, Paul, and Deborah Sawyer. *Walk in the Garden: Biblical, Iconographical and Literary Images of Eden* (Sheffield, England: JSOT Press, 1992).

Rushby, Kevin. *Paradise: A History of the Idea That Rules the World* (New York: Basic Books, 2006).

Scafi, Alessandro. *Mapping Paradise: A History of Heaven on Earth* (Chicago, IL: University of Chicago Press, 2006).

Weir, James. *In Search of Eden: The Course of an Obsession* (London: Haus, 2007).

Chapter 1: The Last Giant Man of Eden

As the first president of Boston University, William Warren had his place in history assured, and his prolific works well preserved. The release of *Paradise Found!* in 1885 drew lots of response from newspapers and periodicals, including the *Boston Daily Globe, New York Times, Chicago Daily Tribune,* and *Washington Post.* The lively anonymous review in the *Atlantic Monthly* in July 1885 first led me to Warren's story. *Paradise Found!* was reissued by Fredonia Books in 2002, and, believe it or not, you can download a version of it on your iPhone. I found Warren's letter to Professor Charles P. Fagnani of October 27, 1909, still tucked inside the copy of *Paradise Found!* in the library of Union Theological Seminary in New York; Warren's 1903 passport application was among the many wonders I unearthed on the genealogy database Ancestry. com. Details of Arctic exploration came from Pierre Berton's *The Arctic Grail: The Quest for the North West Passage and the North Pole, 1818–1909* (New York: Random House, 2001), and from a history of the Greely Expedition compiled by the county historian of Seneca County, New York. All direct quotations from Warren are from *Paradise Found!,* except as noted below.

4 "eminently fitting to postpone"...: William F. Warren, "Scripture Inspiration," in *The Ingham Lectures* (Cleveland, OH: Ingham, Clark, 1872).

6 British explorers continued to wear...: Pierre Berton, *The Arctic Grail: The Quest for the North West Passage and the North Pole, 1818–1909* (New York: Random House, 2001).

12 As tersely reported...: "The March of the Anglo Saxon," *Washington Post*, August 16, 1883, p. 1.

13 "not worth while"...: "Where Is Eden?" *New York Times*, April 5, 1885, p. 5.

15 "rapidly superseding every earlier"...: William F. Warren, *All Roads Lead to Thule: Late Attempts to Locate the Cradle of the Human Race* (Boston University Year Book, 1886), XIII, 19–37.

17 "most beneficent enterprise"...: Ibid.

18 "supremely fitting commemoration"...: William F. Warren, "One Way to Honor Columbus," *Boston Daily Globe*, April 7, 1888, p. 5.

18 "charming spirit of open-minded"...: Review of *Paradise Found! Atlantic Monthly*, July 1885, pp. 126–132.

19 This, too, was a much-rehearsed idea...: Jean Delumeau, *History of Paradise*, trans. by Matthew O'Connell (New York: Continuum, 1995).

20 "The poles are tiresome spots"...: "Modern Discovery Is Dispelling the Weird Delusions about the World," *Washington Post*, March 24, 1912.

21 "Blessed are they that do his commandments, that they may have right to the tree of life"...: Revelation 22:14 (King James Version).

21 "Careful mathematical computations"...: George C. Allen, "Says Garden of Eden was located in Ohio" *New York Times*, January 31, 1921, p. 3.

22 "almost stubbed his toe against"...: Willis George Emerson, *The Smoky God or, A Voyage to the Inner World* (Chicago, IL: Forbes, 1908).

22 "Christ is the central figure here"...: Reverend E. D. Ledyard, "Sunday at Chautauqua," *New York Times*, August 13, 1883, p. 1.

22 "Not one of its multitudinous"...: Warren, *All Roads Lead to Thule*, p. 37.

23 "It rejoices me to learn that you"...: Warren to Professor Charles P. Fagnani, October 27, 1909.

Warren, William F. *The Religions of the World and the World-Religion: An Outline for Personal and Class Use* (New York: Eaton and Mains; Cincinnati, OH: Jennings and Graham, 1911).

———. *True Key to Ancient Cosmology and Mythical Geography* (Boston, MA: Ginn, Heath, 1882).

Chapter 2: The Great Divide

Almost a century after his death, Friedrich Delitzsch was still in the shadow of his father, Franz. Until recently, Friedrich didn't even have his own Wikipedia page. Perhaps because of his embarrassing later "pan-Babylonianism," his first book on Eden is nearly forgotten, and it has not been translated into English. I commissioned translations of passages in *Wo Lag das Paradies?* from Lakshmi Krishnan, Laura Killian, and Alison Cheeseman. There's a flood of newspaper coverage of the 1903 "Babel-Bible" lectures; this coverage provided details worth their weight in gold, like the fact that the kaiser himself had run Delitzsch's slide projections, and that Delitzsch lectured only in German. All direct quotations from Delitzsch, except where noted below, come from the English edition of *Babel and Bible,* translated by McCormack and Carruth, published by Putnam in 1903.

28 "the greatest mistake of the human mind"...: "The German Emperor and the 'Higher Criticism,'" *London Times,* January 14, 1903, p. 3.

28 "entirely heterogeneous"...: Ibid.

31 "advanced thinker"...: "The German Reichstag (from Our Own Correspondent)," *London Times,* January 24, 1903, p. 7.

32 "flashlight of a signal lamp"...: "The Kaiser Gives Offense," *London Times,* January 16, 1903, p. 9.

32 "Deuteronomy is a falsification!"...: Raymond F. Surburg, "The Influence of the Two Delitzsches on Biblical and Near Eastern

Studies," *Concordia Theological Quarterly,* Vol. 47, no. 3, July 1983, pp. 225–240.

34 "Why must Pishon" . . . : *Wo Lag das Paradies? Eine Biblisch-Assyriologische Studie* (Leipzig: J. C. Hinrichs'sche Buchhandlung, 1881).

35 "lonely and lifeless desert" . . . : Friedrich Delitzsch, "Discoveries in Mesopotamia," in *Smithsonian Institution Annual Report* (Smithsonian Institution: Washington, DC, 1901), pp. 535–549.

37 "geographical correctness" . . . : "The Site of Paradise: Prof. Delitzsch on the Garden of Eden," *Chicago Daily Tribune,* November 8, 1882, p. 6.

38 "militate too strongly" . . . : "The Site of Paradise," *Nation,* March 15, 1883, p. 286.

40 "I shall not think that Adam ever used" . . . : "No Faith in Eden Relics: Prof. Lyon Laughs at Alleged Discoveries by Seton-Karr," *New York Times,* August 27, 1897, p. 11.

41 "It is all bosh" . . . : T. W. Goodspeed. "Calls Bible Criticism Bosh," *Chicago Daily Tribune,* January 15, 1903, p. 7.

42 "goes beyond Babel and antagonizes Babel" . . . : H. T. Sell, "Defends the Books of Moses: Chicago Student of Religion Says Prof. Delitzsch Stands Almost Alone in Views," *Chicago Tribune,* January 19, 1903, p. 11.

43 "Religion has never been the result of science" . . . : "Kaiser Explains Own Creed: German Emperor Furnishes Proof of His Orthodoxy," *Chicago Tribune,* February 21, 1903, p. 1.

43 presented copies of it . . . : "The German Emperor," *London Times,* March 6, 1903, p. 3.

44 "'smarting' under his former patron's criticism" . . . : "Kaiser Explains Own Creed."

44 "my audience consisted of intellectual, highly cultured men" . . . : "Says the Kaiser Is Unorthodox," *New York Times,* February 22, 1903, p. 5.

44 he was not an atheist . . . : Ibid.

44 "My dear professor, we have broken a lance" . . . : "Delitzsch's Witty Reply to the Kaiser," *New York Times,* April 12, 1903, p. 5.

45 "blow the horn of anti-Semitism" . . . : Rabbi Kohler, "Replies to Prof. Delitzsch," *New York Times,* July 1, 1903.

Arnold, Bill T., and David B. Weisberg. "A Centennial Review of Friedrich Delitzsch's 'Babel und Bibel' Lectures," *Journal of Biblical Literature,* Vol. 121, no. 3, Autumn 2002, pp. 441–457.

———. "Delitzsch in Context," in *God's Word for Our World: Theological and Cultural Studies in Honor of Simon John De Vries* (New York: Continuum, 2004), pp. 37–45.

Delitzsch, Friedrich. *Im Lande des Einstigen Paradieses* (Stuttgart: Deutsche Verlags-Anstalt, 1903).

Jastrow, Morris, Jr. "Adam and Eve in Babylonian Literature," *American Journal of Semitic Languages and Literatures,* Vol. 15, no. 4, July 1899, pp. 193–214.

Larsen, Mogens Trolle. "The 'Babel/Bible' Controversy and Its Aftermath," in *Civilizations of the Ancient Near East,* Jack M. Sasson (New York: Scribner, 1995), pp. 95–106.

Lehmann, Reinhard G. *Friedrich Delitzsch und der Babel-Bibel-Streit* (Freiburg: Universitätsverlag; Göttingen: Vandenhoeck and Ruprecht, 1994).

Lloyd, Seton. *Foundations in the Dust: A Story of Mesopotamian Exploration* (New York: AMS Press, 1978).

Seton-Karr, H. W. "Discovery of Evidences of the Palaeolithic Stone Age in Somaliland (Tropical Africa)," *Journal of the Anthropological Institute of Great Britain and Ireland,* Vol. 25, 1896, pp. 271–275.

Chapter 3: The Serpent Lesson

Landon West's Eden theory has survived as an amusing footnote to the history of Ohio's Serpent Mound, mentioned at the visitors' center and in any article about new archaeological discoveries there. But to my knowledge no one had dug into it further to see where West was coming from. Randall's article mentions that West was a "Baptist," but there's a world of difference between "Baptist" and "German Baptist," or, more correctly, "Church of the Brethren"—as I learned when I contacted Patrick Kennedy, the local history librarian at the Troy Public Library in

West's hometown, Pleasant Hill, Ohio. Kennedy graciously provided local genealogies, newspaper articles, and *The Brethren Encyclopedia,* issued by the Brethren Historical Library and Archives (BHLA) in Elgin, Illinois (Philadelphia, PA: Brethren Encyclopedia, 1983–1984). Ken Shaffer at the BHLA kindly provided permission to reprint the very rare photograph of West. The Church of the Brethren, in its three divisions, still exists today, ranging from Old World denominations (which to an outsider look like the Amish) to actively engaged, modern Brethren churches. In fact, West's son Daniel would go on to found the Heifer Project, originally a Brethren outreach effort and now a worldwide charity, Heifer International. People in Pleasant Hill had certainly heard of Landon West's theory, though Kennedy's library didn't have a copy of *Eden's Land,* so I happily let the library photocopy mine. Kennedy said that already, several library patrons were interested in reading it. All direct quotations from West, except as noted below, come from *Eden's Land and Garden with Their Marks Yet to Be Seen* (microform; American Theological Library Association fiche 1990-5072. Pleasant Hill, Miami County, Ohio : [s.n.], 1908).

51 "The Bible is our main witness" . . . : West, Landon. *Close Communion; or, Plea for the Dunkard People. In 2 parts, Edition of 1888* (Dayton, OH: G. B. Brethren Book and Tract Work).

53 "China, or Salt Lake City" . . . : Ibid.

56 "fairly intelligent" . . . : "Giants of Other Days: Recent Discoveries Near Serpent Mound, Ohio," *New York Times,* March 5, 1894, p. 5.

59 "It certainly cannot be maintained by any good American" . . . : "Was the Garden of Eden in Ohio," *Elyria* (Ohio) *Reporter,* Vol. 12, no. 34, September 19, 1901, p. 2.

59 "not exactly archaeology or history" . . . : E. O. Randall, "Ohio, the Site of the Garden of Eden . . . The Theory of Rev. Landon West," in *Ohio Archaeological and Historical Publications,* Vol. X (Columbus, OH: Published for the Society by Fred J. Heer, 1902), p. 225.

60 Details about viewing tower . . . : Stephen Kelley, "Tower Stands 100 years," *People's Defender,* May 21, 2008.

62 Hellfire and brimstone . . . : "Brother West in his prime was an orator of no mean ability and fearless in his denunciation of all evil."

Historical Committee, Church of the Brethren, *History of the Church of the Brethren of the Southern District of Ohio,* Editorial Supervision by Elder Jesse O. Garst, A.M., rev. ed. (Millville, NJ: Brethren Heritage Publishing, 2007).

Underwood, Paul. "The Riddle of Ohio's Age-Old Serpent Mound," *New York Times,* October 8, 1967, p. 20.

West, Landon. *Tract: The Life of Elder Samuel Weir (Colored),* 10th ed. (Covington, OH: Tribune, 1909).

Chapter 4: The Salt River

Archibald Henry Sayce may be the best-known of my early twentieth-century Eden seekers, probably because he was amazingly prolific; one might even say he was profligate with his scholarly and popular articles. I first found him referred to by both Warren and Delitzsch and wondered what kind of a person could possibly count these two cantankerous entities as friends. I soon discovered that this was only the beginning: reading his hefty memoir, *Reminiscences,* was an adventure in itself. (And that's where Sayce's direct quotations in this chapter come from, except as noted below.) On every page, Sayce seemed to travel to twenty new destinations and drop fifty names. Despite, or perhaps because of, all this verbiage, Sayce's slippery theories about the Bible, Moses, and Eden were the most difficult to understand and explain. To the extent that I was able to do so, I must credit the following secondary sources: Roshunda Lashae Belton, "A Non-Traditional Traditionalist: Rev. A. H. Sayce and His Intellectual Approach to Biblical Authenticity and Biblical History in Late-Victorian Britain" (dissertation, Louisiana State University, Department of History, December 2007); and Gordon Booth, "Documents versus Monuments: Captain Conder, A. H. Sayce and W. Robertson Smith," http://www.gkbenterprises.org.uk.

70 "exercise his remarkable genius" . . . : "Dr. Schliemann," *New York Times*, November 10, 1876.

73 "what we should now call a plantation" . . . : William Willcocks, Prof. Sayce, John Jackson, L. W. King, and F. R. Maunsell, "Garden

of Eden and Its Restoration: Discussion," *Geographical Journal*, Vol. 40, no. 2, August 1912, pp. 145–148.

74 "self-denial . . . rare" . . . : A. H. Sayce, *Academy*, no. 20 (1881).

77 Description of Nile . . . : Amelia Ann Blanford Edwards, *Thousand Miles Up the Nile* (London, New York: G. Routledge, 1890).

79 "no theological fairy tales" . . . : A. H. Sayce, *The "Higher Criticism" and the Verdict of the Monuments*, 3rd ed., rev. (London: Society for Promoting Christian Knowledge, 1894).

80 "illusional"; "destitute of solid foundation"; "too slight to merit any attention" . . . : S. R. Driver, in Mark Elliott, "Biblical Archaeology and Its Interpretation: The Sayce-Driver Controversy," *Bible and Interpretation Using Archaeological Evidence, 1900–1930* (Ceredigion, UK and Lewiston, New York: Edwin Mellen, 2002).

80 "our popular literature on the Old Testament . . ." . . . : T. K. Cheyne, in Barbara Zink MacHaffie. "Monument Facts and Higher Critical Fancies: Archaeology and the Popularization of Old Testament Criticism in Nineteenth-Century Britain," *Church History*, Vol. 50, no. 3, September, 1981, p. 327.

80 "I pardon his wild tilts" . . . : Anonymous Assyriologist, letter to G. H. Richardson, *Biblical World*, 1916.

82 "As I have been seeking to show" . . . : A. H. Sayce, letter to the editor, "Hermann's a German: A Review of Teutonic Pretensions," *London Times*, December 22, 1914.

Irvine, William. *Apes, Angels, and Victorians: The Story of Darwin, Huxley, and Evolution* (New York: Meridian, 1955).

Moorey, P. R. S. *A Century of Biblical Archaeology* (Louisville, KY: Westminster, 1991).

Robertson, Edward. "Where Was Eden?" *American Journal of Semitic Languages and Literatures*, Vol. 28, no. 4, July 1912, pp. 254–273.

Sayce, A. H. *Monument Facts and Higher Critical Fancies* (London: Religious Tract Society, 1904).

———. *A Dictionary of the Bible: Dealing with Its Language, Literature, and Contents, Including the Biblical Theology*, ed. James Hastings (New York: Scribner, 1898–1904).

————. *Historical Evidences of the Old Testament* (New York: American Tract Society, 1891).

————. *Fresh Light from the Ancient Monuments: A Sketch of the Most Striking Confirmations of the Bible from Recent Discoveries in Egypt, Palestine, Assyria, Babylonia, Asia Minor* (London: Religious Tract Society, 1890).

Chapter 5: Far East of Eden

Tse is fiendishly difficult to search for, because of the numerous spellings of his name—Tse Tsan Tai, Hsieh Tsuan-t'ai, Xie Zuantai, James Ah See. But everything else about his character was out-front and direct. Remembered by Hong Kong Chinese as a revolutionary and an idealistic newspaper founder, he is now examined by scholars of East Asian studies as a fascinating example of East meets West. Rodney Noonan, author of the most biographical of these scholarly treatments, *From Grafton to Guangzhou: The Revolutionary Journey of Tse Tsan Tai*, kindly e-mailed me Tse's otherwise untraceable memoir of the Chinese revolution. Quotations from Tse come from *The Creation, the Real Situation of Eden, and the Origin of the Chinese* (Hong Kong: Kelly and Walsh, 1914) unless otherwise noted.

85 Hong Kong economy . . . : W. H. Morton Cameron, in *Present Day Impressions of the Far East and Prominent and Progressive Chinese at Home and Abroad* (London: Globe Encyclopedia, 1917).

86 "career of Mr. Tse Tsan Tai" . . . : Chesney Duncan, Ibid., p. 583.

86 Cartoon . . . : Wendy Siuyi Wong, *Hong Kong Comics: A History of Manhua* (New York: Princeton Architectural Press, 2002).

88 Grafton description . . . : Rodney Noonan, "Grafton to Guangzhou: The Revolutionary Journey of Tse Tsan Tai," *Journal of Intercultural Studies,* Vol. 27, No. 1-2, February–May 2006, pp. 101–115.

89 "persistently putting my head . . . : Tse Tsan Tai, *The Chinese Republic: Secret History of the Revolution* (Hong Kong: *South China Morning Post*, 1924), p. 35.

90 Protestant missions . . . : *Present Day Impressions of the Far East and Prominent and Progressive Chinese at Home and Abroad*, p. 107.

91 didn't take off until it fired him . . . : "Slow Start, Then Fledgling
Soared," *South China Morning Post,* October 24, 1995, p. 12.

Armentrout, Eve. "The Canton Rising of 1902–1903: Reformers, Revolutionaries, and the Second Taiping," *Modern Asian Studies,* Vol. 10, no. 1, 1976, pp. 83–105.

Hsueh, Chun-tu. "Sun Yat-sen, Yang Chu'yun, and the Early Revolutionary Movement in China," *Journal of Asian Studies,* Vol. 19, no. 3, May 1960, pp. 37–318.

Tsan Tai, Tse. *How to Solve World Depression and the Un-Employed Problem: An Appeal for International Sanity,* reprinted from *Hong Kong Daily Press,* January 19, 1932.

————. *No. 12: Solution of Mysterious Blank in Ancient Egyptian History, and the Age of the Siberian Mammoth,* English ed. (Hong Kong, Shanghai, Hankow, Singapore, Yokohama: Kelly and Walsh, 1914).

————. *No. 11: Solution of Easter Island Mystery,* English ed. (Hong Kong, Shanghai, Hankow, Singapore, Yokohama: Kelly and Walsh, 1914).

————. *No. 10: "Correlativity"—New Theory of the Universe, and Origin of Typhoons,* English ed. (Hong Kong, Shanghai, Hankow, Singapore, Yokohama: Kelly and Walsh, 1914).

————. *No. 8: What Was the Colour of Our Primitive Ancestors? The Real Mountains of Ararat,* English ed. (Hong Kong, Shanghai, Hankow, Singapore, Yokohama: Kelly and Walsh, 1914).

Chapter 6: Practically Paradise

What more can I say about William Willcocks? Reading the lectures he gave before the Royal Geographic Society required layers of knowledge about British colonial politics, societal manners, and irrigation engineering. Willcocks's 1919 *From the Garden of Eden to the Crossing of the Jordan* is one of the books about Eden most often mentioned elsewhere, especially in the 1920s and 1930s. Possibly that's because Willcocks was a self-professed amateur in Biblical studies and as such appealed to a wider audience than did the scholarly Warren, Delitzsch, and Sayce. Though Willcocks is remembered in Mesopotamia, his story really belongs in British-colonized Egypt, where he was a prominent personality for decades, and where he died. Willcocks's feud with the British government in Cairo, which almost put the elderly knight in prison, is a story in itself.

100   "20th century Don Quixote"...: Gertrude Bell, letter of March 21, 1911, accessed from Gertrude Bell Project at Newcastle University, http://www.gerty.ncl.ac.uk.

100   chapter a day...: Courtenay Clifton, "Sir W. Willcocks," letter to the editor after Willcocks's death, *London Times,* August 6, 1932, p. 10.

100   "Politics I have nothing"...: William Willcocks, *Sixty Years in the East* (Edinburgh and London: W. Blackwood, 1935).

104   "Life and prosperity"...: William Willcocks, *From the garden of Eden to the Crossing of the Jordan,* 2nd ed. (London: E. and F. N. Spon, 1920), p. 32.

107   "Irrigation such as we propose"...: William Willcocks, "Mesopotamia: Past, Present, and Future," *Geographical Journal,* Vol. 35, No. 1, January 1910, pp. 1–15.

110   "welcome the possibilities offered"...: Gertrude Bell, quoted in "Mesopotamia: Past, Present, and Future: Discussion, Hanbury Brown, Colonel Maunsell, Gertrude Bell, Colin Scott Moncrieff, William Willcocks," *Geographical Journal,* Vol. 35, no. 1, January 1910, pp. 15–18.

111   "young almond and apple"...: Marie Corelli, *God's Good Man: A Simple Love Story* (New York: A. L. Burt, 1904).

112   "The storm raged high"...: William Willcocks, *From the Garden of Eden to the Crossing of the Jordan,* p. 32.

114   "Studying these questions"...: William Willcocks, "The Garden of Eden and Its Restoration," *Geographical Journal,* Vol. 40, no. 2, August 1912, pp. 129–145.

116   "almost violent"...: "Were There Two Gardens of Eden, or Only One?" *New York Times,* August 25, 1912.

MacMillan, Margaret. *Paris 1919: Six Months That Changed the World* (New York: Random House, 2002).

Philby, H. St. John. "The Eastern Marshes of Mesopotamia," *Geographical Journal,* Vol. 125, no. 1, March 1959, pp. 65–69.

Stewart, Rory. *The Prince of the Marshes, and Other Occupational Hazards of a Year in Iraq,* 1st Harvest ed. (Orlando, FL: Harcourt, 2007).

Thesiger, Wilfred. "The Marshmen of Southern Iraq," *Geographical Journal,* Vol. 120, no. 3, September 1954, pp. 272–281.

Vinogradov, Amal. "The 1920 Revolt in Iraq Reconsidered: The Role of Tribes in National Politics," *International Journal of Middle East Studies,* Vol. 3, no. 2, April 1972, pp. 123–139.

Wilson, Arnold T. "The Delta of the Shatt al 'Arab and Proposals for Dredging the Bar," *Geographical Journal,* Vol. 65, no. 3 March 1925, pp. 225–239.

Chapter 7: The Tree Is Dead, Long Live the Tree

I first saw Norman Wright's 1946 photograph of the Tree of Knowledge at Qurna in Alessandro Scafi's *Mapping Paradise*. It was one of the few photographs in a book of fantastical maps, so I was immediately intrigued. But when I uncovered the *Times* of London's letters to the editor from veterans of the Mesopotamian campaign, which described the circumstances of the tree's breaking, I knew I'd found the heart of the story. I tried like hell to find the original 1919 telegrams received by Cyril Blomeley from indignant locals. My professor, the biographer Patricia O'Toole, kindly added them to her research list on a trip to the British Archives in London. I combed through the archives' extensive Web catalog, and looked in every contemporary travel and political narrative I could find in Columbia's libraries or through interlibrary loan. I never did find the telegrams, but I did find a complete collection of official reports of British political officers in Mesopotamia during and after World War I. Far from being dry and administrative, these reports are full of gossipy details about local sheikhs and heartbreaking statistics about local health. But they didn't actually mention the tree's breaking either, or why the residents of Qurna would be so upset by it. So I was lucky to find Ayub Nuri, an Iraqi journalist studying in the United States, who had traveled all over his country working as a reporter and translator. In a brief conversation on the steps of Columbia's journalism school, he completely overturned my ideas about Qurna—it's beautiful, he said, a very watery place. And his matter-of-fact description of sacred trees—it's his mother who threatened to punish him—provided the "aha" moment I needed.

119 "Tree of Knowledge Dead" . . . : *London Times,* December 23, 1946, p. 3.

120 "But Sir" . . . : Letter from Marmaduke Tudsbery about "Tree of Knowledge Dead," *London Times,* December 24, 1946, p. 4.

120 1563 castle at Corno . . . : Master Cesar Frederick, in E. A. Wallis Budge, *By Nile and Tigris* (London: J. Murray, 1920).

123 "all the theories are reduced to two" . . . : John Philip Newman, *Thrones and Palaces of Babylon and Nineveh: A Thousand Miles on Horseback* (New York, Harper, 1876), p. 66.

123 "the old doxology" in Qurna's date groves . . . : Ibid.

123 "Oh! Shades of one's First Parents!" . . . : Betty Cunliffe-Owen, *Thro' the Gates of Memory from the Bosphorus to Baghdad* (London: Hutchinson, 1925), p. 86.

123 "The few trees, and the little cultivation" . . . : William Huede. *A Voyage Up the Persian Gulf* (London: Longman, Hurst, Rees, Orme, and Brown, 1819), p. 56.

123 "Garden of Hell" . . . : Ibid.

123 "sure didn't need a flaming sword" . . . : Kermit Roosevelt, *War in the Garden of Eden* (New York: Scribner, 1919).

124 "storms in a teacup" . . . : Arnold Talbot Wilson, *Mesopotamia, 1917–1920: A Clash of Loyalties—A Personal and Historical Record* (London, Oxford University Press, H. Milford, 1931), p. 222.

124 Gubashi . . . : J. B. Mackie, Captain (APO Qurnah), "Administration Report of Qurnah and District for Year 1916–1917," *Iraq Administration Reports: 1914–1932* (Farnham Common, UK: Cambridge Archive Editions, 1992), p. 292.

125 sold out immediately . . . : Wilson, *Mesopotamia, 1917–1920,* p. 218.

125 growing dates and weaving reed mats . . . : "Administration Report of Qurnah," p. 420.

125 putting Sheikh Gubashi out of a job . . . : Ibid., p. 282.

125 civil hospital data . . . : "Administration Report of Qurnah," p. 304.

125   plague killed thirty-five people . . . : Ibid., p. 278.

125   eye diseases . . . : Ibid., p. 277.

125   "hopelessly incurable" . . . : L. Wynn Davies, Captain, R.A.M.C., Civil Surgeon, Qurnah in: Ibid., p. 276.

127   so many telegrams . . . : Letter to the editor from Rev. Cyril Blomeley, *London Times,* December 27, 1946, p. 5.

127   projects like building a roof for the outdoor marketplace . . . : "Administration Report of Qurnah," p. 205.

127   "still boasted a few green leaves" . . . : Letter to the editor from R. S. M. Sturges, *London Times,* December 30, 1946, p. 5.

128   Although tree worship . . . : Amots Dafni, "On the Typology and the Worship Status of Sacred Trees, with a Special Reference to the Middle East," *Journal of Ethnobiology and Ethnomedicine,* Vol. 2, no. 26, 2006. Also: Interview with Charles Haberl, March 20, 2007. See also: H.V. Morton, *Through Lands of the Bible* (London: Methuen, 1938), p. 156.

130   Haldane would need as many troops . . . : Mark Jacobsen, "Only by the Sword: British Counter-Insurgency in Iraq, 1920," in *Small Wars and Insurgencies,* Vol. 2, 1991, pp. 323–363.

Cook's Traveler's Handbook to Palestine, Syria, and Iraq, 6th ed., ed. Christopher Lumby (London: Simpkin Marshall, 1934).

Fromkin, David. *A Peace to End All Peace: The Fall of the Ottoman Empire and the Creation of the Modern Middle East* (New York: Avon, 1990).

Oren, Michael B. *Power, Faith, and Fantasy: America in the Middle East, 1776 to the Present* (New York: W. W. Norton, 2007).

Wallach, Janet. *Desert Queen: The Extraordinary Life of Gertrude Bell, Adventurer, Adviser to Kings, Ally of Lawrence of Arabia* (New York: Nan A. Talese/Doubleday, 1996).

Interlude

The ongoing life of William F. Warren was of course meticulously documented in the Boston and New York newspapers of the day. Gertrude Bell's phenomenal letters (cataloged and made accessible online by Newcastle University; Google 'The Gertrude Bell Project') provided the anecdote about Sayce and the tablets, and I heartily thank Michael Janeway for introducing me to Susan Friend Harding's *The Book of Jerry Falwell* and its fascinating history of the Scopes trial in terms of the fundamentalist exile.

133 Sayce's visit to Iraq . . . : Gertrude Bell, letter dated March 24, 1924, accessed from The Gertrude Bell Project at Newcastle University, http://www.gerty.ncl.ac.uk.

135 "Mr. Bryan, do you believe" . . . : Scopes trial transcripts, excerpted by University of Missouri Kansas City Law School, accessed at: www.law.umkc.edu/faculty/projects/FTrials/scopes/scopes.htm.

136 "There stood the man" . . . : H. L. Mencken, "William Jennings Bryan," *Baltimore Evening Sun,* July 27, 1925.

137 they went into . . . : Susan Friend Harding, *The Book of Jerry Falwell: Fundamentalist Language and Politics* (Princeton, NJ: Princeton University Press, 2000).

Chapter 8: The Location Committee

The Urantia Book, like the Bible, is easy to find and read in its entirety. (See the Urantia Fellowship's online edition at http://urantiabook.org.) So is a highly skeptical account of the writing of the book, the exhaustive *Urantia: The Great Cult Mystery* by Martin Gardner. To help me form characterizations of the people involved, however, I relied on the Urantia Book Historical Society's fascinating online database of photographs, biographies, and histories (www.ubhistory.org), including sworn affidavits in various court trials, which discussed the group-writing process. With its transformation from an anomaly during the progressive era to a New Age icon, the Urantia Book has survived, slowly passed along from reading group to reading group nationwide. Jennifer Michael Hecht's *Doubt: A History* provided an enjoyable overview of the progressive era, and Michael Lesy's *Murder City* another angle on Chicago crime and politics at the time. Quotations of *The Urantia Book* are from The Urantia Book Fellowship's Complete English Text, at http://urantiabook.org/newbook/index.html. For the Urantian creation story see Martin Gardner, *Urantia: The Great Cult Mystery* (New York: Prometheus, 1995), p. 194.

141 Sunday session setup ...: Dr. Meredith J. Sprunger, *20th Century Renaissance Heroes: Dr. William S. Sadler,* Truthbook.com, "Discover Jesus and the Urantia Book," www.Truthbook.com. See also "Sunday Tea," Urantia Book Historical Society, http://www.ubhistory.org/UBHS/SundayTea.html.

142 Sadlers' credentials ...: "Lena and William Sadler," The Urantia Book Historical Society, http://www.ubhistory.org/UBHS/StoriesandPeople/Lena&WillSadler.html.

143 "I do not approve of ministers" ...: Katharine Kelley, "Religion Fosters Mental Health, Doctor Asserts: Sadler Talks at Church Workers' Conference, *Chicago Daily Tribune,* January 3, 1935, p. 7.

144 Lecture on mediums ...: William S. Sadler, *The Mind at Mischief* (New York: Funk and Wagnalls, 1929), pp. 382–384.

147 leaves a hole in the believer ...: Martin Gardner, *Urantia: The Great Cult Mystery* (New York: Prometheus, 1995), p. 406.

149–150 fondness for numbers ...: Ibid., p. 190.

151 Rowley story ...: "Stories and People: Marian F. Rowley," ubhistory.org.

154 World's Fair booth ...: "Dr. Bertha Van Hoosen, the Michigan Petticoat Surgeon," Urantia Book Historical Society, http://www.ubhistory.org/UBHS/CenturyofProgress.html.

154 no secret of their plagiarism ...: Ted Glasziou, "Science, Anthropology and Archaeology in the Urantia Book, Part 3: Who Wrote the Urantia Papers?" Urantia Book Fellowship Web site.

155 1920s Chicago ...: Michael Lesy, *Murder City: The Bloody History of Chicago in the Twenties* (New York: Norton, 2007).

158 Promotional ideas ...: Martin Gardner, *Urantia: The Great Cult Mystery*, p. 319.

Encyclopedia of Psychology and Religion, ed. David A. Leeming, Kathryn Madden, and Stanton Marlan (New York: Springer, 2009), p. 934.

Kendall, Caroline. "William S. Sadler: Skeptic, Believer, Inspiration," *Holiday Social,* December 9, 2006.

"The Peculiar Sleep: Receiving The Urantia Book," in *Sacred Traditions,* ed. James R. Lewis (Cambridge: Cambridge University Press, 2008).

Sadler, William S. *Theory and Practice of Psychiatry* (St. Louis: Mosby, 1936).

Chapter 9: Mother Eve's Great Decision

Elvy Edison Callaway, in the best tradition of lawyering, left an impressive written record of his own philosophical and political evolution in his two books: *The Other Side of the South* (1935), and *In the Beginning* (1971). But his personal journey was full of gaps, which I tried to fill using the public record: documents showing his marriage, draft deferment, divorce, and move to Bristol. Like Landon West, Callaway had the foresight to choose for his Eden an exceptional natural wonder, which has since been turned into an official preserve where his story survives as a footnote. Steven Cutshaw of Torreya State Park in Bristol, Florida, was an extremely helpful virtual guide to the landscape, as were Gloria Jahoda's *The Other Florida* and Harry Crews's *Florida Childhood.*

160 "proves beyond all doubt" . . . : Thomas Morrow, "Want to Get into Garden of Eden for Buck, 10 Cents?" *Chicago Daily Tribune,* February 14, 1956, p. A2.

160 It began with a girl . . . : Elvy E. Callaway, *The Other Side of the South* (Chicago, IL: Daniel Ryerson, 1934), p. 61.

162 "strongest evidence of evolution" . . . : Ibid.

163 "If we can ever have religion and reason" . . . : Ibid., p. 51.

163 "like a cow in the woods" . . . : Elvy E. Callaway, Letter to the editor, "Comment on the Pepper Victory," *Washington Post,* May 11, 1928, p. x8.

165 "It appeared that there was nothing for me to do" . . . : Elvy E. Callaway, *In the Beginning: The Four Greatest Recorded Events of This Earth* (Dayton, OH: ITB Associates, 1971).

166 *Torreya taxifolia* goes by many names . . . : See http://www.torreyaguardians.org/torreya.html.

166 gopher wood . . . : "Gopher-Wood," at jewishencyclopedia.com.

167 "pious pilgrimage" ... : Gloria Jahoda, *The Other Florida* (New York: Scribner, 1967).

169 "evolution won the battle" ... : Callaway, *In The Beginning*, p. 51.

173 opened Garden of Eden Park in 1956 ... : Morrow, "Want to Get into Garden of Eden for Buck, 10 Cents?"

174 "Mr. and Mrs. F. W. Wentworth" "aging serpent to raise a family" ... : Ibid.

174 Goldwater ... : Jahoda, *The Other Florida*, p. 70.

175 "surprising number" ... : Ibid.

175 "tourist boon" ... : "Visit the Garden of Eden," *St. Petersburg Times,* July 29, 1973, p. 177.

175 When the *New York Times* came ... : Martin Waldron, "Ecologists Battle for Idyllic Florida River," *New York Times,* October 7, 1972, p. 35.

Chapter 10: Back to the Land

Thor Heyerdahl was the one Eden seeker I had heard of before I began this project. His iconic *Kon-Tiki* voyage had made him a hero to the idealistic postwar generation, including my parents. Heyerdahl's later escapades in the Middle East and Africa are less well known than his work in the South Pacific but perhaps even more fascinating, as they took place against the backdrop of disastrous cold war maneuvering, and the escalation of dictatorship in Iraq. Reading Heyerdahl's account of the Tigris expedition next to his later autobiography *In the Footsteps of Adam* revealed the tragic gap between his ideals and his reality. Christopher Ralling's *Kon-Tiki Man* gave a particularly illuminating account of Fatu-Hiva and Heyerdahl's early life; and Gary Knoll's *America's Ocean Wilderness* put the *Kon-Tiki's* voyage into fascinating cultural context. Quotations of Heyerdahl are from his account of the voyage, *The Tigris Expedition: In Search of Our Beginnings* (London: Allen and Unwin, 1980), unless otherwise noted.

177 "it would have to be all the way back" ... : Christopher Ralling. *Kon-Tiki Man: Thor Heyerdahl* (London: BBC Books, 1990).

178 "no geographical location" ... : Thor Heyerdahl, *In the Footsteps of Adam: An Autobiography,* trans. Ann Zwick (London: Little, Brown, 2000).

179 all things Polynesian ...: Gary Kroll, *America's Ocean Wilderness: A Cultural History of Twentieth-Century Exploration* (Lawrence: University Press of Kansas, 2008).

180 Norman C. Wright biography ...: Ralph W. Phillips, "FAO: Its Origins, Formation and Evolution 1945–1981" (1981). Accessed at FAO Corporate Document Repository, Knowledge and Communication Department, http://www.fao.org.

Heyerdahl, Thor. *Fatu-Hiva: Back to Nature* (London: Allen and Unwin, 1974).

Chapter 11: An Evolving Creation

Creationism is an ever-changing and enormously complicated topic. Frances FitzGerald's extended profile of Jerry Falwell in her 1987 *Cities on a Hill* was immensely helpful, as were her 2009 lectures at the New York Public Library on the future of evangelicals in politics. Susan Friend Harding's *The Book of Jerry Falwell,* included invaluable descriptions of ICR and the early creation museums. A 2007 PBS documentary on *Kitzmiller v. Dover* put faces to the otherwise dreary parade of show trials. At one point I was reading Jeff Sharlet's *The Family,* Sarah Vowell's *The Wordy Shipmates,* and Tony Hurwitz's *A Voyage Long and Strange* simultaneously for three very different accounts of Puritanism and where it went after Plymouth. The heart of this chapter was my visit to the Creation Museum in 2008, and interviews with Dr. Lee Meadows, whose book, *The Missing Link,* provided a complement to our conversations. I'm very grateful to Professor Ronald L. Numbers, author of *The Creationists,* for his deep knowledge and helpful comments.

201 *Inherit the Wind* ...: Susan Friend Harding, *The Book of Jerry Falwell: Fundamentalist Language and Politics* (Princeton, NJ: Princeton University Press, 2001), p. 211.

204 Kent Hovind ...: "Evangelist's Wife Follows Him to Prison," *St. Petersburg Times,* June 30, 2007.

204 1991 Gallup poll ...: Harding, *The Book of Jerry Falwell,* p. 213.

205 he was in the first generation to experience ...: Lee Meadows, personal communication, January 8, 2010.

206 $100 million . . . : Harding, *The Book of Jerry Falwell*, p. 212.

206 uneasy truce . . . : Ibid., p. 211.

206 *The Genesis Flood* . . . : Ibid., pp. 213–214.

206 Having a $1 million year . . . : Frances FitzGerald, *Cities on a Hill: A Brilliant Exploration of Communities Remaking the American Dream* (New York: Simon and Schuster, 1987), p. 140.

207 flurry of antievolution legislation . . . : Harding, *The Book of Jerry Falwell*, p. 211.

207 Liberty Baptist v. ACLU . . . : Ibid., p. 218.

210 "reporters were just amazed" . . . : Ibid.

211 *Kitzmiller v. Dover* . . . : NOVA, *Judgment Day: Intelligent Design on Trial*, PBS, November 13, 2007. Transcript at http://www.pbs.org/wgbh/nova.

212 contributions of $100 or less . . . : Peter Slevin, "Creation Museum Inspires Belief," *Washington Post,* May 27, 2007.

215 "bathtub-size" recreations . . . : "The Bathtub Ark," http://www.answersingenesis.org, June 15, 2002.

217 "we do not know where it was" . . . : "Answers Daily" podcast, Vol. 46, http://www.answersingenesis.org, Or read the discussion on Eden at http://www.answersingenesis.org/docs2003/1021eden.asp#_ftnref3.

Gentry, Leland H. "Adam-ondi-Ahman: A Brief Historical Survey," *BYU Studies,* Vol. 13, no. 4, (Summer 1973), pp. 553–576.

Matthews, Robert J. "Adam-ondi-Ahman," *BYU Studies*, Vol. 13, no. 1 Autumn 1972, p. 32.

Numbers, Ronald L. *The Creationists: From Scientific Creationism to Intelligent Design,* Expanded Edition. (Cambridge, MA: Harvard University Press, 2006).

Chapter 12: The Once and Future Eden

I tried to let this chapter unfold as much as possible from primary sources, but the history of Joseph Smith and his church is a story that needs a lot of mediation, and I'm grateful to Duane Jeffery for providing a reality check on my assumptions about Missouri, and for recommending a unique book by Alvin R. Dyer, *The Refiner's Fire,* a meticulous catalog of Mormon Missouri lore. Quotations from the sacred texts of the Church of Jesus Christ of Latter-day Saints, including the *Book of Mormon* and *Doctrine and Covenants,* come from the church's official editions, available at http://scriptures.lds.org. Hermana Cameron and the staff of the LDS visitors' center in Independence were gracious and helpful. Joseph Smith's commandment to his followers to keep records is alive and well today, and I'm thankful for the many online repositories of historical documents.

222 "in the Middle East somewhere!" ...: Hermana Cameron, LDS visitors' center, Independence, Missouri, July 19, 2008.

222 a hub for methamphetamine abuse ...: "Rural Missouri Becomes Capital of a Deadly Drug," *Philadelphia Inquirer,* July 15, 1997, p. A1.

223 not about creation ...: Doctrine and Covenants, chap. 93, verse 29. For these and all LDS scriptural references, see http://scriptures. lds.org.

223 "only rarely did I have a student" ...: Duane Jeffery, e-mail communication, May 4, 2007.

223 "the Lord did not intend" ...: Robert J. Woodford, "'In the Beginning': A Latter-day Perspective," *Ensign,* January 1998, p. 12.

224 "having no joy, for they knew no misery" ...: Second Book of Nephi, 2:23.

224 "Zion will be where Eden was" ...: From the hymn "Adam-ondi-Ahman" by W. W. Phelps, LDS Hymnal.

226 "but a wilderness and desert" ...: Joseph Smith, *The Evening and the Morning Star,* Vol. 1, no. 2, July 1832.

226 "stone and stick" ...: Ezra Booth, "Mormonism Unveiled," *Ohio Star,* November 17, 1831, accessed on saintswithouthalos.com.

227 "All heaven seemed enwrapped" ...: Joseph Smith, *History of the Church of Jesus Christ of Latter-day Saints, Period 1,* Vol. 1 (Salt Lake City, Utah: Deseret News, 1902), p. 439.

228 "established the foundations of" ...: Joseph Smith, *Doctrine and Covenants,* 78:15.

228 "This earth was once a garden place" ...: From the hymn "Adam-ondi-Ahman" by W. W. Phelps, LDS Hymnal.

229 "valley"...: Smith, *Doctrine and Covenants*, 107:53.

229 "named by the Lord Adam-ondi-Ahman"...: Smith, *History of the Church*, 3:35; *Doctrine and Covenants*, 116:1.

230 "one of the most beautiful places I ever beheld"...: Whitney, Orson Ferguson, *Life of Heber C. Kimball* (Salt Lake City, UT: Kimball Family, 1888), p. 221.

230 Mormon war...: See Missouri State Archives collection of primary sources on the Missouri Mormon War at http://www.sos.mo.gov/archives/resources/mormon.asp.

232 litmus-test questions...: "Romney's Mormon Question," *Time*, May 10, 2007.

233 "Some doctrines are more important"...: Church of Jesus Christ of Latter-day Saints newsroom, May 7, 2007, http://newsroom.lds.org.

234 "what he was hunting for"...: Alvin R. Dyer, *The Refiner's Fire: Historical Highlights of Missouri* (Salt Lake City, UT: Deseret, 1972), p. 212.

234 this Mormon generation is suspended between...: For examples of the debate going on among believers, see the extensive commentary in the following two online articles. Nate Oman, "The Challenge of Adam-ondi-Ahman," *Times and Seasons*, September 13, 2004, www.timesandseasons.org; Kevin Barney, "Was the Garden of Eden Really in Missouri?" *By Common Consent*, July 4, 2007, www.bycommonconsent.com.

Cline, Eric. *From Eden to Exile: Unraveling Mysteries of the Bible* (National Geographic Books, 2007).

In Search of Eden, Discovery Communications, Santa Monica, CA, 2002, distributed by Artisan Home Entertainment.

Rohl, David. "The Road to Paradise," *Express*, February 8, 1999.

———. *Legend: The Genesis of Civilization* (London: Arrow, 1998).

Chapter 13: The Beginning or the End?

The genesis for this chapter was the 1987 *Smithsonian* article on Zarins's theory, and it led me to several other primary sources on his work. Eric Cline's *From Eden to Exile* provided a framework for my analysis, and I appreciate the responsiveness of Zarins, Cline, David Ilan, and Michael Sanders to my queries about Biblical archaeology. All quotations from Zarins not otherwise cited come from a telephone conversation I had with him on February 28, 2010. Conversations with the Middle Eastern studies scholar Charles Häberl also shaped my knowledge on this topic.

236 "roll their eyes" . . . : Eric Cline, "Raiders of the Faux Ark," *Boston Globe*, September 30, 2007.

237 Ubar . . . : John Noble Wilford, "On the Trail from the Sky: Roads Point to a Lost City," *New York Times*, February 5, 1992, p. A1.

237 "frankincense trail" . . . : John Noble Wilford, "Ruins in Yemeni Desert Mark Route of Frankincense Trade," *New York Times*, January 28, 1997, p. C1.

237 "Atlantis of the sands" . . . : David Roberts, "On the Frankincense Trail," *Smithsonian Magazine,* Vol. 29, issue 7, October 1998, pp. 120–135.

237 "People always overlook that" . . . : NOVA, *Lost City of Arabia,* PBS, October 8, 1996.

237 "made a movie about you" . . . : Patricia Corrigan, "Discoverer: Missourian Scores in Oman," *St. Louis Post-Dispatch,* February 6, 1992, p. 1a.

238 "condensed and evocative" . . . : Dora Jane Hamblin, "Has the Garden of Eden Been Located at Last?" *Smithsonian Magazine,* Vol. 18, no. 2, May 1987.

238 ahead of the bulldozers . . . : Dora Jane Hamblin, "Treasures of the Sands (Saudi Arabia's Fossils and Relics)," *Smithsonian Magazine,* Vol. 14, September 1983, p. 42.

238 Abdullah H. Masry . . . : Hamblin, "Treasures of the Sands."

239 heirs to its natural bounty . . . : Ibid.

241 seas beyond Mesopotamia began to rise . . . : Juris Zarins, "The Early Settlement of Southern Mesopotamia: A Review of Recent Historical, Geological, and Archaeological Research," *Journal of the American Oriental Society,* Vol. 112, no. 1, January–March, 1992, pp. 55–77.

242 "I believe they literally did" . . . : Hamblin, "Has the Garden of Eden Been Located at Last?"

242 landlocked town of Amara . . . : Zarins, "The Early Settlement," p. 60.

242 "reasonably plausible" . . . : Eric Cline, *From Eden to Exile: Unraveling Mysteries of the Bible* (National Geographic Books, 2007), p. 14.

245 "literal veracity" . . . : Calvin R. Schlabach, "The Pishon River— Found!" focusmagazine.org/articles/pishonriver.htm.

245 "new Edenists" movement . . . : Tibor Krausz, "Paradise Found," *Jerusalem Report,* February 1, 1999, p. 38.

245 "non-practicing Catholic" . . . : Ibid.

245 "just like the writings of Herodotus" . . . : Ibid.

246 "extra-biblical" . . . : David Rohl, "Genesis and the Followers of Horus," on Ginna Lewis's "Freely Speaking," September 26, 1997, Geneva International Radio 74, http://www.solami.com/a1.htm.

247 "no reason to connect" . . . : See "Adam and Eve" cylinder seal at www.britishmuseum.org.

247 "reluctant to pay great attention" . . . : "Paradise Found? Archaeologist Claims the Home of Adam and Eve Was in Iran," *Pittsburgh Post-Gazette,* September 27, 1999, p. A10.

247 "Eden in Jerusalem" conference . . . : Krausz, "Paradise Found."

247 "play ball" . . . : David Ilan, e-mail communication, November 17, 2007.

247 "no more probable" . . . : Cline, *From Eden to Exile,* p. 10.

247 "wrong end of the Euphrates" . . . : Charles Sennott, "Scholar Claims Paradise Lost Is Found," *Boston Globe,* September 20, 1999.

249 "Jones is better looking" . . . : Mike Sanders, in: Peter Sheridan, "Real-Life Indiana Jones Michael Sanders is Risking Life and Limb in the World's Trouble Spots to Unravel the Mysteries of the Old Testament." *Express,* March 15, 2001, p. 44.

249 "scientific rational pursuit" . . . : Ibid.

249 "people have looked for 2,000 years" . . . : Matthew Kalman, *Daily Mail* (London), January 17, 2001, p. 34.

249 "not pleased"...: Mike Sanders, e-mail communication, December 19, 2007.

249 "The problem with Zarins"...: Ibid.

Chapter 14: Last Tree Standing

My "return" to Qurna was made possible entirely by the many intrepid journalists who traveled to southern Iraq in the wake of both the Kuwait war and the American invasion. All quotations of residents came from reported accounts, particularly those of the *Times* of London. I tried to do for Qurna as a place what I attempted for the other central characters in this book, that is, to gather the many small stories written about a footnote or novelty, and throw this background story into the foreground. Descriptions of the current state of the tree can also be found in Bruce Feiler's *Walking the Bible;* and Rory Stewart's *Prince of the Marshes* gives an amazing firsthand account of life in southern Iraq after the invasion.

253 adventurous travel companies...: Geoff Hann, "Voices on Iraq," *Guardian Unlimited,* May 21, 2003.

253 Associated Press, Qurnah, Iraq. April 30, 2003.

253 Adam's Ice Cream Stand...: Bruce Finley, "Personal Diplomacy," *Denver Post,* February 13, 2000, p. A1.

253 "about as far from idyllic"...: David Blair, "Garden of Eden Covered in Concrete," *Daily Telegraph,* October 28, 2002, p. A12.

253 Human and animal feces...: Sarah Oliver, Pooled dispatch from Al Qurna, Iraq, in *The Mail.* (Associated Press) April 12, 2003.

253 contaminated battlefield...: Andy Kershaw, "A Chamber of Horrors So Close to the 'Garden of Eden,'" *Independent,* January 12, 2001.

253 Qurna's hospital was thoroughly looted...: International Medical Corps press release, Nasiriyah, Iraq, April 15, 2003.

254 "Down with the U.S.A.!"...: Blair, "Garden of Eden Covered in Concrete."

254 prayer dais, bomb shelter, wishing well, stars, bleached tree...: Sarah Oliver, pooled dispatch from Al-Qurna, Iraq, in *The Mail,* Associated Press, April 12, 2003.

254 removed the helpful sign . . . : Associated Press, Qurna, Iraq. April 30, 2003.

254 "at least 2,000 years old" . . . : Sammy Ketz, "In Paradise, War Never Ends," *Agence France Presse,* February 4, 2003.

255 "this is a part of paradise" . . . : Anthony Browne, "War Takes Its Toll on the Garden of Eden," *London Times*, May 28, 2003.

255 "Every generation was taught" . . . : Oliver, pooled dispatch.

255 "no place for uniforms and weapons." . . . : Oliver, pooled dispatch.

256 took over the abandoned Garden of Eden Hotel . . . : Browne, "War Takes Its Toll on the Garden of Eden."

256 "It's only history" . . . : Ibid.

256 Zahra rode the local bus . . . : Ketz, "In Paradise, War Never Ends."

257 "protect us from every disaster" . . . : Ibid.

257 "specially put here" . . . : David Blair, "Garden of Eden Covered in Concrete."

257 "significant to all religions" . . . : Ibid.

257 rebuilt it without fanfare . . . : Browne, "War Takes Its Toll on the Garden of Eden."

257 just a decaying stump . . . : Mark Lacey, "After the War: Paradise Lost; It May Once Have Been the Cradle of Humanity, but It's Far from Eden Today," *New York Times*, May 30, 2003, p. A14.

257 "had been dead for decades" . . . : Anthony Browne. "War Takes Its Toll on the Garden of Eden."

Acknowledgments

At the end of the process of writing this book, I started looking to escape New York City and finish the last four chapters somewhere peaceful, quiet, and stress free. Like Vermont. I applied to the Vermont Studio Center, and was thrilled to receive a fellowship for a month-long residency. With my acceptance letter they sent a brochure describing the Center, in Johnson, Vermont, "along the banks of the Gihon River." Wait, what?

Immediately, I tried to explain away the coincidence. *Oh, that's why they accepted you. They saw that the Gihon plays a prominent role in your project.* I went back to my application. I'd sent them the Qurna chapter, which, it turns out, does not mention that particular river of paradise, the four of which have been coursing through my brain for the past three years: *Tigris, Euphrates, Pishon, Gihon.*

Then I thought: there must be some other reason to name a river Gihon. Nope: it's a Hebrew word only mentioned in Genesis 2:10–14. Maybe there were dozens of Gihon Rivers all over the country? I searched, and found . . . Johnson, Vermont. There was no getting around it: Eden had found me.

Of course I knew I was obsessed with Eden, just like the seekers I was writing about. But I still thought mine was a strictly intellectual pursuit. It wasn't until I was accidentally invited to go live by the Gihon River that I realized I had been missing that little flash of magic, that little spark of "well, maybe" that defies logic, just like the Gihon River coincidence defied my attempts to reason with it. Despite my repeated claims of objectivity, there was no way I could extricate myself from the search. I had, after all, grown up on Mount Desert Island, Maine, an exquisitely beautiful idyll surrounded by water, mountains, and trees, whose largest town, Bar Harbor, was actually named "Eden" until 1918. How had I missed that?

To the extent that I was able to get that tiny spark of Eden magic onto these pages, then, I have others to thank. First, my father, Henry Lanford, not only for the original tip that started my research, but for passing on his insatiable curiousity and sympathy toward seekers everywhere. My mother, Sheila Wilensky, has always been behind me 3000%. My brother Ethan's kindness and support as a fellow writer meant everything to me. I completed most of the research and writing of this book while I was a student in Columbia University's nonfiction writing program, an Eden in itself on 116th Street. Many people at Columbia helped me bring this book to fruition, but the book wouldn't exist without the unwavering support of the fantastic Patty O'Toole. She introduced me to the joys of research, and offered her always spot-on guidance for this book and its writer at every stage of the process. I was equally privileged to receive the close attention of the remarkable Richard Locke, whose care and curiosity bestowed me with the determination necessary to keep going through numerous false starts. Michael Janeway's courses in criticism opened up whole new worlds for me, and I'm honored by his kind advocacy for this book.

Paul Elie, Lis Harris, Margo Jefferson, Darcy Frey, and Stephen O'Connor all helped put the project in context. Kindred writer Josh Garrett-Davis was so in tune with the spirit of this book from the beginning that he dreamed up its title, for which I owe him many cases of beer. Abby Rabinowitz's astute readings of the last section could not have come at a better time. I want to thank every single one of my fellow students who read numerous versions of this project, especially Glenn Gordon, Christina Rumpf, Starre Vartan, Annie Cobb, and my fellow thesis workshoppers in the Fall of 2007. Nell Boeschenstein and Rachel Reiderer very kindly recommended their German-speaking friends, Laura Killian and

Lakshmi Krishnan respectively, who graciously provided original translations of Friedrich Delitzsch's Eden book.

Phoebe Sheftel and "the other" Dallas Sherman kindly answered my queries out of the blue. Goran Djordjevic and Charles Haberl talked me through the big picture. Patrick Kennedy went way beyond the local librarian's call of duty, driving me around Reverend West's hometown of Pleasant Hill, Ohio, while laying out the history of German Baptism. Rodney Noonan scanned and e-mailed me Tse Tsan Tai's otherwise-unavailable memoir. Ayub Nuri provided essential insights on Iraq and trees. Soon-to-be Dr. Louisa Pyle was the missing link between me and Lee Meadows. Jorunn Buckley, James Marshall, and Susan Pederson helped put me in touch with the right people. Thanks to Duane Jeffrey for his astute Adam-ondi-Ahman observations and his kindness in sharing them. Juris Zarins patiently fielded my call out of the blue from Oman, as he had with so many other seekers. Thanks to Andrei Codrescu, who first published Chapter 5 of this book in his *Exquisite Corpse Annual #2*; it's an honor to join his roster. Michelle Legro of *Lapham's Quarterly* and Nathan Schneider at *Killing the Buddha* helped me work out ideas from this book in their pages. Thanks also to *Triple Canopy*, *The Faster Times*, the Earshot Reading Series, Rachel Aviv, Montana Wojczuk and Julia Schaffer.

I'm grateful for the support of the Maine Community Foundation, the Hertog Family Foundation, the Arthur J. Harris Memorial Prize, and the Vermont Studio Center, whose generous fellowship funded by the National Endowment of the Arts made it possible for me to finish the book along the banks of the actual Gihon River. My thanks to its founding Eden-seeker, Jon Gregg, and to Gary Carter, Sebastian Matthews, Jennifer Acker, Beth Schuman, Tania Aebi, Jeremy Lloyd, Timothy Brandoff, Michael Leslie and all the other Maverick Writers for their warmth and friendship. Kitty Hoffman gets a special shout-out for accompanying me to Eden, Vermont, on her birthday. This might be a good time to acknowledge those Edens that I explored but did not include: General "Chinese" Gordon and the Seychelle islands, that means you. The Hollow Earth people really need their story told; so does the crew of Biosphere 2. S. P. Dinsmoor in Lucas, Kansas, deserves his own book. And of course there's my own "home Eden," in Maine, about which Richard Sassaman (author of my favorite book, *Bar Harbor Police Beat*) knows everything there is to know. Thanks to the good people of Tremont and Southwest Harbor, Maine, especially Weslea Sideon, Curtis Wells, Lisa Howley, Vicky Haynes, Ellen Gilmore, and all of the Ozettes. It takes a village.

Nathaniel Jacks of Inkwell Management was a dedicated supporter when he first heard about this project, and became an astute reader, agent, and advocate throughout the publication process. Thanks to my editor, Jamison Stoltz, for his enthusiastic collaboration and trust, and everyone at Grove/Atlantic for their thoughtful shepherding of my first book. Copy editor Heather Angell saved me from many embarrassments. Rosamond Purcell, Austin O'Driscoll, Rob Verger, Murwarid Abdiani, Sara Marcus, Stephen Prothero, Jeff Sharlet, Peter Manseau, Benita & Colin Eisler, and Aura Davies generously offered their help in getting the word out. Thanks to J. C. Hallman, Ronald L. Numbers, Andrei Codrescu, Paul Collins, Philip Zaleski, David Farley, Les Standiford, A. J. Jacobs, and Patty O'Toole for their extremely kind words. Thanks to all of my many employers, especially Joanann Scali, James Bradley, Jen Shotz, Amanda Pennelly and the rest of the crew at the *People* copy desk, the best nighttime day job out there.

Writing this book was a life-changing process that began in 2005, and I can't thank enough the people who led me to it. Jennifer Mackenzie and Amy Wilensky took the leap first; Hollace Beer talked me through everything; and Jim Mairs taught me how to really look at books. Thanks to Sunny Daly and William Myers, and Mika and Matthijs Braakman. I am tremendously lucky to have the friendship of Alison Cheeseman, reader, translator, baker, and avid fan. She and my fabulous Inwood team of Marie Nguyen, Steven Bell, Xuan Bell, and Anna Fewell, followed three years' worth of unsolicited digressions on obscure Biblical topics while keeping me sane and well-nourished. Gianmarco Leoncavallo may not have known was he was getting into, but he took the leap anyway, and I'll always be grateful for his savvy and single-minded dedication. Finally, thanks again to my family for their beyond-unconditional love and enthusiasm. Keep looking for Eden, and let me know when you find it.